D1538574

NO CRYSTAL STAIR

Lynell George

NO CRYSTAL STAIR

African-Americans in the City of Angels

———◆———

LYNELL GEORGE

ANCHOR BOOKS
DOUBLEDAY
NEW YORK   LONDON   TORONTO   SYDNEY   AUCKLAND

For My Family

AN ANCHOR BOOK

PUBLISHED BY DOUBLEDAY
a division of Bantam Doubleday Dell Publishing Group, Inc.
1540 Broadway, New York, New York 10036

ANCHOR BOOKS, DOUBLEDAY, and the portrayal of an anchor
are trademarks of Doubleday, a division of
Bantam Doubleday Dell Publishing Group, Inc.

No Crystal Stair was originally published in hardcover by Verso in 1992.
The Anchor Books edition is published by arrangement with Verso.

Library of Congress Cataloging-in-Publication Data

George, Lynell.
No crystal stair : African-Americans in the City of the Angels /
Lynell George. — 1st Anchor Books ed.
p.   cm.
Originally published: London ; New York : Verso, 1992.
1. Afro-Americans—California—Los Angeles—Social conditions.
2. Los Angeles (Calif.)—Social conditions.   I. Title.
[F869.L89N328   1994]
305.896'073079494—dc20   93-46285   CIP

ISBN 0-385-47411-3

Copyright © Lynell George 1992

ALL RIGHTS RESERVED

PRINTED IN THE UNITED STATES OF AMERICA

FIRST ANCHOR BOOKS EDITION: July 1994

10   9   8   7   6   5   4   3   2   1

CONTENTS

ACKNOWLEDGEMENTS

Versions of 'Waiting for the Rainbow Sign', 'Guns No Butter', 'Sometimes a Light Surprises', 'Freedman', 'I Can Be Reached Here Anytime', 'Going Between', 'Set This Tangle Straight', 'African-American Me', 'Long-Distance Runner', 'This One's for the Ladies', 'John Carter Blows Hot and Cool', 'Precious Memories', 'Notes from a Native Son', 'I Heard It through the Grapevine', 'My End of the Bargain', 'The Spook Who Sat by the Door', and 'Who's Your People?' first appeared in the *L.A. Weekly*. 'One Man's Family', 'Family Album', and 'The Black Gallery' first appeared in *L.A. Style* magazine. 'City of Specters' appeared in David Reid, ed., *Sex, Death, and God in L.A.* (Pantheon Books).

For their wisdom, inspiration and assistance, I'd like to thank: Mike Davis, Anne Fishbein, Kristin Hohenadel, Lorna Anozie, Rubén Martínez, Kit Rachlis Judith Lewis, David Davis, R. J. Smith, and the *L.A. Weekly* support team, Debra DiPaolo, Ted Soqui, Howard Rosenberg, Cynthia Wiggins, Steven Hiatt, David Reid, Jayne Walker, Levi Kingston, Frank McRae, Kamal Hassan, Cynthia Hamilton, Kay Elewski, Emily White, Wanda Coleman, Michele P. Clinton, Meri Nana-Ama Danquah, Lisa Teasley, David Dante Troutt, Sarah Lazin, Bob LaBrasca, Robert Lloyd, Susan LaTempa, Michael Ventura, Ginger Varney and Barbara Morgan.

Photos credits are as follows: 'Behind the Veil' by Cynthia Wiggins; 'Waiting for the Rainbow Sign' by Anne Fishbein; 'Guns No Butter' by Anne Fishbein; Ward African Methodist Episcopal Church by Anne Fishbein; Ward AME ushers by Robert Malone; Nelson Mandela by Ted Soqui; Levi Kingston by Anne Fishbein; Halford Fairchild, Dennis Westbrook, Jan Sunoo, and Marcia Choo by Ted Soqui; 'Set This Tangle Straight' by Debra DiPaolo; Meri Nana-Ama Danquah, Mazisi Kunene by Cynthia Wiggins; Charles Burnett by Howard Rosenberg; Yo-Yo by Debra DiPaolo; John Carter by Anne Fishbein; Marc Anthony Thompson by Anne Fishbein; Storyteller by Anne Fishbein; Roland Charles by Anne Fishbein; 'City of Specters' by Anne Fishbein; 'My End of the Bargain' by Anne Fishbein.

MOTHER TO SON

Well, son, I'll tell you:
Life for me ain't been no crystal stair.
It's had tacks in it,
And splinters,
And boards torn up,
And places with no carpet on the floor —
Bare.
But all the time
I'se been a-climbin' on
And reachin' landin's,
And turnin' corners,
And sometimes goin' in the dark
Where there ain't been no light.
So boy, don't you turn back.
Don't you set down on the step
'Cause you finds it kinder hard.
Don't you fall now —
For I'se still goin' honey, I'se still climbin',
And life for me ain't been no crystal stair.

Langston Hughes

INTRODUCTION:

LIVES BEHIND THE VEIL

Despite grim prophecy, travelers still come to glimpse the city myth. I've often wondered why. Certainly they must know that this city is barely a glimmer of what it once was. And what it once *was* never quite measured up to those early reports from vantages atop arroyo-gashed hills or in the shadow of a barren valley. But they arrive as they have for a good portion of this century, mementos, histories, hope, all tied tight to the top of a car; loads heavy enough to buckle a roof under the weight of abstract expectation.

African-Americans have come for years, just like this. First escaping the Jim Crow South, then the ravages of the Hawk, then bent toward the very edge, the long journey toward the western extremity, into Los Angeles. Vast space and mild days could ease the sting of hard times. So far from home, no one had to know about it if you had failed or lost yourself along the way. Racism, on the coast, wasn't as persistently visible or pernicious as in the South of the night-riders or of the 'strange fruit' dangling from the trees that Billie Holiday sighed about, yet it could be as red and as unexpected as the savage desert winds.

In 1784, twenty-six out of the forty-four *pobladores* who settled in *Nuestra Señora la Reina de Los Angeles* identified themselves as mixed-race or black. These mysterious figures – Quintero, Gertrudis, Camero, Petra, Rubio, Mesa, Moreno – were often lost in local schoolroom history books. Their long journey toward a better life laid the sturdy groundwork for a city that grew out of red rock and sand.

With the westward drift of the rest of the country's population, drawn by gold and the luxury of space, the possibilities for these Angelenos of color were soon eclipsed, and subsequently guaranteed to be kept in check by laws that summarily regulated presents as well as futures – from restrictive housing covenants to unconscionable employment stipulations. City streets were full of black emigrés who held professional degrees garnered from prestigious universities countrywide relegated to jobs waxing radio station floors after-hours or wheeling steamer-trunks as railroad station redcaps.

Amid the casualties, strong figures emerged. Biddy Mason purchased her freedom in 1859 and became a model of strength and perseverance. Much later, Vada and John Sommerville's Dunbar Hotel played host to a parade of visiting black dignitaries during the golden age of Jazz Street, the dazzling strip of Central Avenue in the thirties.

Langston Hughes, Chester Himes, Countee Cullen, and W. E. B. Du Bois made frequent visits to the coast, rested their hats on someone's sunny kitchen table, pulled out a pen and made some notes. They liked the cast of the light, the shimmering sea, the half-speed pace. But none felt the inclination to stay, to lay sturdy roots in what was seemingly only sand. They weren't blinded in the sun.

My mother broke away from the Jim Crow South; my father, the Hawk.

My mother left Louisiana for college and larger prospects. But lecture halls frequently grew silent when she entered. Her presence at an off-campus Journalist Society Tea prompted incredulous stares. When she attempted to put her observations into words, constructing a sober editorial that compared the nature of racism on two coasts, the professor, from the lectern, marveled at the size and weight of the 'chip' on her shoulder.

My father grew up in Pennsylvania, then served his country, mopping up in Korea. After leaving the army he arrived in Los Angeles via Route 66, joining his brothers, mother, and sister in a rambling craftsman near USC. They referred to it proudly by its street address, '1660' – no apartment numbers or letters; no halves, quarters or eighths – all hard won and entirely their own. My father was looking for a smooth transition on his way to a California teaching credential, then a graduate degree. Police work provided stability. So he did his training in the hills above Chavez Ravine, receiving a starched black uniform

MAY 1, 1992

and silver badge for his efforts. But this was Police Chief William Parker's force, where nobody wanted to be paired with a 'nigger', or were always primed and ready to 'go get one'. Consequently, my father, eyes set dead-ahead in his task, walked his skid row beat alone. In a year he walked out, and always looked upward.

'No limit to your . . . possibilities', W. E. B. Du Bois promised in a 1913 issue of the NAACP magazine *The Crisis.* It was difficult to resolve this inequity, interpret this empty promise. A climate of unremitting denigration takes its toll: Needs unmet, voices unheard; corporations, supermarkets, assembly-lines, teen-posts firmly shuttered, one after another. Old structures stand and rot in the sun. There's seldom anything to replace them. In 1965, Watts blew in a fury; the seventies saw the advent of a more savvy and militaristic style of street gang, who left its mark on freeway overpasses and walls and began bringing their anger as well as their guns to school.

For L.A.'s African-American population, those who didn't gain momentum on the tail-wind of white flight and rise out of the inner city, there are the remains to sift through: decrepit schools, poorly funded community services, inadequate health services, jammed low-income housing. It is the fallout that has firmly secured the media's eye, not the abundant reasons for it. What is engendered by this neglect plays as universal icon – desperation and hopelessness.

When L.A. was wild in flames last spring, I supposed this time the world outside expected placards. Sit-ins. Candlelight vigils. Mumbled Bible verses and hands clasped tight in private prayer. Maybe an angry display downtown at LAPD headquarters in Parker Center, some objects thrown, a few arrests made. To test the boundaries of civil disobedience, possibly a boisterous (but organized) demonstration in front of the courtroom in Simi Valley, or a rally at the front doors of each and every one of those twelve jurors' homes. . . .

But people get weary.

This rage's kindling was fatigue. It was stoked by generations of ostracism, fortified by neglect, the long fuse lit by a baffling justice system that did much more than support the status quo. This jury's verdict implied, more explicitly than it realized, what African-Americans have surmised all along – that in the eyes of white America, 'a black life ain't worth a damn.'

In the aftermath, amid the trail of fire-gutted buildings, a sad handprinted sign fashioned from an old bedsheet that implores, 'Mr. Busch (sic) I need help.'

Los Angeles as fetching multicultural melting pot was said to be the place where those of all races could happily co-exist under the sun. But within the brief span of the first few days of May, under the hot pressure of mounting violence and the emotional peaks and valleys of fear, Southern California was far from the romantic vision to which it has aspired. 'L.A.?' I heard one woman quip during the first moments of dead calm: 'Everybody knows what that really stands for – "Lower Alabama".'

As the city burned, it became a startling flashpoint, its embers scattering, settling off new conflagrations, if not blazing physical effigies: maybe it simply set a psyche on fire. Yet for weeks afterward in the inner city, where the acrid odor was still omnipresent, where it took clever planning to determine the easiest way to procure a quart of milk if you didn't have a car, people hadn't softened into a half-dream state of relief. Things certainly weren't 'back to normal'. They were worse. The reality of pre–April 29 life remains: no jobs, no resources, no rosy promises for the future.

Standing at the threshold of not simply rebuilding L.A., but considering the at once intimidating and exhilarating thought of reinventing it, residents know that carefully reassembling this puzzle will take much more than a magic incantation, or the smooth politics of the city's recently named Great White Hope, Peter Ueberroth. People have become more optimistic about the possibilities because of the brief sparks of unity emanating from within: the scuttlebutt of a black gang truce; an east-side Latino gang that worked to keep their home-turf market guarded and safe from harm; and the presence of a new police chief who, unlike the old chief, will pause and bend to listen.

Los Angeles has been, as Langston Hughes once wrote, 'no crystal stair', full of 'tacks' and 'splinters', but the journey upward hasn't been hopeless or for naught. This body of work is an attempt to offer an alternative vision, radically different from the mainstream media's careless commentaries full of 'theys' and 'thems' peopled by 'thugs' and 'packs', a race made that much more one-dimensional by the outside's sheer ignorance of the city grid, an unschooled view that renders the deep, dark thicket south of Pico, south of the I-10 Freeway, the heart of 'the community', the interzone known as South Central L.A.

Black Los Angeles isn't just the chaos one tunes in to every evening at six and again at eleven. It is as well a 9-to-5, a bungalow, front lawns. It is family, perseverance and resilience. It is a collection of eloquent voices, wise and striking faces. These teachers, musicians, community organizers, visionaries, preachers, filmmakers, civic leaders, students, *griots,* authors and photographers have shared their stories, have over the years become an extended family of sorts, an inspiration. They are just a few of many out there sinking their roots into rich soil, not sand. They make it easier for me to realize why people still come to wrestle with the ugly beauty that Los Angeles has become, but more important, they help me slowly to understand just why it is so imperative to stay.

Los Angeles, August 1992

REPORTAGE

CHAPTER 1

WAITING FOR THE RAINBOW SIGN

By midnight, no one phoning long-distance bothers with hello. Instead they just ask, 'Is it as crazy as it looks?'

I want to say, 'It started long before all this. . . .' Long before this afternoon's bewildering decision left me less astonished than strangely numb. Long before George Holliday ran tape capturing Rodney G. King's struggle and submission. Long before Latasha Harlins, Eulia Love and Marquette Frye became cautionary symbols. Long before Watts shouted its existence into the sky in 1965, sending up searchlights in the form of flames.

They want me to make sense of the footage I'm mesmerized by, of the faces that register anger giving way to elation. Sirens. Police in riot gear. Familiar landscape altered by skewed aerial views and flame. I try to put into simple words what I've seen and heard in the last few hours of the day.

Until I can see it up close with my own eyes, I'm relying on sound-and-video bites as if they were air: first the radio reports of an 'intentional' accident at Florence and Normandie; 100 to 150 people sprinting through intersections at rush hour; the new, bloody chaos at Normandie and 70th. Mayor Tom Bradley, whose face doesn't seem able to accommodate any more fatigue standing solemn at the pulpit at First African Methodist Episcopal Church, trying not to flinch when pelted with boos. Local ministers use their melodious baritones to frantically implement 'Operation Cool Head'. Too late. By sundown rocks and bottles sail toward the windshields of passing cars, through store windows, at nothing in particular. Random debris jams the city works.

I'm in a press of traffic motoring east on Washington. It thins dramatically when I swing south on La Brea to Adams. *My* wide stretch of boulevard, gateway to black L.A.'s Sugar Hill of the forties. Old churches, big trees, even bigger houses. A place that seldom before surfaced for the world as representative of Black L.A. But no doubt the world will see it now.

At Crenshaw, I see what has been sketchily described on the radio for the last couple of hours: figures rendered to silhouettes, occupying the street, advancing randomly. Shouting, laughing, they drift on foot into traffic, into the beams of headlights, as if truly invincible. My tires eat glass, trundle over big, splintered husks of plywood, of brick and clods of dirt. On my left I see a waterfall of glass. I don't hear the sound of it breaking: this scene has no soundtrack, no narrative line to hold on to. Out the other window I watch six pairs of hands pry apart white iron security gates. Here I see an ironic twist on the multiethnic coalition that local community leaders have been talking about for years, but not successfully implementing: black and Latino teenagers coming together to lift a sofa out of a furniture store's showcase window, onto shoulders, then down the sidewalk.

As a reflex, I'm already speedily taking notes, as if the act of writing down what I see and hear will bring about some sense of order. Clarity. But my handwriting turns out looking like angry, spiky hieroglyphics. Automatic writing. Subjects without predicates. Issues without resolution.

I don't head toward First AME for answers. I know that right now there are none to be had. Maybe the warmth of others equally confused, or moving toward sadness or rage, will thaw my numbness. When the decision was passed down, I wasn't sure how to process the information; I didn't know how to respond to officer Powell's smile, to interpret Daryl Gates's barely suppressed grin; to understand my own emptiness.

Closer to the church, spectators have left cars all over, along red-painted curbsides, in driveways, in loading zones, abandoned at the center of the road. Those of us circling for parking places are told to move on. Since the streets have quickly heated up, the 24-hour vigil has been canceled. Praying in public tonight is too dangerous. I smell alcohol in the air, strong, oozing out of broken glass that has met pavement. Then come the stones. Random. They thud against the thin metal of the car. I begin to understand that this is the heat of chaos.

CLEAN-UP, FRIDAY, MAY 1, 1992

I wind back to Adams. At the corner of Western, where looms the Golden State Mutual Life insurance company (an early monument to African-American business ingenuity and tenacity in Los Angeles), two men set fire to a wooden bus bench. The first flames are weak. They egg it on with words first, then look around for something to stoke it – paper, wood, maybe a piece of their own clothing. I watch transfixed for too long as the fire leaps, changes in color. I remain because I know that tomorrow I will not recognize this corner. I want to preserve what still stands. Over static, City Councilman Mark Ridley-Thomas is on the radio composing his thoughts carefully: '. . . we haven't recovered from Watts yet. . . .' I conjure a picture of my own familiar city routes, down Martin Luther King, Arlington, Jefferson, other wide central city 'business' corridors, looking at row upon row of run-down nothing. Dilapidated facades with decaying or neglected interiors. Never been rebuilt, no plans to even begin. My foot trembles as I lift it from the brake, to place it on the accelerator, heading east, heading home. It tremors, I realize not with fear but with rage, and I'm relieved that I finally feel something. Problem is, as always, I don't know what to do with it, or who will hear.

Go home, stay home. Lock your doors.
KFWB 980 AM, Thursday, April 30

I've already seen the look.

Driving through the Silver Lake hills to avoid Sunset Boulevard's panicked snarl, I climb along the incline. People are out jogging and walking their dogs, even though fires have moved closer, are no longer a distant TV hell. The higher I climb, the more I see residents take note of my car's make and color; they mentally record the license number, but most importantly my unfamiliar deep-brown face, any distinguishing marks. They look at me as if they will at any moment join together to form a human barricade if I make a wrong or abrupt move. Later, across town, a blond man in the next lane looks over L.A.-pickup casual, then quickly lifts his smoked glass window.

The same video feeds that have inspired their terror have fueled my own curiosity, augmented my pain. For hours I've been transfixed, watching childhood landmarks swallowed up in the surprisingly liquid aspects of billowing smoke and flames – stores, streets, memories, futures. I'm watching my old neighborhood blister, turn to embers, rendered entirely foreign. I hear the fear in the voices of my relatives and friends who've been trying to track the course of the flames, guess the trajectory of anger.

'If you've got your ass out here you might get shot', one seen-it-all on-looker tells me. We're standing near the corner of Walton and Jefferson looking at the remains of a corner Mom & Pop still smoldering, a single red flicker looking like some eerie twist on an eternal flame. 'Brothers getting busy', and he backs it up recounting the staggering list of firearms he's seen the past week, from shotguns to .357 Magnums to Uzis. 'They shut everything down early last night. I went down on Arlington, everybody started hitting the pawnshops. It was kids, old women, not just like criminals, like they've been sayin' on TV. It's like a free-for-all. Get it while you can. Let's roll and see what's poppin'', says my newly self-appointed guide.

'The message was there, but the method was wrong', offers one of the playground prophets chillin' at the Denker Recreation Center. 'We've inconvenienced ourselves now', he says, looking into the sulfur-tinted sky. Fires loom around us, sirens scream, puddles of water left by pumper trucks look more like polluted lakes. 'Folks are gonna start getting real hungry down here. RTD shut down, people don't have cars.'

'It's sad to me 'cause I grew up here and now they're burning it down', says the office manager from a Century City law firm. He has his hair cut into a neat, close fade and is still wearing his pink shirt and paisley tie with a square knot; a pager is clipped to his belt. 'I had to drive over and check on my relatives', he explains. 'I don't agree with the looting, but I understand the frustration.'

'I'll put it in two words', a woman strolling by and looking at my notebook tells me: 'FUCKED UP'. She wants to make sure that I've underlined the words, that they stand out somehow from all the rest on the page. 'Two words, "fucked up". We hurt our folks the most. *We* deal with that. People scared to walk out on the street.'

As the burned-out buildings multiply, look more disfigured, more abstract as they collapse upon themselves, the stories become more tragic. Like the little boy who's decided not to leave the cement backyard behind his house because 'I don't want to get caught by no police. I don't want to have to go through that.' There is Francis, bewildered, who stands in front of the Church of God of Prophecy on Western, watching his electronics business smolder: 'What . . . do . . . I . . . feel?' he asks the dead space before him. 'What do I feel now? Upset. Angry. We as black people have been told that we could achieve anything if we put our minds to it. Now, because of a couple of days, it's going to take twenty or thirty years before we can achieve anything again. People here complain about South Africa. It is no better here.'

'The arrogance of Gates, I believe, caused the whole thing', a security guard tells me as we watch a van pull up full of teens, loading up bottles of soda and alcohol. One offers me a cool drink. I decline with a shake of the head. 'They've created a monster', the guard continues. 'Now they have to feed him.'

It's now 7:30. If you're on the street now you're breaking the law.
KFWB 980 AM, Friday, May 1

I've seen a number of objects lifted out of open windows of automobiles in motion. Brandished with a purpose. Each day it's been a different symbol. Wednesday it was a baseball bat shaken belligerently to the down-deep beats of DJ Quick as a long yellow Cadillac took St Andrews Place at an estimated eighty mph. Thursday it was a clenched fist raised to all passers-by on the Crenshaw strip. On Friday, snaking down Stocker, it was a well-worn broom.

Crenshaw Boulevard traffic is sluggish since all the signals are out for blocks after exiting the freeway. No one has the time to direct traffic, so crossing the intersection requires steely determination. The pace, however, gives a driver sufficient time to read the hastily scrawled signs making desperate pleas: 'Black Owned. Black Owned Business. Employs Black Young Mothers'. Some of the messages are a bit more sinister than others: 'Black Owned/Not Korean Owned' – the 'O' in *Korean* filled with a frowning face. Tags on shells of buildings read, 'It's a black thang'; little boys loot a wig store on a dare, then sport their spoils. This revolution has become unfocused, its battle cry cacophonous.

When I see the National Guard's Humvees I'm reminded of the passed-down memories of 1965. Of the tanks that trundled authoritatively down Crenshaw, of my grandfather, in his suspenders and stingy-brimmed fedora, on his first visit to L.A. from Louisiana, wandering away. On foot, he took his own discovery trip, his expedition lasting long after curfew. He was returned to us, telling tales, by a uniformed escort. Now I'm realizing that I worry my loved ones as well because I need to see for myself. I need to understand.

Crenshaw is now lit with a different spark. The hard-won Lucky's Supermarket at the corner of 39th Street remains sealed behind Alexander Haagen's trademark fencework. A Louis Farrakhan recording plays from the loudspeaker of a corner bookstore. And when about five members of the National Guard make a fast break toward 39th with guns at the ready, I follow their gaze and the tilt of their upraised guns . I see nothing, except it's the first time I notice that the sky is almost blue.

'I basically wanted to help my community', says Brandi Younger, a thirteen-year-old student at Bancroft Junior High. She's got a push-broom in hand and is working on her little piece of the Child and Adult Health Group Urgent Care building, its collapsed and untidy skeleton spilling onto the sidewalk. 'I got tired of people calling us "animals" on TV. I didn't want our community to look bad, I didn't want people to say bad things. All I've seen is looting and violence. I really haven't seen anything positive.'

Lancelott Keith is taking a break when Marla Gibbs arrives with trays of catered food from her supper club, Memory Lane, to feed the crew of about fifty and growing who have gathered here with their brooms, rubber gloves and rakes. They've come from around the corner and across town, dispatched by radio DJs, ministers, their own consciences. 'Problem with the young men is that they have no work', says Keith. 'No jobs. Those are the things that make you feel worthwhile. Even pushing a broom. There's been a void for too long. People have to have a purpose.'

'I know people who didn't plan for the revolution', writer/performance artist Akilah Nayo Oliver tells those assembled in the circle. She looks at a food-distribution list, then sends it around the room for those willing to participate to sign.

'Toilet paper and milk. Two things in a riot that go the quickest', suggests Wanda Coleman, recollecting her experience during the 'old rise in sixty-five'.

Across town in Venice, a fifteen-minute freeway ride from the clean-up crews on Crenshaw, in the few hours before curfew an ad hoc collective of black artists meets to discuss ideas for immediate relief. What comes out are the first raw emotions voiced in the first moments of calm, the public articulation of what has been swarming around in everyone's brain. People wouldn't burn down something they cherish, something that they perceive as truly their own. The violence of the last forty-eight hours has taken us far away from the monotone reading of the leaden verdict, the crumpled mass that was barely discernible as Rodney G. King. Now it's been the stark reality of no food, of dead or absent family, of no power, of the acrid smell that clings to the clothes, the hair, the nose. 'What does this signify? What kind of phoenix is gonna rise out of these particular ashes?' asks Coleman. 'This didn't come out of a vacuum.'

'I don't want anybody to explain it in *their* terms', says Keith Antar Mason, barely suppressing his tears and the tremble in his voice. 'This happened to *me*. Now it's beyond Rodney King. It's beyond 1619. There ain't no explanation for this.'

'All my life I've been called an "animal". All my life I've been called "sub-human"', testifies a woman from across the room, throwing her thoughts into the circle. 'We have to be careful of the language. The "thugs", "rats", "packs" and "hoodlums". I pay close attention to the words, so it's been hard for me to watch TV or read the newspaper.'

'If this was happening in another country, they'd talk about the repressive government', says poet Meri Nana-Ama Danquah. 'Pay close attention to what these people were stealing – food, diapers, toys. No one mentioned economics.'

A woman in T-shirt and jeans echoes the inchoate thought that has most occupied my own mind. 'We've been trusting too long', she says quietly. 'We trusted the jury to do right. I'm so mad at us for trusting. . . .'

I'm looking out the window, listening, but thinking about the sun. About the thin light we're quickly losing, about the urgency of heading back east to beat the night. I'm thinking about the nightmare that became our lives for hours into days, about the biblical 'rainbow sign' sent after the flood, wondering how it will make itself known this time. As I drift further, what wanders in from the circle of angry voices is a stray thought, a fragment, offered up as a single puzzle piece of a larger explanation: 'Maybe it had to burn . . . like how sometimes you have to burn a field. To make something new. . . .'

May 1992

CHAPTER 2

GUNS NO BUTTER

with David Dante Troutt

Los Angeles is wonderful. Nowhere in the US is the Negro so well and
beautifully housed. . . . Out here in this matchless Southern California there
would seem to be no limit to your opportunities, your possibilities.
W. E. B. Du Bois, The Crisis, 1913

. . . We have these no-good, miserable sons-of-bitches out there, which
society allows to continue to roam the streets.
L.A. Chief of Police Daryl Gates, September 1988

Mary Davis is a single mother. She has two teenage children: a daughter, sixteen, a son, fourteen. She works for the county of Los Angeles as an eligibility
evaluator for the Department of Social Services, a job she has held for a little
over two years. One Friday evening last April, she went to pick up her
daughter from the home of a friend. Stepping outside of her apartment building, she was 'swept up' along with hundreds of other Southland residents
suspected of being drug dealers or gangbangers.

'First they tried to say that I was a gang member because I was "fraternizing
in a cocaine area". *Mind* you, I know they sell drugs around here, but economics
predict where you live. "Well, you were there", the transporting officer told
me. "This wouldn't have ever happened if you hadn't been there."' Police took
her to the L.A. Memorial Coliseum. There she was fingerprinted and booked
under harsh stadium lights and herded into a crowded bus that served as a
makeshift holding cell. The media came later, the playing field a tangle of wire
and cable, and were told about 'Operation Hammer' – the police's attempt to
make the streets safe. But Mary Davis has a different memory: 'It's sort of like

being enslaved. They mark a little number on your hand and then they ask you if you're a gang member or not. "You no longer have any rights", my arresting officer told me: "I'm your master; your rights are gone."'

Inspired by the accidental killing of Karen Toshima – an innocent bystander caught in an exchange of gang gunfire in Westwood last January – these citywide sweeps are the LAPD's ongoing attempt to 'take back the streets' and 're-establish police authority', especially in South Central L.A., where the sweeps are concentrated. The real aim of these 'emergency efforts' is to squelch a more than fifteen-year-old problem: Los Angeles youth gangs.

Although South Central residents initially welcomed the idea of more police in their district, the reality of sweeps rapidly proved to be crude, brutal and unsuccessful. Drug dealing stayed profitable; the gang killing continued, up 15 percent over the previous year; and very few gang members were convicted of serious crimes. Meanwhile, innocent people were being arrested by the thousands, victims of the 'the police authority' concept of government. The lesson was clear: gang sweeps are not just firepower against gangs – they're war against an entire community.

The Gang Problem isn't simply a story of male teens in lowriding Levi's and roomy white tees commanding city street corners. It is the evidence of the failures in a socioeconomic structure that disenfranchises the poor and the non-white. This indicates that that the Gang Problem is not, at bottom, a police problem. The notion that violent sweeps are the answer is viewed by the black and Latino communities as a way of blaming and punishing victims for their difficulties, denying racism and continuous economic depression.

Police intervention may not be the solution, but gangs have nevertheless become *big* business for law enforcement. The City Council last July apportioned $6.4 million in additional overtime monies (sweep funding is computed as overtime), with approximately $2.2 million earmarked specifically for sweeps. Police Chief Gates puts the cost of 1,000-officer sweeps at $150,000 per evening.

Even as money was found for police overtime, in 1988 the city appropriated only $11.9 million for those programs that help to fight poverty. That is, the money found just for sweeps, however ineffectual, is almost one-fifth of the money available for health services, community improvement and recreation, education services, day care and other programs. It's a full two-thirds of the $3.5 million human-services appropriation for South Central.

FIFTH AVENUE, L.A.

The large corps of people working with the thousands of at-risk youth in South Central are frustrated and angry about the way public dollars are being spent in their community. They want to know why, at the peak of the gang crisis, their agencies and organizations face all-time funding lows. They want to know how, after nearly a decade of federal cut-backs and Proposition 13 devastation, public officials are finding millions to pour into police overtime.

'If I don't live in your house, how am I going to come in and tell you what color to paint your bedroom?' asks V. G. Guinses, since 1968 the executive director of Save Every Youngster Youth Enterprise Society, Inc. (Sey Yes). Like many, he is enraged by the arrogance of outsiders who want to tell his community what to do with its children. 'I *live* here, I walk these streets and I'm raising a sixteen-year-old son. In L.A. they will not give a black program credit, period. All the so-called experts are white.'

Those who live and work in South Central know that the area's problems have deep historical roots. The beginning of this century saw an influx of blacks emigrating from the oppressive conditions of the Jim Crow South. The golden and expansive West, with its mild, cloudless days, eucalyptus trees and bending palms, symbolized the utopian concepts of unconditional freedom and absolute equality. Housing and entrepreneurial opportunities appeared plentiful and endless. For a while the city seemed to live up to their dreams. The number of black families settling in the Southland increased throughout the thirties and forties. Black doctors, lawyers and businessmen continued to prosper. Their offices lined Central Avenue, black L.A.'s major thoroughfare, known as 'Harlem West' – a literary arts and music center blooming with jazz clubs and soft-lit salons.

Around the time of the Watts rebellion in 1965, middle-class black families began to abandon the area for safer hilltops and outlying suburbs in an exodus that continues today. In the late seventies, South Central was abandoned again – this time by federal and state dollars and area plant closings – and many youth programs were either killed or stunned in their tracks while unemployment mounted. Young baby-boom blacks were caught in a squeeze that was made worse by waves of immigrants from Mexico, other parts of Latin America and Southeast Asia. Many were shut out of the high-tech manufacturing sector due to lack of technical skills.

Despite the vast numbers of families whose sons and daughters don't join gangs and whose parents hurry to work every morning, from the Santa Monica Freeway to Rosecrans, from La Cienega to the Alameda corridor, there are mile-long stretches where one finds no supermarkets, coffee shops, dental offices or boutiques. Major arteries are dotted instead by liquor stores, storefront churches, laundromats and fast-food joints. Most parks and schoolyards are unsafe. The Grape Street Crips preside over Grape Street and 103rd, a stone's throw from three of the city's largest and poorest housing projects. According to 1980 Census figures, their 'turf' was home to 900 families: 40 percent had incomes below the poverty line, a third had no workers at all, and about half were headed by single women. Two-thirds of the sixteen-to-nineteen-year-olds out of school had dropped out and were not in the job loop. Many of them were already in gangs. But the gangs didn't really become explosive until easily available and low-priced rock cocaine began to flow over the Mexican border around 1983.

'Our kids have been made sick with unemployment, drugs and despair', says Michael Zinzun, who heads up the Coalition Against Police Abuse, a ten-year-old organization that sprang up in reaction to a wave of police-related shootings in black and Latino communities during the early seventies. 'Society is responsible for giving guidance and support to our young people. A lot of the community services have been shortchanged, they've been operating with one hand tied behind their back.' As the problems have continued to multiply, the community has continued to lose money, attention, and respect. This neglect is reflected in many aspects of daily life, from the absence of updated textbooks and tenured teachers in community classrooms to the more visible need for street cleaning and traffic-light repair.

Gerald Ivory, a fourteen-year veteran L.A. County probation officer, says that the tension within the community, symbolized by heated, violent episodes between gang sets, in many ways parallels the series of events leading up to and culminating in the Watts uprisings: 'This is the same thing – destruction of the community – just a different posture. They just burned it down in sixty-five; now it's guns and drugs. These kids are operating from a survival standpoint: they are doing what they have to do to survive.' They've fallen through 'the safety net'.

A language barrier divides the people who work with at-risk youth from those who arrest them. To law enforcement, the passwords are 'gangs', 'gang intervention' and 'drug prevention'. Community workers rarely refer to gangs, speaking instead about the need to provide 'options', 'outlets' and 'alternatives' to children on their way to adulthood. The city calls it 'human services', and nothing in the city charter obliges it to provide any. Mayor Tom Bradley has never pursued an aggressive program to help fight poverty. This became a crisis when the Reagan administration began slashing federal poverty programs, especially those designed for prevention. The Comprehensive Employment Training Act (CETA), whose L.A. funds peaked at $120 million in 1979, was eliminated and replaced in 1983 by the Job Training Partnership Act (JTPA), with a $42 million budget.

And the city has done very little to take up the slack. According to Sue Flores, director of the human services division of the Community Development Department (CDD), her department now contracts with 126 nonprofit groups in the city to provide everything from programs for seniors to programs for the infants of teen moms. The allocations are low and the competition is stiff: This year the twenty-six agencies even remotely serving youth in South Central will receive funds totaling only $51.7 million.

'The majority don't get funded because we don't have enough money', not because their programs aren't deemed worthwhile, Flores concedes. 'The other question you have to ask is, of the ones who do get funded, do we fund them high enough? The answer is no.'

This would hardly come as news to those who have dedicated their lives to working in, and improving, their community. Erma Patterson knows exactly what underfunding means. She directs operations at Kazi House, which from 1977 until November 1988 sat in an innocuous little building near the corner of Manchester and Broadway. Her facility is one of only two drug treatment centers in all of South Central where low-income, black and Latino drug abusers can get help. Since founding Kazi House, she has watched the neighborhood grow poorer, the number of gang-afflicted patients grow larger and her funding diminish.

'We have a lot of really motivated clients', says Patterson, smiling through her visible exhaustion. 'Most of them have hit rock bottom. They've smoked up their houses and cars. If beds are cut, they're going to be out there again, committing crimes to support their addictions. But they want to get off drugs, they want to get out of gangs, and they want to change their lives. There are a lot of people like that, but the waiting lists are too long.'

Five years ago, the wait averaged about one month. Since that time there have been no funding increases, though demand has more than tripled. Patterson recently moved to a 40,000-square-foot facility in Compton that can accommodate 135 patients instead of just the 71 available spaces at her old location, although this new space has restrictions: 'I only have a conditional-use permit because Compton doesn't want to accept that it has a drug problem.'

Without help from the county, she partially paid for the relocation with personal loans taken out by herself and her friends – a move that threatens her with personal ruin. Kazi House has not paid bills for three months and Patterson admits to being broke. Patterson's perseverance stems from her belief that her agency serves a unique function. 'We don't rehabilitate. We habilitate. People with money can go to private centers; I'm trying to help kids/adults who didn't have anything to start. Teaching these kids to replace drugs with something else is tough when they come to me as junkies and drugs are *all* they know.'

The county seems prepared to write off the current victims of drugs. In late May, a motion sponsored by Supervisor Deane Dana proposed redirecting $6.7 million out of drug rehabilitation and into the sheriff's SANE (Substance Abuse and Narcotic Education) and the LAPD and school district's DARE (Drug Abuse Resistance Education) – drug and alcohol prevention/diversion classroom programs that stress self-esteem building. While it was temporarily defeated, Richard Dixon, the chief administrative officer for the county, immediately proposed diverting $800,000 from drug treatment to SANE, a move that appears indicative of the county's new funding mood: to give money for school-based prevention by the police rather than rehabilitation and treatment by community groups.

'They [the police] shouldn't be leading the community. People here don't trust the police [to lead]. And why should they? Not very much has been done to improve relations. There is a "police-against-us" attitude throughout the community', Michael Zinzun explains. 'If you live here you are immediately a suspect. When those kids are picked up during sweeps, scars are left. It's not only degrading at the moment, but it puts a stamp on their lives.'

Patterson, who has weathered one budget storm after another for fourteen years, sees many holes in the funding process. 'The people that do the work – nobody ever consults us. If they did, they would find out what was really happening. But I'm not sure they want to know.'

The fight for city funding is much the same. Sey Yes's V. G. Guinses is one of the experts who trains the 'experts' in how to detect early signs of gang involvement. Since 1972, he's had training contracts with hundreds of schools, the California Youth Authority, the Los Angeles Police Department, the US Department of Labor, Job Corps and church and parent groups, as well as delegations from China and Nigeria. For people desperate to avoid becoming 'another L.A.', Guinses is the first ounce of prevention.

Guinses's love is working one-on-one with the youths themselves – gang members or not – whom he thinks of as his children. His future, like theirs, is constantly threatened by lack of funds for proven programs. His staff, which once numbered sixty workers – including twenty-two full-time job trainers, counselors and presenters – is now down to thirty-five, with only seven employed full time. Once an all-volunteer organization, Sey Yes initially received both state and federal demonstration contracts for its work in reducing gang hostilities and directing high-risk, sometimes violent youths into jobs, sports and counseling. After federal cutbacks in 1982, Sey Yes lost much of its street presence. Today the staff of job trainers, counselors and lecturers works mainly in the schools, holding rap sessions, sponsoring drill teams and teacher workshops. Neighborhood watch programs and parent workshops help communities identify gang and drug characteristics and interpret graffiti. More than an aid to law enforcement, Sey Yes planned to become an outpost for youths who wanted to turn around, but had no place to go.

Chronic financial instability, says Guinses, reduces his effectiveness: 'In the past five years you have had no new prevention money in the black community. But you have more law enforcement. If you put every one of these kids in jail, you'd still have gangs. Unless you earmark the money for community-based organizations that can be held accountable for their prevention programs, you'll continue to have gangs. If we could work six months to a year without hassling about where the money is coming from, we could really be a good program. We could really expand.' Guinses (who received $59,000 in 1988 for Sey Yes from the CDD) figures that his program would require only a fraction of the funding law enforcement receives to have a greater impact. He puts it succinctly: 'The city hurts itself by ignoring what's working in this district.'

Leon Watkins feels the same way. Tucked away in a basement across town, his organization, Family Helpline, specializes in coordinating various efforts to help motivated kids leave gangs. Last June, it put on 'Ceasefire for LIFE', an outdoor event at the Ujima Village housing project featuring the rappers Run-D.M.C. Family Helpline received 100 calls a day immediately following the show – and for this and a decade's worth of efforts Leon Watkins has garnered much laudatory press. City and county public officials have congratulated him with plaques. He even met with President Reagan at the White House last spring. But despite all the acclaim, Leon Watkins can't get the funding he needs. His offices are quartered in a cramped two-room space donated along with a phone by his upstairs neighbor, the Brotherhood Crusade. 'Sometimes I look at my situation and wonder how I'm in it. I appreciate all the rewards', Watkins says, shrugging his shoulders. 'But I don't see any money.'

Family Helpline, the only black-oriented service of its type in the state, serves as a community troubleshooter and referral network – offering job placement, crisis intervention, housing and substance-abuse assistance. 'People call in with a problem and we try to set them up with the *best* service or program for them', Watkins says. To the hard-core gang member who has been out of school and is *sincerely* committed to leaving the gang and changing his or her life, Watkins poses a list of questions: Did you finish school? Did you get a GED [General Equivalence Diploma]? Are you interested in trade school? Community college? 'We help and place them one way or another. Get them involved in something else.'

Watkins can't explain why he hasn't received funding. 'I've approached everybody: you know – city, county, federal. I could see it if we weren't successful. Can't we get a *piece* of the millions? I get *so* frustrated because time is wasting. I'm not in it for the glory, I'm just doing it to save a life. But I've been doing it so long that I don't think I can go on much longer.'

Like many of the South Central organizers who are struggling for funds, Watkins is reluctant to give specific figures or make trouble by pointing fingers at individual city officials. He says only that his requests are small: he wants a secretary to handle calls, stipends for volunteers, emergency funds for families in trouble, a toll-free number, an answering machine, a van.

'I spoke to a group in the San Fernando Valley a little while ago. They were ready to form a committee to see the mayor *for* us. They want to know why politicians haven't done anything about getting us some money. They don't think any blacks are down here doing anything because *that's* how it is in the paper. How could they know?'

With funding virtually nonexistent, some have taken alternate routes. MAGIC (Mothers Against Gangs in Communities) has been operating for a little less than a year. An entirely *privately* funded organization, it boasts a membership of over 900 that also includes men. The emphasis is on job training and placement as well as counseling for parents and their children. MAGIC's founder, Patricia Patrick, is set on making a dent in the problem without the assistance of governmental funding. 'I feel that we can be stronger that way. We want to be able to go all the way with what we have. We don't want to sit around wondering if it's going to come or if it isn't.'

Project BUILD was a personal dream of Assemblywoman Maxine Waters. Started in 1985 and funded by the state, it has centers in all six of South Central's housing projects. More than 2,000 youth participants have received job training. Resident coordinators with an average of ten years of experience counsel, tutor and train youths from the area.

'We have a beautiful and dynamic community full of people who really want to do something with their lives out here', says Sonny Walker, executive director of the Nickerson Gardens Project BUILD. 'For different reasons, there are some people out here who really can't turn away from gangs. But there's a percentage, if given options and alternatives, who *would*.' Walker feels fortunate to have received financing. But he would like to see Project BUILD provide transportation for apprentice youth workers employed by the Century Freeway construction project or bring child care to the housing projects themselves. Project BUILD would like to be both employer *and* teacher to his participants, and to receive maintenance contracts from the city and county. But as with many others, Walker's ideas cost money that Project BUILD does not have.

Recognizing the child care problem, Waters has already worked to set up facilities that are now about ready to open. It took her two years of winding through the bureaucratic maze to obtain the funding. Child care, says Waters, is crucial to the program placing more single parents in jobs. She realizes that you can't get everything at once ('We're piecing it together', she says), but adds that her problems raising money have deep social roots: 'What has happened here is that the inner cities have been dropped off America's agenda. These kids created their own reality – discovered that they have more power through guns and dope. They took over these housing projects and they run them.'

She agrees that the system needs an infusion of many things – 'not just law enforcement'. Her larger plan, which included development of a comprehensive neighborhood watch and block club organization as a way of creating local power – was rejected by the city council. 'The police opposed it', she explains. 'They said, "We do that and we do a good job of it." I also wanted to set up a crime-prevention commission. Give it a place in city government like building safety or the arts. Set up the commission to include business people, law enforcement, community leaders, juveniles – to oversee and thereby become advocates for their communities. To organize and empower people to utilize existing resources and make them work for their community. You're going to get crime prevention when you get *that* kind of activity going.' Waters hasn't abandoned hope. She spends her time, when the legislature is not in session, performing some of the job-training lectures herself. 'This is my one-person journey. I know *how* and *what* to do if I had the money and the people working with me.'

In the eleven months since the slaying of Karen Toshima' in Westwood, the city has been bombarded with gang summits, sweeps, conferences, task forces, and legislative bills. It has seen haunting, grainy-print images of tearful mothers, hovering over the prone bodies of children gunned down in drive-by shootings. Rabid politicos have suggested sending in the National Guard. Dennis Hopper has had a hit movie with *Colors*. Nighttime network news has streetwise gangbangers 'running it all down'. The whole country has looked at South Central – from the outside.

Looking from the inside, one thing is clear above all else: local government's whole policy toward South Central has been a failure – even the (much ballyhooed) war on gangs. And even if this policy had worked, sweeping the streets free of 'rotten little cowards' (as Chief Gates has tagged them) would be no positive answer. Solutions to problems as old and intricate as these don't come quickly: they are complex and costly; they involve setting people free rather than locking them up. And that means helping people in the community to help themselves, rather than sending in a battalion of cops and experts.

'Nothing constructive is coming out of the sweeps', says probation officer Gerald Ivory, who speaks for the South Central majority when he adds, 'It's a negative situation. The political climate is not supportive. . . . Any politician who is *supposed* to be serving my community has failed me.'

January 1989

CHAPTER 3

SOMETIMES A LIGHT SURPRISES: THE LIFE OF A BLACK CHURCH

CHOIR PRACTICE

Lately, when I head east of Adams between La Brea and Hoover, curiosity has led me to count the churches I pass along the way. This stretch of road has always been house-of-worship heavy. These days I total out at ten, and that includes the shabby storefronts with frosted glass as well as the corner monoliths with intricately carved cornices. But in pursuing my tally I miss my turnoff. I will be late again. I realize that getting to church on time will always be an impossibility for me.

At Hoover, pedestrians fill the sidewalks and spill out from buses. Latino men in heavy-soled brown boots, with blue workshirts tucked into darker blue trousers, gather at the corner. Teenagers – black, Latino, Asian – push off from the curb with schoolbooks tucked under one arm and precious boomboxes or mates cradled in the crook of the other. A group of middle-aged Latinas in white uniforms sit, not speaking, on bus stop benches within the shade of a building.

Moving back down 25th, I brake suddenly as a trio of older black women wander out from between parked cars. They fail to notice me till the driver behind me slams on his brakes, nearly sideswiping the row of automobiles. They stop in the middle of the street to smile and wave apologetically. Balancing heavy red and brown leather Bibles stuffed to bulging with sheets of loose papers, they are uniformed in suits, stockings, patent-leather pumps – Sunday morning attire on a Wednesday night. A security guard with a walkie-talkie pressed to his hip monitors the parking lot at the corner of Magnolia and Adams. He watches as they hurry toward the sidewalk, climb three steps, and disappear behind a pink iron gate.

A Toyota eases out of a space about half a block down and I squeeze in. Outside my car, I can already hear the voices. They overpower all the sounds on the block: the tambourines from Templo Pentecostes Rio Jordan, the Latino church across the way; traffic along Adams; the Spanish emanating from neighboring front porches; radio static slipping through kitchen screen doors. The security guard trails my steps until I reach the gate. And as the sun begins to disappear, the white neon letters that climb thy building's spire flicker on. At the top, above the lighted 'Ward AME', sits a single white cross.

Heading east, you can see the cross from Interstate 10. It rises above stocky palms and shaggy eucalyptus trees. It isn't an elaborate landmark, but it dutifully performs its function. The cross has marked the home of Ward African Methodist Episcopal Church since 1951, when pastor Frederick D. Jordan led his flock in their Sunday best on a march along Adams Boulevard from 1250 East 25th Street to their new church home here on West 25th.

Wednesday is Family Night. At 6:15 Bible study begins and the younger choirs rehearse. At 8 o'clock, kids file in for Bible class, while parents and other adults assemble for rehearsal. The basketball game, which has been going on downstairs in the Fellowship Hall, breaks up, and I hear an agitated young mother chastising her son for being late. She walks a brisk five steps ahead of him and turns: 'You won't be playing next week, y'understand me.' He offers a string of excuses; when they don't work, he attempts elaborate apologies. His tag-along junior posse stifles giggles with two hands.

Ward's Minister of Music, William Marshall – 'Brother Bill', as he's known around the church – sits with me under the skylight in the church sanctuary. Appointed six years ago, Marshall oversees Ward's five choirs as well as the church's on-site music school (named after African-American composer William Grant Still). Our conversation is interrupted by a steady stream of urgent questions and requests. Sunday's soloist is troubled over the piano's tuning. A choir member has an appointment conflict with the next rehearsal. A choir director laden with a stack of books and papers deals Marshall a worried look. To each he smiles and shrugs: 'We'll take care of it.'

Marshall's duties, he admits, extend beyond the music. He is choir confidant, he is late-night adviser to his choral directors, and lately he has been working hard to develop a strong silent connection – what he calls a necessary 'sixth sense' that links him to the new pastor, Howard S. Gloyd. Marshall admits that he doesn't have much free time. 'My calling was to be part of the support ministries', he explains to me. 'Because I'm a minister's son, I know the role. The importance. And that was where I wanted to be.'

The choir, and the music rising from it, rests firmly at the church's spiritual center. Known widely for its theology of survival and hope, the black church remains the heart of African-American culture. Its songs of worship and praise – the spiritual – are its purest expression. Much of the music was born of suffering or sadness, though classifying spirituals as merely 'sorrow songs' is limiting if not erroneous. The singing provides a release, the strength of the voices embodying vitality and commitment, fervor and endurance. Spirituals, as Langston Hughes wrote, are like roots of trees or rising shafts of mountains – they're 'something strong to put my hand on'.

The choir ignites the church, lifts the congregation to a new level of praise. 'It's a spiritual phenomenon', says Marshall. 'Sometimes during the service, I just feel a particular song or a particular hymn as if God has picked it. You have to be in tune with the spirit of worship.' You have to be in tune with your congregation as well, he points out. And Ward has changed over the years. When thirty-year-old Frank Reid became Ward's minister in 1980, he attracted a younger, more politically active congregation. Members still speak in awe of Reverend Reid, who left Ward last year for a church in Baltimore. He eased the church back into its traditional role – serving the community – by setting up or strengthening existing programs that ranged from an adoption service to substance abuse. In the process, Ward, with its camera-friendly facade and interiors, became a bit of a media darling. When you're inside, you can understand why. It feels safe, solid and unpretentious – warm wood, high beams, white walls, worn red carpet.

'People have been steeped in different musical diets', says Marshall. 'Different religious experiences. We try to present music to the younger crowd that Ward has attracted, the contemporary gospel style, but I would like to teach them how to appreciate the spiritual anthem as well. Not only here at Ward but within the AME church as a whole. We should go back to that traditional music. The anthem hymn.'

WARD AME

During rehearsal, Marshall, as he warned me, loses his quiet demeanor. He strikes the piano sharply, plumbing for blue notes and chords. I wander in late on the heels of a little girl in pigtails and take my seat on a metal folding chair along the rear wall of the classroom. People smile a silent greeting. Spread before me is the choir, out of its loft and out of its robes. The room, lit with bright, flickering fluorescents, is filled mostly with women draped in wool shawls, tightly curled, fresh-from-beauty-shop hair tucked beneath felt berets or cloth caps. The trio who crossed in front of my car sit with the rest of what look to be the choir veterans.

Marshall calls for altos, then tenors: 'Thank you, Jesus', they sing. In black slacks and a salmon-colored pullover, he stands over the piano with his back to them. He calls out: 'Altos. Problem with the altos. It's "All praise be to the King of Kings", and then you breathe. Come on, BREATHE.' They try. Shaking his head, he demands again: 'BREATHE.' The sopranos fill the soundscape with wispy hallelujahs. He stops them and asks for another. Putting his hands on the keys and beginning to play, he turns toward the choir and smiles over his shoulder: 'Let me see how much of this one you remember. He starts them out: the first few bars are sung loudly, boldly. They then suddenly blur into an unsure, slurred jumble. Everyone breaks up. Marshall simply shakes his head.

Ward's reputation throughout the community, despite a carefully guarded (by Marshall himself) low profile, is that it cradles a strong collection of voices. An organist from a United Methodist Church down the street stops in some Wednesdays to listen. A couple of musicians I know sometimes settle in the back rows for Sunday service. I've heard first-time experiences described as 'startling', yet even that seems an understatement for the elated voices that coax and rouse even the most discouraged spirits Sunday morning. There are sixty to eighty selections that make up the department's basic repertoire. They cater to the spirit, singing selections that mirror or drive home the events or topics that have transpired during the service. The choir directors – John Marshall, Rachel Griffin and Ron Burwell – tell me that sometimes, days later as they're wandering the aisles of SavOn or Boys Market, someone will tap them on the shoulder and say, 'Aren't you from Ward? Well, I *shouted* on Sunday.'

The AME order of worship calls for three specific choir selections. The first should offer praise and adoration; the second should be a song of discipleship, followed by a selection building on the morning message. Ron Burwell explains that in these general slots they try to present three different styles. 'We might do an anthem, which feeds a different group. Then we like to do something in a spiritual range or light gospel, which feeds another group, and then the high-praise gospel.'

'When people walk in the door', says Rachel Griffin, 'you've got to meet them where they are. Everybody that walks in is not ready for an intellectual sermon. Everybody is not ready for people dancing, either. Being able to feed everybody is important. It is our responsibility to make sure something is different when they walk out. Because if they are the same person they were when they came in, then you just kind of feel that you have not done your job.'

John Marshall, William's brother, agrees: 'She isn't talking about wrecking the church, having folks yelling and screaming. We're talking about being able to sing or direct or handle harmony to the best of our capabilities. And sometimes that's a tough row to hoe Sunday after Sunday.'

Choir affiliation undeniably grants prestige – a bit of high-gloss glamour at the local level. Despite my own faded church memories, I can still conjure images of the processional – choir and pastor working their way up the center aisle, the whispering satin trailing the scent of mothballs. At service's close, it is the young soloist to whom the flock is drawn. But for most community choirs singing for fame (let alone money) is not the goal. If it is, says William Marshall, the heart is in the wrong place and, he insists, choir life isn't as glamorous as people might think. The robes get hot in summer; call rehearsals can be frequent; and Sunday's congregations can present a sea of confrontational faces.

'You get a myriad of expressions', John Marshall admits. 'Some sad, some evil, some grumpy, a few happy – and some: "Okay, I'm here, now y'all do what y'all gonna do. Now you gonna move me? Move me!"'

A mediocre voice coupled with a 'good and willing' spirit is preferred over a strong voice and 'haughty' spirit. 'You don't know who you could be killing spiritually by rejecting them', says Ron. 'This is not a professional choir, and we've had voices that should not stand alone. But because of their dedication, because of their spirit and interest, they are an important part of our organization.' That's how William Marshall sees it. The key is to complement – not upset – the flow. 'Pastors and ministers of music have to develop a connection. That "sixth sense" I was telling you about. Pulpit and music, one moving, one supporting. I always watch the pastor. Follow him. We are there to support. And there are times that we should be silent and just sit back.'

After choir rehearsal, Marshall appears as energetic as he was when the two-hour practice began. 'Y'all don't have time to get tired', Marshall calls out toward the assembly, and I knew he was speaking of himself. When the rehearsal finishes, the members cluster around him, and I remember a wish Marshall expressed during our conversation: to be on the sidelines for just one Sunday service. 'I'd like to sit up in the balcony and watch it all happen from there. To look down and see where it's all going, just how everyone else sees it.'

To hear the voices rise.

PUT THE DEVIL IN HIS PLACE

There is a story that Ron Wright will sometimes share. About how his body was almost discarded in the weeds beneath a neglected freeway overpass. About how close he came to dying of a heroin O.D., to becoming an anonymous police statistic, backpage news copy for the morning papers.

His version of the story consists of fragmented recollections gathered from onlookers who, in this case, were lucid enough to take action. He was taken by the shoulders and shaken awake. He was showered with containers of ice water. But even after mouth-to-mouth resuscitation, his irises continued to drift heavenward, then disappeared.

Panicked, someone suggested loading him into the trunk of a car, driving him to another part of L.A. and dumping his body. Another suggestion – rather, the last resort – was to inject black coffee into his veins. 'It saved my life', Ron tells me as we cross the parking lot to Hunan Taste, a Chinese restaurant located in a refurbished House of Pies building in the Fairfax district. 'It's the truth', he adds. I don't doubt him. Ron Wright is small-framed but has a deep, intimidating voice edged with a rasp. After a while he relaxes, calls me 'Sis', unfastens a generous smile that softens an otherwise stern, even menacing face. But it isn't too difficult to visualize him as he used to be.

On Sundays Ron Wright, an associate pastor at Ward AME, slips into a black satin robe and sits at the right of the pulpit. His bellowing 'Amens' and 'Hallelujahs' punctuate the pastor's words and scattered calls from the congregation. During the first hymn of the morning his voice rides the crest. He walks a straight line back and forth between his chair and the pulpit. Eyes closed and hands raised, he allows the Spirit to fill and move him.

On Monday evenings, in sweats and sneakers, Ron Wright paces before a roomful of recovering addicts and alcoholics who sit in folding chairs or lean against the walls. The session begins with the welcoming of newcomers and attempts to put them at ease. There are no dues requested, no offerings or donations expected for the food – bananas, apples, crackers, cheese, cookies, sliced raw vegetables that have been laid out on the back tables. 'We didn't want people saying, "Yeah, I went over to that meeting at the Church and they're just passing the Plate." We wanted to make it different', Ron says. 'We wanted to make it more appealing. The price was already paid two thousand years ago, by Jesus on the cross.'

Freedom Now, Ward's own twelve-step substance-abuse program, is part of a network that hooks up churches around Southern California. Ron has watched it grow from a discouraging handful of curious but silent drop-bys to full meetings numbering forty to sixty enthusiastic attendees a week. 'There was some closed-mindedness at first', Ron explains, 'some archaic feelings about teaching substance-abuse in the church, some people who saw addicts as just sinners or losers. But the community is dying; we *had* to do something.'

Because many black churches today sit so conspicuously at the center of struggling or impoverished minority communities – communities beaten down by crime, unemployment, drug addiction, homelessness and gang warfare – they have often been accused of turning their backs on their flocks. Or, as Ron Wright puts it, 'If there's no outreach, the church is simply serving itself. We have to be doers of the Word, not just hearers.'

As rapidly as the neighborhood around Ward has changed – as single-family dwellings have become multifamily households, mostly Latino – so has the church itself. It has been difficult to maintain numbers, in terms of attendance as well as financially. It's been difficult to bring people back home. As inner-city neighborhoods crumble from the inside out, church leaders nationwide have been taken to task for wringing their congregations dry of funds and doing little or nothing to change the quality of their lives.

Victims of city violence are often included in the congregation's prayers, yet no matter how much the church may seem a protected oasis, the fear, especially as the evening hours approach, is sometimes palpable. Leaving Ward one evening after choir rehearsal, I hear my name shouted out in the darkness. 'Where are you parked?' One of the directors appears beneath a street lamp. 'Just down the street', I tell her. 'Now you be careful', she warns. 'I'll be watching you.'

At dinner Ron orders some old favorites – barbecued chicken, a plate of spicy shrimp, fried rice. The waiter recognizes the order. 'Are you a friend of Frank Reid?' he asks. 'When you speak with Frank, please tell him hello.' Rev. Reid has moved to Baltimore, to another church, but it was his persistence that got Freedom Now off the ground in Los Angeles. That, and his faith in Ron Wright. 'Oh, he *stayed* on me to organize it. It was my project. He kept saying that we needed to have some kind of meeting down at the church, but we didn't know what kind.'

Eighteen years of Ron Wright's life don't easily fall into place. There are too many loose or dead ends, thanks to alcohol and drugs. 'Things had gotten really bad. I shot up in jail when I could, drank "pruno", the wine they make in prison. I was messed up. When I got out in seventy-eight, I ran into a guy who told me about "the rock", how he had made $90,000 in two months selling crack.'

In February 1984, Ron, who had been arrested for possession and for the sale of cocaine, checked into the Beverly Glen Hospital, where he became involved in A.A. and C.A. programs. 'My wife had had it with me. She had burned the wedding license and flushed the ring down the toilet.' He tells me that it was while working through this 'program' that he first felt he was 'getting in touch with God'. In March 1984, his first Sunday out of the hospital, his wife took him to Ward AME. The sermon that Sunday, Ron recalls, was 'Put the Devil in His Place'. It sparked something in him. 'I thought my wife had told Reverend Reid all about me, told him I was coming. But she hadn't. I ended up joining right then.' Later, she told Ron, 'You know, I can see you in the pulpit.' Ron smiles. 'I said, "What are you talking about, woman? One step at a time." But it turned out to be prophecy.'

Life took a sharp turn and things became clearer, more manageable. Ron enrolled in courses at UCLA in drug and alcohol counseling, then took a job as a recovery counselor at the Castle East Drug Program. Then he decided to preach the Word himself.

Valerie Harris was part of Rev. Ron Wright's original flock. We are sitting in the living room of her new apartment in Sherman Oaks. There are boxes to be unpacked, and the walls are still mostly bare save for a few finger-paintings signed by her three-year-old daughter, Victoria. Valerie is wearing shorts and a 'Property of Jesus' T-shirt; Victoria brings her dolls and stuffed animals by, introducing them to me one by one.

Valerie entered the Main Street Wagon Alcohol Program (now known as the Castle Substance Abuse Program) a little over two years ago. It was there that she first met Ron Wright: 'He would come by and get us to go to church on Sunday. He had the church van and would leave early services to pick us up. On our way to Ward, he would tell us what the early service's message was. On the way back, he would test us. We would have to pay attention.'

An addict for seven years and clean for the past two-and-a-half, Valerie now shares her past with ease. 'I thought I'd be embarrassed at meetings', she says, 'but I wasn't. I know my story will help others.' A high school honor student, Valerie had earned a full scholarship to the University of Southern California, but a few years later she was stealing regularly from her family, was turning tricks, and eventually had to pawn her car to support her habit. She took her first pill in her senior year: 'White – I liked the up.' From pills to booze to weed to angel dust, Valerie's life took a predictable turn. 'It was all about low self-esteem', she says, shaking her head as she watches Victoria pitch plastic flies into a battery-operated rotating frog's head.

Living from high to high, Valerie wandered in and out of receptionist jobs, but would lose them almost as quickly as she landed them. Spotty attendance and a 'bad attitude' would generally send her back to running a red pen through the want ads. 'I would put rock in my cigarette, put the boss's calls on hold, lock the door, and smoke.' After a series of personal and professional catastrophes, she finally considered seeking help. 'For me, Ward provides the spiritual fellowship that the others – A.A., C.A., and the rest – don't', Valerie tells me. 'I'd never been particularly religious, but I find that I need that now. And Ward addresses my needs.'

'No matter what happens, it's important not to forget where you came from. People have a tendency not to want to remember the bad things. They think, "Oh, I wasn't that bad." But sharing isn't talking about the time you got high with Richard Pryor. It's talking about recovery. The message. The bottom. Your climb back up.'

At tonight's meeting, two 'birthday' cakes are presented to members who've succeeded in remaining sober for another year. After the evening speakers have finished, Ron asks us to stand and form a circle. We join hands as people in the circle call out names for us to pray for: addicted mates, mothers, children. They pray for strength, and for Ron Wright, and for programs like this one.

We close our eyes. Ron begins the prayer in a soft voice that steadily builds in volume and intensity. Random shouts burst out from around the room. There are upraised palms, bowed heads, faces tipped up toward the ceiling, trembling bodies, stomping feet. There is an intensity to these prayers that I haven't heard before. It's not like the prayers Sundays in the sanctuary, nor is it like the ones that close the lay ministry meetings Saturday afternoon. Not even close. These are the private testimonies of troubled souls. Here are people who have stumbled through the darkness in the valley of the shadow, and now they slowly out. They are simply asking to remain among the living.

KNEE BOWED AND BODY BENT

The Sanctified Church is a protest against the highbrow tendency in Negro Protestant congregations as the Negroes gain more education and wealth. It is understandable that they take on the religious attitudes of the white man, which are as a rule so staid and restrained that it seems unbearably dull.
Zora Neale Hurston, from The Sanctified Church

Shouting is not enough. There is a difference [between] shouting and Praising God. It becomes necessary to remember the words of the Scriptures: 'Be still . . . in the silence, God came . . .' (Galatians 6:1–10). We need a balanced religion. Religion is not Either/or; it is Both/and.
from the Ward AME Annual Report, 1983–1984

As a child I wasn't allowed to clap my hands in church. Foot-tapping was discouraged as well – whether in time to the music or in response to a well-rendered solo. A stern stare would force my hands to flutter to my sides; a gentle palm placed on my knee would command my foot to rest. Church was not a place for 'carrying on'.

In the church of my childhood, there were no soloists whose round, resonant voices would (or probably even *could*, for that matter) 'wreck' a church. No one would 'fall out' or dance out into the aisles. No one was 'seized by the Spirit', and no one, while I was present anyway, ever spoke in tongues.

Black worshipers may have leapt and shouted from the pages of James Baldwin, yet such scenes were as alien to me as they were to my curious classmates in grade school (and, later, in college), who occasionally asked to attend my church, as if Sunday morning services in a black church would provide the shocks and novelty found at a circus sideshow.

But our United Methodist congregation was sedate, if not quite cool. Good sisters smiled and nodded toward latecomers, who quietly filled the rear and side pews. Pockets of polite conversation formed within the foyer in the last moments before the processional. On special Sundays, the frailest of the old ladies would ease down from the choir loft, steady herself at the pulpit, tap the head of the microphone and, in a reedy, sorrowful voice, sing 'Onward, Christian Soldiers'. I never doubted that love and joy filled that small sanctuary on Sunday mornings. But the prayers came in whispers, in silence, with heads bowed in decorous stillness.

Within the walls of Ward AME I find a different world. 'We need a Holy Ghost revival', shouts Pastor Howard Gloyd. It's a cloudy Sunday morning, 8 a.m. He stands before his congregation in a flowing blue moire robe accented with thick black braiding. His hair is smoothed back from his face to show off the soft salt-and-pepper waves. With his words, open palms shoot up like summer wildweed. Shouts of 'Praise Jesus!' rise from the four corners of the sanctuary. Minister of Music William Marshall runs the organ keys, notes screeching out through the pipes above the altar. He watches Pastor Gloyd's every step, his slightest gesture. 'That's what you call *praise!*' the pastor smiles. 'Praise is *good* for you!'

The applause intensifies as the organ emits a deep, heavy pulse. The wood floors rumble and quake under the weight of scores of stomping feet. Pastor Gloyd smiles out at his assembly, at the Ward 'family'. 'God', he assures us all, '*is* in charge'. The church is 'lifted'. The band – drum kit, saxophone, electric bass – launches into a jazz-tinged vamp. Up in the loft, a few choir members now stand sweating, smiling out at the faces that fill the floor and balcony. Some have unzipped the fronts of their ivory robes to cool down as the heat rises; others fan themselves with the blue mimeographed announcements. One member, tears dampening her cheeks and neck, paces back and forth along the loft's side aisle. 'Love you, Jesus!' she calls out, hands upraised. 'Love *you*, Lord.' I sit watching this church in motion – I'm amazed, and smiling, yet my hands remain neatly folded in my lap.

Richard Allen, a former slave who earned the money to purchase his freedom by hiring out as a blacksmith, became a minister in 1780. He was soon invited to preach in St George Methodist Episcopal Church, a prominent white church in Philadelphia. Allen, now a local novelty, attracted large groups of visiting blacks from adjacent burgs; they were assigned special seating along the rear and side walls. One Sunday in 1787, as St George's began to fill up, the blacks seated downstairs were forced from their knees during prayer and ordered to relocate to an upstairs gallery to make room for late-arriving white worshipers. 'We all went out of the church in a body', he later recorded in his memoirs, 'and they were no more plagued by us. . . .'

Along with fellow clergyman Absalom Jones, Richard Allen formed the Free African Society, which gave birth in 1816 to the African Methodist Episcopal Church, setting the framework for a new tradition. The Methodist Church, Allen believed, was the form of worship that best suited African-Americans' spiritual needs. In the teachings of Methodism's founder, John Wesley, exalting the Holy Spirit took precedence over all other observances. Modeled after the white fellowship from which it broke, the AME Church spiritually strengthened black Americans by stressing the importance of self-reliance. The founding fathers preached not only about racism and suffering, but about the dignity and pride attained through survival in an oppressive world.

In the first decade of the nineteenth century, black communities used the AME Church as a model for their own. Denominations quickly divided, then subdivided as blacks sought to shape and direct their own futures. Those who were drawn to the Presbyterian or Episcopal churches were more inclined to quiet worship and to intellectual sermonizing than were those who were first attracted to the Methodist (and Baptist) churches, which had comparatively 'freer' pulpits.

Ward AME has gained prominence in recent years as one of the churches most responsible for the rebirth of African Methodism across the country, building one of the largest, most enthusiastic black congregations in Los Angeles. Over the last few weeks, I've been meeting people who speak reverently of their 'callings', of 'sacrifice', of giving of their time and talent for God.

Put simply, worship at Ward is a celebration of the gift of life. Yet here, unlike at the church services of my youth, it is joy unbridled, undirected and unrehearsed, spontaneous enthusiasm set ablaze. Services touch, but don't dwell on, life's atrocities; or, rather, they praise what comes to pass and what's yet to come. Within the AME Church, the order of worship is flexible, leaving the local minister room to amend or experiment, to etch his or her signature on the weekly proceedings. At the same time, AME unity ensures that church members will feel at home in any AME church, anywhere in the world.

'You just don't find many churches like Ward', says Pastor Gloyd. 'Ward is different. You could walk into some other AME church and if somebody said "Amen", everybody would turn around and look at them strangely. It's not a denominational thing. There are bishops in the church who would be *extremely* critical of Ward's style, but they can't appeal to any AME *norm*. People here are praising the Lord; they're gracious and thankful, and they express it. A handful of Ward members going to another church with that same exuberance would probably disturb somebody. But I think it's a sin to come to church and not embrace or speak to somebody. But a lot of churches don't do it. Some people want to be left alone, they want to come from the humdrum and hassle of daily life; they just want to sit somewhere and be quiet. They've got a right to that, but I just think it's ridiculous if you come to church and don't share your joy.'

Ward is different – in style, in spirit, in approach. It has broadened into a pivotal institution in the movement toward black socioeconomic power. 'Plan the work, then work the plan' – the church's motto – is a constant reminder to members that there is no time to sit complacently. There is a church to build, a community to embrace, families to house, children to nurture, the gospel of life to teach.

This Sunday, Ward members reach across the aisles, raise clasped hands toward the ceilings, linking the sanctuary end to end. They hug their neighbors, look into their eyes, and tell them that they love them. I've yet to work my way up to tapping my foot in time with the bass line, but I know that this service isn't just about shouting – or as the good sisters from my church at home would say, about 'carrying on'. It's about a church that works. Hard. Or, as one Ward sister lets me know as we start down the front steps into the late morning sun just breaking through the clouds, 'It's about turning your religion into reality. That's what Pastor Gloyd said last week, and girl – dontcha know – I *love* it.'

LEARNING TO FALL AND GET
BACK UP AGAIN

Ron Johnson sits out a minute. He squats next to the folding chair that only moments ago two little boys placed for me at the gym floor's foul line. He isn't ready to answer too many questions. Instead, he matter-of-factly pelts hard stats my way.

'By the year 2000, seventy percent of black men in America won't have jobs and never will. They now make up forty percent of the population in prison. Forty-four percent of black America can't read; another seventeen percent is semi-literate. A black boy between the ages of eighteen and twenty-one has a one-in-five chance of being arrested; between twenty and twenty-four, it's one in three. If you're a black man, the number one killer is homicide. The most dangerous period of a black man's life is between fourteen and twenty-five, when he has a one-in-twenty chance of being shot. So I'd say we're in bad shape, wouldn't you?' Before I can find words, or record all of this on the page, he's across the gym on bare feet to greet some of his students. I write '70 percent' in broad blue characters in the top margin of my pad. After a moment, I go back and underline them three times.

From where I sit inside Ward AME's Fellowship Hall, I can see and hear the weekend progress outside on 25th Street without us. Low-riding sedans glide by, snatches of thudding bass and cocksure boasts slur past the open doors. Just before leaving her post as church secretary, Maurine Anderson had been doing extra duty, playing an odd mix of college adviser/travel agent at my request. She carefully selected my activities: 'This is something you might want to check out', or 'This might give you a better feel for . . .' Tonight it's a jujitsu class, part of one of the outreach programs offered through Ward's Family Life and Education Center. I watch boys and girls dressed in white *gis* – four white belts, one yellow – warming up with jumping jacks, situps, pushups on a blue mat beneath a basketball net.

Johnson bearhugs a latecomer, cups the back of his head within the palm of his right hand: 'Hey man, how ya feel?' With one arm, he almost lifts him off the ground. Ten smaller boys with close-cropped hair sit cross-legged at the sidelines watching the older ones practice rolls and falls on the mats. They learn to fall, one mother tells me, so that they can learn to get back up and fight.

Behind an observation like this one, there is the hidden, deeper story that has grown dispiriting. Not the television or print news, which on any given day, week or month choose either to ignore, misinterpret or exaggerate the events transpiring in any predominantly black neighborhood around the city (neighborhoods that mysteriously, no matter the location, fall conveniently under the far-reaching, ever-broadening circumscription: 'South Central L.A.'). It's the news that Ron Johnson brought in with him this evening that's got everyone on edge. Two young men Ron had just met – one fourteen, the other sixteen – were shot this week; it's made him and those with whom he's shared it jittery. Ron explains that within these neighborhoods and within these four walls as well, his students learn that it will be brutal from womb to tomb: 'They *have* to learn. They will have to learn early: black *boys* die.'

He gets them Friday nights and in the dead-heat of a long Saturday afternoon; critical hours, generally open and unstructured. He thieves away their prime hanging out time. He works them till they sweat and whine, till they cop attitudes or drop from fatigue. In their few hours together he tries to teach them that it is their minds that control their bodies, that survival means fighting. At the end of each session, if he is at all successful, they should desire only sleep.

Saturday classes are followed by a series of what Ron calls 'respect workshops'. They cover basics – manners, study habits and test-taking skills. Ron holds them in the church gym. Later on down the line each pupil is expected to design and deliver his or her own workshop. At the end of each meeting, before they're dismissed, they form a unity circle and pray.

Five years ago, Ron Johnson, who has worked as a teen counselor all of his professional life, started out with twenty-eight students; a few weeks later he was left with only half a dozen. These days, there are about forty boys and girls – a combination of neighborhood and church kids who wander in and out on weekends. The classes attract the bored and curious as well as the serious and the committed. For some, it is what introduces them to the church. For others, it introduces them to God.

'You burn 'em up, get the ones out who are there because *sensei* [teacher] is cute, or because "My mother made me come". They're looking for somebody to keep a foot in their behind and make 'em do right.' There are certain kids whom Johnson refuses to let go of, no matter what. The ones who stay home

Friday night just to see if he may notice. He'll play the game; he'll take it one step further and show up at their door with a stern-faced reprimand. 'A lot of them believe that if a person doesn't act angry toward them that he or she doesn't care. So at least I show a response. If you hug them and talk to them and show them a full range of emotions it shows them something. Sometimes you feel like cussin' them out because they piss you off, so you cuss 'em out. But better them take it home than you.'

By age thirteen the eye is errant, and Johnson admits that, even with all his years of work with kids, he still finds it difficult to keep them occupied or interested, especially if they've had a taste of sex, drugs, alcohol or 'kickin' it' on the corner. 'They come down here and there are girls in this class who give them an erection and they're distracted, but at least they're in an environment where they can learn to control that. And to think with the big head, not with the little one.'

'We're in bad shape, and people are running around trying to work with high school students, and high school students are damn near in a coma. This sounds real cold, but it's true. If you have limited resources, you put the money where the best bet is. The best bet isn't on high school students – it's on elementary and junior high kids.'

Weeks later, the bold, blue '70 percent' still looms large. It's the one I find myself throwing out in conversation, then gauging the reaction. When I ask Devron Lewis about it, he takes some time to answer. 'I think it's negative, though realistic. But if each and every black man sets a goal for himself, they can have a hand in changing the statistics. Just because you're in that category doesn't mean you can't move out of it. You can change it. You at least have to try.' He's a polite, quick-witted eighteen-year-old, with thoughts and opinions that trip nostalgic, yet don't play as blindly optimistic. He knows, in many ways, that he's been lucky in bucking the numbers stacked against him. Though Devron lives five minutes from Ward, his mother had him bused away to Pacific Palisades through the school district's Permit With Transportation Program.

This fall Devron headed to Prairie View A&M in Texas to study fire science and pyrotechnics: 'I'll learn how to set them, then I'll learn how to put them out.' He's just graduated from Palisades High, where he was a member of the Afro-American Awareness Club and played three years as defensive end for the

Palisades Dolphins, an experience that he says educated him about life. 'It teaches you that a lot of big, dumb, muscle-bound guys *have* to become a family on grass. Playing defense takes a lot of courage, determination and a lot of heart, like life does.'

It is a résumé by which Ron Johnson would be heartened.

At Pali, Devron didn't have to sweat the campus crack wars; he didn't cower because he chose not to flash colors and signify. But there above Malibu's palm-lined strand, the consumption of drugs (mostly weed and coke) and alcohol by Palisades students, he says, is high. It's passed around at parties; you can buy or borrow in the halls between periods or at lunch. Pali's problems have been the topic of local radio talk shows and network evening news magazines. Devron says it takes self-discipline, lots of it, to ignore it. To get home in one piece. Does it make him feel out of place? Sometimes, yes. A little awkward, too, but he's gained, he says, a lot of his strength through Ward.

When he talks about church, the joking stops. His voice lowers, his pace slows. 'You shouldn't make a habit of going to church if you don't get a thing out of it. To be a Christian, to be a good, devoted Christian, is where the maturity comes in.' Inspiration should call a young man or woman to church, is how Devron explains it to me.

Devron became a member six years ago. 'Before I knew it, I was walking up to the altar to join. It really happens, just like that.' Trying to explain makes him stop dead to search for the concrete. He instead settles for similes: 'It's like a ride at Magic Mountain or probably what people experience with drugs – a euphoric feeling that moves up and down the spinal cord. It's a rush. I've experienced it, but not to the degree I've seen at church. People filled with the Holy Ghost screaming and jumping up and down, just inches from hitting people.'

Devron isn't so much an anomaly as an anachronism. Church on Sunday, for many black children, used to be an unconditional duty. You took time out to thank God for what little you had. But as 'the distractions', as Ron Johnson terms them, multiply and life becomes more complex, sitting on Sunday seems pointless or irrelevant when you feel that there is little or no sign of a God traversing your world.

For Devron, though, who estimates that he probably misses only one Sunday a year, church is fundamental. As a member of the Youth Usher Board and the Young People's Department, he gives his time as well. He finds his strength in 'the preaching of God's Word, the singing of His Gospel, the teaching of His Book.' He adds, 'For me, when something goes wrong, if I'm alone a long way from home, there's God to push me on. So I'm not afraid. He has gotten me through a lot.'

Devron says that Palisades tested him: 'A lot of my classmates have a system of values that is almost totally different from mine.' He says, watching what happens around the city – death, the gangs, the drugs, homelessness – that he's often amazed by what some of his schoolmates see as problems. 'If the typical Pali child doesn't get the car, the sharkskin suit, that he/she asked for, well then, they run away from home until they do. With me, things like that I know are out of my mother's financial grasp. It's something that doesn't occur to me to ask for.'

Passing on that sort of strength, Ron Johnson says, is not like shuffling paper eight hours a day. 'They have it. They know they have it. They have to prove it. And along with their relationship with God they'll get through. . . .' He points out at the bodies skidding across the mats before us. 'You see, when they put them down, how they come back? How they fight harder?'

I watch faces set in determination. Though the breaths are hard and the footing somewhat unsure, there is a frown that denotes not frustration but confidence. 'Come on, reach back for the heart. . . .' Johnson coaxes from the sidelines. 'See, God allows them to give you back little pieces. When you meet boys who don't smile and all of a sudden they're smiling every day, feels good. The guys that used to beat on your students, now defend your students. You feel *good*. I can sit down sometimes and watch my students teach other students things I've taught them, and they sometimes teach them even better than I taught them. See, you don't lose and you die happy.'

From the sidelines, I watch the evening's final battle progress: graceful legs and arms silently cut the air; the quick jabs exchanged are swift, sharp jolts. When the opponents pull apart, brush themselves off and rise slowly to their feet, I expect to see one last furious blow.

Instead I watch with a smile as two boys slowly bow, then embrace.

DO I DO MY BEST IN SERVICE

'We've had one of the worst churches, and we have had one of the best. I'm telling you the good as well as the bad, because to me the truth is the light.' Josephine Griffin pushes through boxes of loose photos and crumbling newspaper clippings from the *L.A. Sentinel* and the long-defunct *California Eagle*. She is trying to find 'the best one'. Nestled near the white borders of black-and-white snapshots or standing in the background of newspaper society photos, she is forever captured in stylish hat and patent-leather (though sensible) shoes. It isn't what you've done, though, she tells me, it's what you're doing.

'When the church moved to 25th and Magnolia the neighborhood was mostly white, then black, 'cause the white folks moved out when they saw us coming. Now it's mostly Hispanic. I think there's a lot more that we could do in the community. I take it that people are too busy to see it, though. The fact that it's run-down as it could be is because they allowed it to get that way. See, a lot of our members used to belong to the neighborhood. They don't now so they don't care anymore. They all moved out, and so it's just gone down. There is lots of crime – car thefts in the parking lot. One of the sisters had her hubcaps stolen Sunday last. Those pretty wheels – took them off while she was sitting in the church. It's a terrible neighborhood. It's changed to the point that you want to put an electric fence around the church, and you *can't* do that.'

Mrs Griffin, or 'Mama Jo' as she's known around the neighborhood, lives with her husband, John, in a small wooden bungalow with red-brick trim a few blocks east of Crenshaw Boulevard. When I arrive, John Griffin is working in the yard. Inside, the air smells of old perfume and flowers. Small paintings of Jesus stand on a mantel and on low, carved dark-wood end tables; paper roses rest in porcelain vases near a window. Mrs Griffin sits at the edge of the sofa cushion, back straight, hands folded tightly in her lap. As she speaks, she occasionally adjusts the hairpins hidden in a careful silver chignon.

Though you wouldn't guess it by the speed and enthusiasm with which she speaks, Mrs Griffin doesn't have as much energy as she used to – a piece of information she imparts reluctantly. These days her involvement is restricted to local missionary work and her September Club (an activity group comprising church members born in September). And, of course, there is always Sunday service. An active Ward AME member for close to sixty years, she says that if people in the church need help, they know whom to call.

'When I got to Los Angeles, I wanted to work in moving pictures, but they said I was too light to do that. They wanted me to play a maid or some sort of character like that. My mother used to invite the MGM people over and make them oyster suppers, but it didn't help. I went back to work at the drugstore until I married.

'I met my husband in church. We're Ward's oldest couple. My grandmother sent me over to ask his mother if she was interested in joining some of the church clubs. John was sitting there next to her. One Sunday the two of us went over to [the] first church [the old building on Eighth and Towne] for Sunday school. The reverend was reading the visitor cards, and he got to John's and slipped: "Mr and Mrs John Griffin", he said. Predicted right. The two of us just got real close. I was really sweet on him. He was real cute.

'John's been devoted from the time we started going out. He works as the finance man on Sunday mornings after 8 a.m. service. At 8 a.m. he plays his sax in the church band. He plays tenor, alto sax and baritone clarinet, but he won't play anything but the alto in church. It is his sacred horn. Some weekends he used to come in 2, 3 in the morning from jazz shows, get up and go to church, then go to the post office to work.

'I've worked in all phases of the church, and if anybody asks, they get help from me, because that's the way I was brought up. That's all I know. And, see, that's what's wrong with Ward today. So many of the new people that have come along since my time are just elevating themselves, getting the best thing that they can get out of the church. I never charged for anything I ever did — from cooking to conferences on down. My husband and I believe in that. So many of our young people, so many of our older people as well, are trying to see what they can get out of the church, instead of putting all they can into the church. I don't understand that kind of Christianity, because really the church does so much towards making you what you are in life.

'If they come up and sing a solo they want you to pay them; if they come up and play an instrument they want you to pay them. I lose all sense of reasoning when I hear about that. We used to run and get our friends to come and sing for us, and they didn't charge us, but now everybody feels that the church is a place to go begging. I won't say it like that. They're not really begging, but they want pay for whatever they do.

'Seems to me that once in a while there ought to be something in your life you want to give to your church. Your talent, your time, your money is what the Bible means when it says give your tithes, it does not all mean money. Because God gave you the talent. Instead of doing to the glory of God, they are doing to the glory of "myself". Want everybody to see them. Get active if there are big shots around. They want to be right up front. I try to duck all of that, because y'know, after all, God sees me and that's all that matters. Kills me when I see people trying to be greater in the eyes of the minister, and minister can take them *nowhere*. The minister can't take them to Glory.

'People seem to forget that they are not serving man, they are serving God. We've had three splits because of pastors or decisions made by bishops. Maybe it's because I'm a pastor's daughter that I speak boldly with and about pastors. But I remember in the forties, after we worked hard to save money for a new church, Reverend Price used the money to buy a house. He said he deserved it. I loved that man, but that really hurt me. We deserved houses, too. We worked hard for that money. When he left he took half the congregation with him, took my young friends.

'They brought in Reverend Harry White afterwards – that was 1948. He just didn't know what to do. When you're down at the bottom of the sack, you've got to punch your way out. We worked double, triple, quadruple time. We started putting together fundraiser dinners – fish dinners, chicken, and spaghetti socials. We had to raise money. The congregation grew. Then the bishop decided to move the church to where we are now. It really tore us apart. I remember asking my grandmother: "Where are you goin', mama?" "It's too far for me to get there", she said. "I want to stay at my little church. I can walk to it. Don't have to put anyone else out to get me there." A lot of people felt the same way. You don't split up a church like that. It was *wrong* to split people up who have gone through so much together. I will never understand that.

'The same with moving ministers to churches in the same city. You don't do that. When the bishop decided that Reverend Ford had overstayed his time and moved him to Price Chapel in 1959, that of course split the church again. With half of the people leaving with him, it left it kind of hard for us to make the big notes and things. We came to Sunday worship one morning and the doors were locked. We were going to be foreclosed on. We were in a whole mess of trouble. One choir member was so angry, she tried to hit Reverend Thornhill with her purse.

'I'd say our greatest growth was under Reverend Ford. We have never seen anything like that. He was a young man and really he brought the young people in such a way. He brought young people in from everywhere and a lot of them stayed. Every Sunday we had chairs down the aisle, the balcony, the whole building was full. We were before the public all the time. If we were sneezing loud at Ward, people knew about it.

'Reverend Reid was a real power in the eighties for bringing your people back into the church as well. Second largest following after Ford. But I think sometimes he kicked the old people aside. There was nothing for the old people to do, and he didn't have anything to do with old people, their clubs, their functions. He went where he wanted to go. I just don't think that he understood old age, that God *blesses* you with old age. I don't think he fully understood that we were the bridge that brought him here.

'Church just isn't as important as it used to be to people. It would be beautiful if it was, but it is not. People are so busy with other things. Everything is replacing it. Dope, drinking, partying, all that sort of thing is taking over where the church used to be. You can hardly get young people away from television, away from the shows, the discos, y'know? Church used to be our society. The meeting place. It used to be in all phases of our life. We didn't have all these other things.

'We've gone away from the real church. The real purpose of the church. There is a tomorrow and yesterday that we have to think about. But I'm happy to say that it seems that some of us are coming back. We are getting more and more young people in Ward, and I imagine the other churches are doing the same. So I hope that this is a turnaround.

'I'm committed to duty wherever I find it. You see a need, you take care of it. I didn't go to college, so I did the best I could with what I have. I've lived to be three-score ten – past seventy. I've had a happy life, and as my husband says, we're living the icing on the cake.'

AT THE PULPIT

The Pastor is running a little late this morning. Maurine Anderson, the church secretary, apologizes. As I take a seat on one of the steel-legged office chairs grouped against the wall, she asks me if I would like coffee, tea, or maybe just some ice water, before hurrying back to her impatient telephones.

This Tuesday morning is so grim and overcast that it is easy to miscalculate the hour. The sidewalks along 25th and Magnolia are the stillest I've seen them; the silence in the church courtyard and halls is broken only by one voice, Mr Shaw, a church maintenance man, who removes his cap before calling out: 'Good morning, young lady.'

The hallways burst suddenly with heavy, booming voices – preacher voices – deep, resonant, melodic. Their laughter echoes through the halls. I catch glimpses of suits and ties, shiny black shoes marching quickly across waxed floors. At the end of the hallway, I hear a piano and soon those same heavy voices soften into song. After the hymn, they whisper in prayer. Moments later, Ward AME's Rev. Howard Gloyd, nattily dressed in a beige cashmere sweater, silk hose, soft leather loafers, rushes into the office, smiling sheepishly. He quickly greets me, then turns to Maurine: 'Are they still having devotion?' Without waiting for an answer, he asks me to follow. I'm ushered into a class-room where men and women are relaxing into chairs. Ministers without robes or ceremonial sashes are dressed in polyester flares or cotton leisure wear; others are in silk business suits or somber black jackets and turtlenecks.

These are the voices who every Sunday morning lead Los Angeles's African Methodist Episcopal congregations: First AME, Walker Temple, Grant, Bethel, Price Chapel. They gather once a week to discuss the issues affecting their community, to re-examine the traditional worship service, read from the *AME Church Discipline*, run checks on 'pulpit ethics'. First AME's Rev. Cecil Murray, one of L.A.'s most prominent and powerful ministers, addresses practical strategies to end city gang violence. 'If African Methodism doesn't take the lead [in action], the Muslims will', he warns. Someone else announces that a blue-ribbon task force of small businesses struggling in South Los Angeles is looking to the ecumenical community for help; another mentions a career-counseling and job fair at the renovated Baldwin Hills-Crenshaw Plaza; still another, a church-sponsored community health fair. One pastor encourages the others to monitor their health, to take days off for rest: 'Pastors get so busy working for the Lord and the church that they don't take time to get a checkup themselves.' He settles into a story (with shades of a testimonial) about a friend whose body was 'eaten up with cancer' long before anyone could do anything, the story's end marked by a somber round of 'Amens'.

When the ministers head outside toward their cars, toward the week ahead, Pastor Gloyd shakes hands and claps backs; he stands at the door of his office checking his watch. ('Got your keys? Got your wallet?' Maurine asks.) 'Are you finished with me, for today?' He turns in my direction. Putting on a Fila baseball cap, he pulls it forward until it completely shades his eyes. He is on his way – running.

There are some Sundays when it seems that Pastor Gloyd really 'gets on' his parishioners, when he must pull, or better, wrench responses from them: 'Praise got to shake you up a little bit, can't sit there dignified . . . you have to sweat and shout.' He comments on the suits and ties and the stern faces hovering above them – unmoved and unmoving. His style is aggressive; today he is prodding agitator. Opening the doors of the church for membership, the acceptance of Christ, he asks that the 'Ward Family' be seated. Those left timidly standing he sometimes coaxes to the altar. ('Hope you visit more often, like every Sunday.')

Pastor Gloyd shouts, he sprints, he sweats, some Sundays he even sings, in a sonorous scatting baritone that skims just beneath the other sanctuary voices. The words tumbling from his mouth seem to propel his body. Immersed in the message, he is swept up by the delivery. As the church heats up, the easy saunter becomes a complex combination of steps that look more like carefully choreographed moves.

Writers have for decades tried to 'fix something of him', of the 'old-time Negro preacher', as poet James Weldon Johnson put it. Johnson traveled throughout the United States in the twenties, listening and taking copious notes on black folk sermons for a book of poems he titled *God's Trombones*. Many ministers were good orators, he concluded, but many more were accomplished actors. The key hinged on delivery; the rhythmic progression of words and the liveliness with which they were presented: 'I have witnessed congregations moved to ecstasy by the rhythmic intonation of sheer incoherencies . . . [the pastor] was master of all modes of eloquence. He often possessed a voice that was a marvelous instrument, a voice he could modulate from a sepulchral whisper to crashing thunderclap.'

Pastor Gloyd sees his preaching style as more evangelical preacher than pastor – not just actor but grand showman. 'I'm loud, I'm noisy. You've got some ministers in the AME who are *high, high* on the liturgical bit, go for all the pageantry, the robes . . . and if somebody said "Amen" during one of their

WARD AME: PREPARING FOR OFFERING

services, everybody would look at them strange. I don't know what I would do if I had to whisper, "Yass, and the Lord said . . ." If I was in one of those churches, I guess I *would*. I would have to feed that flock and', he adds, smiling, 'I would imagine that I'd have to do all of my rejoicing and shouting at night, at home. But it's got to come out. If it doesn't come out you could have a stroke.'

If you listen to your people all week, he says, you know pretty much what to talk about on Sunday morning. African-American pulpits have historically been concerned with life experience, relating the Scriptures to the day-to-day. Pastor Gloyd uses his own life to shade and shape his sermons, to give his flock a sense of direction, of hope. Sometimes, he admits, he doesn't know what he's going to say until the message meets air. 'It encourages us to do a lot of reading and to be sensitive to the congregation and their needs. Listen to them – they talk to you.'

When Pastor Gloyd finally slows down, it's weeks later. Up until now, I've been having my own problems trying to 'fix something of him' on the page. He settles behind his desk with his pipe and a cup of hot tea. 'This is unusual, what we're doing now, pausing this long', he tells me. As I pull out my pen I notice a large, formal color portrait of a shaggier, darker-haired Rev. Dr Howard Gloyd standing behind a seated Rev. Jesse Jackson, both sleek in dark suits and wide striped ties. Jackson looks dead-center into the lens, smiling; Gloyd somber, eyes focused on a point just above.

He tells me that there is no such thing as a typical week. 'Already we have a case where a mother's nineteen-year-old son got killed, the mother is at her wits' end, all kinds of problems. Yesterday a drunk came in and was laying on the floor right down here', he points to a spot behind my chair. 'Day before that another drunk laid down right in the courtyard. I mean, just problems. Teenagers don't know which way is up. About eight different young couples trying to get a divorce – they don't know why. You've got problems ranging from the insurmountable to the very minor – what do you do with a five-year-old who tells a lie? On the other hand, you've got people who are traumatized by retirement. You've got every organization in town raising money for this or that, wanting to talk with you. And in an attempt to stabilize our community you've got to champion every cause that makes sense to you. People are always looking to you for the right answer or at least for a reasonable one, and sometimes you don't have that for your own day-to-day life. My *God*, it forces one to stay in prayer.'

It's been just about a year since Howard Gloyd took over Ward's pulpit. He had only one Sunday to tell his flock in San Francisco that he was moving on. The next Sunday he was standing before the congregation at Ward. 'So what do you say? You don't have a kit where you have the sermons for the first time you appear at a church. You don't have a kit that tells you how to go into a congregation whose former pastor was *extremely* popular and they loved him dearly and all of a sudden he's gone and here *you* come. I mean, how do you *follow* Frank Madison Reid III? Absolutely a tremendous preacher, teacher, thirty-nine years old when he left here.'

Rev. Frank Reid has been a shadow hard to shake. The son and grandson of bishops, he attracted such big-name visitors as Jesse Jackson, Desmond Tutu, Louis Farrakhan. His 10:45 a.m. services eased well into the afternoon. In his eight-year stay, Rev. Reid built one of the strongest and most zealous black congregations in Los Angeles. And even though it has been a year since he left, his name echoes persistently.

'I've never followed a Frank Madison Reid III, and that's a good experience. An opportunity for a person who's been in this for thirty-seven years to grow some. I've known Frank all his life. His dad was a good friend of mine. Frank followed a giant, too, when he followed John Bryant in Baltimore. He had to face the same thing; the man who replaced me in San Francisco, the same thing. You just don't walk in each other's shoes – what you do is walk in your own.'

Nonetheless, sharp comparisons came quick, and people watched closely as Gloyd took Ward's pulpit. He says his approach was careful; it was – quite simply – different. In San Francisco, Pastor Gloyd chose to 'externalize' his activities. Involving himself in community affairs, he was a civil-service commissioner for six years, and ran Jesse Jackson's Northern California campaign in 1984 and again in 1988. He made the dailies, appeared often on TV news.

Since arriving in Los Angeles, he's kept a low profile. 'My particular role in terms of visibility might confuse some people, but I have to first of all dig in here. At Ward there is a specific need. This congregation needs a church and we're going to build it. That's creating a problem with me in terms of extending myself too far beyond this task.' The construction required is extensive. The education building and church offices must be razed and rebuilt to meet earthquake safety standards. The 700-seat sanctuary will be refurbished and expanded to include space for 300 more members and guests. The estimated cost: between $6 million and $10 million.

The community makes its own demands. Gloyd counts the issues on his fingers: drugs, housing, hunger, teenage pregnancy. 'They're all here and they all need to be addressed, and we are addressing them through the various ministries of the church. I know the problems. I mean, my God, in San Francisco I might have given forty hours a week to my church, but I gave eighty to my community. Now it's ten years later and that means that I'm ten years older, and we've got a twenty-year-late job to do. Doesn't suggest that I have a lack of energy, just means that my style is quite different. I made an effort not to get into the way of the movement at Ward, not to say: "Stop now until I get in the front." I just don't have any *need* to be in front of a TV camera. What I want to do is push somebody else out there in front, and do what I came here to do: build people and build this church.'

As Pastor Gloyd sees it, when many blacks achieve success, too often they leave the church. 'A great many of them have become politicians, got there on the back of the black church. That's all over America. Athletes, bankers, physicians – they leave the church. All of these people are usually the first to say that the church isn't doing enough for the community. Ward is struggling with the question of how to raise millions to build a church. The church has been doing more with less. They [black people] need to come back home. Black folks usually try to cut the umbilical cord. That's not 100 percent, but that's a large part of the problem you see in the black community. They see church as a Sunday-morning event. They fail to realize that it's twenty-four hours a day, seven days a week, or that most churches out there *are* doing something.'

A humid Sunday morning in early September. Attendance is light. There's no one in the balcony. The section of the sanctuary beneath the skylight is slow to fill. Pastor Gloyd is preaching 'as if they are hanging from the rafters', the man seated next to me says. The choir isn't wearing their robes; instead, they wear starched white blouses and shirts open at the collar. Still, they have worked up a good sweat. Gloyd prowls. He gesticulates and smiles. A young couple brings a baby girl in a frothy white dress up to the altar for christening, her pudgy brown legs poking out from the frilly layers of skirts. One of the stewardesses stands close by with a white towel. Pastor smiles and teases, then sprinkles the child with holy water. She cries.

Gently raising one hand, Pastor Gloyd slows the pace; the organ becomes one long, ambient sigh. Scanning faces scattered across the sanctuary, his broad smile disappears. The face becomes cloudy, almost fierce. 'Breaks my heart seeing Bush picking up black babies to demonstrate his "concern" for urban problems, thereby painting those problems black', he tells his congregation.

'If all those people who went out to explore the possibilities in America would bring those resources back to the source of their spring into success', he tells me several days later, 'maybe the church would be in a much better position to do some of those things that people talk about. Then, too, you would not need George Bush going out to hug black babies. We need to pick up our own black babies.'

Now more than ever.

September–November 1989

CHAPTER 4

FREED MAN

'Do you have your *Kente* and your crown?' Malikah Salaam asks. 'You'll need your *Kente or* a crown for Friday', she insists. Today, Thursday, is Malikah's first day of business, and her retail rap is flawless. Early afternoon, she had strategically set up her goods right outside of the Nelson Mandela Reception Committee offices on Degnan Boulevard. She had been working as a volunteer inside, answering phones, processing a steady flow of paperwork, but everyone, she explains, kept stopping by her desk, asking her about her 'Freedom Man/Nelson Mandela' pins ('The small ones are $5') and T-shirts ($15 today, but they'll be $25 tomorrow'). After awhile, getting any work done became close to impossible.

So now that the heat has eased out of triple digits and into the low nineties, she stands with a straw pith helmet arranged atop her cornrows and beckons anyone in sight to her folding table draped with a vibrant *Kente* sample of cobalt blue, green, gold, and crimson splashes. It is loaded with T-shirts, pins, leather bracelets, sashes, earrings the color of Africa's flag, and regal Kufi crowns. Men and women wander out of the reception committee offices into the bright sunlight squinting hard at their blue-and-white Coliseum tickets. More often than not, Malikah catches prospective customers off guard and places a high crown on unsuspecting passers-by. 'Ah, she has a face like a queen! Yes? Like an African queen.'

Inside the Reception Committee offices, project coordinator Brenda

A PIECE OF MANDELA: CITY HALL

Shockley casts a sharp stare at her support staff's freshly coifed heads, 'Nobody's had any sleep, but everybody's found time to go to the beauty shop.' Laughing, she adds, 'Including me.' Earlier, Gwen Green, the office manager, and I head outside to escape the bleating phones and the buzz of office chatter to talk. We watch a barrel-chested doorman in iridescent tails, tuxedo shirt, bow tie and opaque shades explain to the steady stream of ticket-buyers approaching the door that they'll need a cashier's check or money order to make a purchase. With a tilt of the head, he efficiently directs them to the Liquor Bank or the Great Western on Crenshaw a few blocks away. 'It's been all segments of the community – church folk, labor, activists, teachers, students – helping out', says Green. 'For me, doing this is my way of saying thank you. I worked for King, and if I was with King there's no way I would miss this. Mandela is a world leader, a role model with strong principles. Maybe this visit might help us get *our* community together.'

This stretch of Degnan Boulevard, which empties out at its southern end into a grassy triangle dotted with leafy shade-trees, has been enjoying a renaissance the last few years. Galleries, artists' studios and a performance space called the World Stage have sprouted up along this quiet artery that looks more like an isolated European village than a mid-city shopping mall. Medgar Evers's son, Darrell, keeps a studio space along this corridor, and actress Marla Gibbs recently purchased a stretch of property from 43rd Street to the Watchtower Theater, which faces the park. Gibbs, several committee staffers remind me, donated the workspace to the Committee. Late Wednesday afternoon the actress ducked in to check up on things and pat a few backs.

Brian Breyé, who runs the Museum in Black down the street, has been helping out – providing everything from art to spruce up the office's beige walls to sweeping the street at the end of the day. But he's quick to spell out his reservations about the hoopla. 'Some of these people didn't support the ANC before all this. Some of them didn't *know* about the ANC. Now everybody wants to be on the bandwagon. It's the up-to-date "bourgie" thing to do.'

Masamba Diop, an art dealer and exporter from Senegal, has decided to sit out the Coliseum event. 'Even if you don't go to hear Mandela you can support him. The best way to support him is to support his freedom-fighting. It's not giving him money or inviting him to the White House. There's got to be follow-up afterward. After he goes home, I'm just afraid that people are just going to go back to doing whatever it is they were doing before he arrived.'

'Everybody wants a piece of Mandela now', Lisa Neeley, one of the student outreach coordinators, insists. Since taking a leave from her job with a computer software company in Berkeley, she has been working on the youth march planned for Friday night. 'There've been so many changes around the world in the last year and a half, and we're right in the middle of all of it. I want to be standing on the right side of history. We need something, someone to rally around, and if it's not Mandela, then who will it be?'

'When you hear him speak', Marcel, an art student from Howard University, explains, lowering the volume on the cassette player pumping out the new Public Enemy, 'it's almost like magic, the feeling inside you.' Marcel's been charged with preparing the banners for Friday's march. In faint but careful pencil strokes, he has reproduced Malcolm and Mandela, and now begins to shade and shape the features, alternating among the stubby remains of gray, white and black pastels. Marcel says that he took Mandela's image from a videotape of his *Nightline* appearance. He found a moment he liked – it flickered on pause as he sketched – but now he's worried about the likeness, about what he hasn't captured in the eyes.

As camera crews, photographers and reporters jockey for position along a barricade, an LAX employee announces, 'We sure don't see this kind of turnout when Bush comes into town.' Along with Assemblywoman Maxine Waters (chairperson of the reception committee), the mayor and his wife, we're waiting for Nelson Mandela's plane to arrive. After receiving news that there's going to be a three-hour delay, a few photographers take bets on exactly when the plane is going to land. When it does, they don't have more than five minutes to shoot him. Mandela goes through the official receiving line, and then, to accommodate the photographers, strolls beside the barricade. But it is the reporters who break the code of objectivity and show their emotions. Several of them stop scribbling and reach out and try to touch him.

The Reception Committee printed 400,000 flyers (40,000 in Spanish) and distributed 10,000 posters to publicize the events, from the City Hall welcome to the Coliseum rally. But a lot of the posters were taken down. 'They're pretty nice', says logistics coordinator Mike Murase. 'I suppose people wanted them for themselves.' Around City Hall, while waiting for Mandela to show up, I don't see any posters, but a lot of people are carrying red-and-white pieces of cardboard with Mandela's name. It's not until I have left and am several blocks away that I see people rescuing them from *Los Angeles Times* vending machines.

Out of earshot of the City Hall festivities taking place beneath the white tent, there is a collage of confusing voices. A black woman in her early thirties, elegantly turned out in an ivory suit and open-toed sandals, patiently explains to her white co-workers that 'the white man has always been free. You can empathize, but you'll never *really* understand.' A young black man in jeans and straw hat carrying a voter registration clipboard shouts at a smirking homeboy in a black Raiders cap: 'You're a young man, use your power as a young man.' A woman with blue hair travels the crowd's perimeter, selling satin flowers whose buds are fashioned from green, gold and black folded swatches. Two tables wage price wars over bootlegged 'Simpsons Go Funky Reggae' T-shirts, with Bart sporting an impressive stock of dreadlocks.

Despite the wall of bodies obstructing the view, the numbers seem embarrassingly small. Nothing like the crowds in Harlem, Detroit or D.C. The figures gathered and compared conflict – ranging from 4,000 to 15,000. One quick look around the assembly convinces me the tally is closer to the low end. 'But the number of people who *have* shown up says *something*', says Linda A. Brown, a member of the Westmoreland 200 Voice Gospel Choir, which performed as part of the afternoon festivities. 'People around the world are searching for some kind of leadership. I think many are hoping to find it here.'

When Nelson Mandela, in ash gray suit and forest green tie, takes the platform, two homeless men who have been tirelessly working the crowd, passing around large cardboard boxes for spare change, pause. They stand atop their sooty bed-rolls to get a better view. 'That's the man', says the smaller one, pointing toward the stage. 'He's the man', the other nods, squinting up at the dais, and smiles.

A group of waiters in white waistcoats and black slacks pour out of a bus, then jog toward the Armory in Exposition Park, where a splashy $1,000-to-$5,000-a-plate dinner is scheduled for early evening. Party planner Yvonne E. White of Catering by Yvonne and Company has prepared the food for the $5,000-a-plate reception, as well as Nelson and Winnie Mandela's personal meal. 'I did research to learn more about what he liked. We prepared sweet pepper herb chicken, wild rice and grilled vegetables. He doesn't eat any bread or butter, hardly any sugar, since it wasn't available in prison. He's still trying to adjust to it. He eats a little bit of red meat and seafood, but prefers chicken.' (After the event, Yvonne's mother told me that the Mandelas were so overworked that they didn't finish their vegetables. She took them home in a plastic bag instead – a piece of history for her refrigerator.)

Outside the Coliseum, the more downscale celebrations feature cold chicken, fresh fruit and cookies in picnic baskets; 'Free Nelson Mandela' echoes through the trees from portable tape players on spread-out blankets. Special A.K.A.'s Rhoda Dakar's voice lifts up, expands her plea, as ardent as it was six years ago. Inside, twelve ANC flags stretch the length of the stage. A perfect half-moon hangs above the stadium. With 71,000 in attendance, there hasn't been a more elegant collection of drapes and head-wraps since Louis Farrakhan held sway at the Sports Arena six months ago. 'He represents our heritage, our freedom', says Deval Parkinson, a native of Jamaica, who spots my press credentials and stops me in front of the snack bar. 'African-Americans are looking for a symbol, a change', adds Deval's friend, Aaron Lawson. 'He sticks to his guns. I've been following him on TV. He eats them up and spits them out. He was too much for them. He talks through his beliefs, though they do not want to hear.'

As dusk settles, evening explodes into a celebration of blackness, of Pan-Africanism. Behind me, toddlers stand and wave clenched fists to the cadence of African talking drums. Even the weary press section comes to life as a crew of rappers led by Ice-T, DefJef and Tone-Loc storm the stage. A fired-up Jesse Jackson steps back to remind all that 'we can't just admire [Mandela], we must follow him.' And with a smile and a sigh, comedian Marsha Warfield resolves: 'It's good to be black nowadays.'

By the time Mandela arrives, it's 10:55 p.m. The crowd, which had been waiting for three hours for this moment, bursts into cheers. 'We will not give up until apartheid gives in', Mandela says, and the crowd roars again. He and Winnie raise fists in a gentle power salute. 'Amandla', they cry, and thousands of voices echo the call. 'It's like a shot in the arm', an African-American journalist confides. 'Told my editor that objectivity went out the window on this one. I just feel too good.' As I hear these words, I spot an African, draped in flowing blue and violet robes, tall Kufi hat askew, elated by the crowd, by Mandela, by the moment. He's standing in the middle of the aisle waving brilliant red, black and green banners. He's one more person welcoming Mandela to L.A. It didn't seem to matter to him that he barely had a chance to say hello.

July 1990

CHAPTER 5

'I CAN BE REACHED HERE ANYTIME'

Even when you press him, Levi Kingston can't say how many miles he walks in a day. It isn't nearly as many, he insists, as everyone seems to think. But an imposing mythology has grown up around his daily constitutional; about the collection of hats he selects from before departing; about the sheer deliberateness of his gait. People who have known Levi for a long time measure the years by the succession of hats. Ed Bereal has known Levi for four hats – that translates to thirty-five years. Bereal met Levi during the sixties – the decade of the sombrero.

Lately, since a wandering pain in his leg forced him to give in to a slight limp, Levi Kingston – a veteran community organizer who's been fighting the education battle and the homelessness battle and, more recently, the drugs and AIDS-awareness battle in his corner of South Central for two decades now – has been shuttling around more and more on the RTD. 'See, you don't really see L.A. on one level unless you walk or ride the buses. We can talk forever about eighty-five languages being spoken in Los Angeles, but if you're in a car, you don't see the people. You just conjecture that they are here.'

Neighbors often see him around: in gray fedora crossing the quad at USC for morning meetings; strolling the stretch of Hoover between Jefferson and 32nd with a Tams Stationers bag in hand; stopping a moment to catch up – quick-fast – with the security guard installed near the crowded corner of 36th and Western. He always makes it a point to speak. At Sid's Cafe on Exposition, when they hear his laugh – a low titter that suddenly bursts hysteric – a waitress heads over with a plastic basket overflowing with saltines for his filé gumbo; at Jack's on Western, they never ask him if he needs a menu.

For twenty or so years (the exact numbers escape him), he's been working these streets, roving these carefully selected blocks and organizing the people who live within them: Vernon at the south, Washington at the north, Arlington at the west, and Main at the East – the whole a perfect square on the map until Washington Boulevard slopes south into Woodlawn Avenue, just a few blocks before it becomes Main. 'I deliberately work in a manageable area. I don't believe anybody who tells me they're working "South Central L.A." I don't see how', Levi says.

Born in L.A., Levi grew up in the Pueblo del Rio housing projects fronting the railroad tracks just outside of the City of Vernon. Curiosity and the desire to travel – but no money – led him to books; he preferred philosophy, particularly Bertrand Russell. After graduating from Los Angeles High in 1957, Levi traveled around the world as a merchant seaman until a dispute over wages altered his plans. He started organizing the sailors around the issue and ended up cooling his heels in a Dutch jail.

Before he skipped out overseas, Levi had been involved with various Left groups throughout the city – the Independent Student Union, the Woolworth's sit-ins. He moved in and around social and political circles, served as liaison between splintered, warring factions. Pogo's Swamp, the coffeehouse Levi owned for a year in 1962 on Melrose at Heliotrope, entertained a motley community mix – LACC students, Venice beatniks, musicians. 'You had it all – civil-rights activists, socialists, the Left, the New Left – a lot of old lefties there too. I was the new kid on the block to all that stuff.'

But Levi was a quick study. He borrowed a *Conscientious Objectors* handbook from one of the regulars, then started up the Freedom Draft Movement. 'There wasn't anything happening for blacks in terms of providing draft options. They were fair game during the Watts Rebellion. During the war, there were three blacks to everyone else. *We* were fighting the war and nobody knew their options.'

'Levi held a unique position', remembers Ed Bereal. 'He was one of the people who could function fairly well with various groups who were at odds with one another. He was a walking Demilitarized Zone. It wasn't anything that he tried to master, it's just how he was. Everybody knows Levi – he had his own political outlook; it was bigger than any one particular outlook, and it seemed to make sense. He does what he does, and really frankly I don't know what that motivation is. And what that's all about is he's been out there for many, many years and he's probably going to die out there.'

L.A. [wasn't supposed to] really have any of the 'problems' that they had on the Eastern Seaboard. We didn't have 'our Harlems'. It was a crock because then, and now, South Central doesn't have. It's elementary. What they don't have is what we don't have – an economic base. Now things have changed institutionally, even. At one point L.A. had a reputation of having nothing wrong. No racism, nothing. Bed of roses. And then when Watts happened it was like a brand-new day. I for one was glad to see that people could see through the smoke screen.

I think Malcolm was significant because he addressed a lot of things that were peculiar to blacks at a time that it was necessary to express some anger. I think it's important to express anger. You know, it's not all about grinning and bearing it. That's what a lot of people do. And now it's not fashionable to really talk about what ails you.

I'm not coming out of an ethnocentric perspective, either. I'm not a cultural nationalist. I'm concerned about children and youth because they represent the future. And we may not have one. And some people don't care whether they have one or not.

The Hoover Intergenerational Child Development Center, a proud neighborhood landmark in shades of pale mesa, cactus and sand, sits a few feet back from the busy street from which it takes its name. It is wedged between the Hillel Foundation and 32nd Street Magnet School and across the street from USC's University Village, an open-air mall catering primarily to Trojan coeds. It took twelve years for the HIC to move from Levi's first vision to its dedication in 1988. Though it is a living symbol of more than a decade of work, his most significant accomplishments tend to blend into the landscape.

Travel along any of the wider north/south thoroughfares within Levi's boundaries will reveal block upon block of boarded-up businesses flanking either side of the boulevard. Old nightclubs fronted by broken neon martini-glass shingles and 'Hi-Fashion' boutiques whose protective accordion gratings rusted long ago provide glimpses of past prosperity, a Los Angeles still vivid in Levi's memory.

Now in a quick stroll the needs present themselves: joblessness, homelessness, drugs. The terrain is 'L.A. Melting Pot': – African-American, Latino,

LEVI KINGSTON

residual white, transient student. 'He has a great ability to cross cultural lines, to bring people together – all kinds of people', says Councilman Robert Farrell, the northern end of whose 85th District is Levi's territory. 'And from his humble base and means he is able to get other people working.'

The Rev. Dr Thomas Kilgore III met Kingston back in 1973 while Levi was working with architect Eugene Brooks in a project called the Urban Workshop. Kilgore helped with the organizational and funding aspects of HIC, and lent guidance in establishing Levi's umbrella organization, the Community Consortium, in 1982. 'He has a great capacity for holding on', Kilgore says. 'He's very tenacious when he has an idea that he wants something, some program that he wants to get over. He'll bug you to death, but that's the kind of person to get things done.'

'This has been one of the most fragmented areas in the city', says Rev. Brian Eklund, pastor of St Mark's Lutheran Church on Vermont Avenue. Eklund shared his church space with Levi in the early eighties, while the city prepared nervously for the Olympics. The church offered a cold drink and some shade to weary tourists while Levi and Consortium members assembled a bilingual newsletter that kept community residents visible at a time when City Hall was trying to sweep them under the carpet. 'Levi does see things as they appear', says Eklund, 'sees issues and raises them for all to see. Whatever rolls into the neighborhood. Whatever needs arise. He goes after them.'

Over the years, he's watched the bottom fall out: elaborate community improvement plans significantly altered, community agencies obliterated, and government funding dollars run bone-dry. Nonetheless, without making false or lavish promises, he has boosted and maintained a spirit of advocacy and optimism in a community that seldom sees concrete signs of progress or hope. 'There are a lot of [black] people leaving South Central', Levi explains. 'And they're scared, a lot of them. But they also move into situations where they don't have any political representation. That's another dilemma. . . . I hear a lot of black people talking about "The Problem" the same way white folks do. No different. But if I'm not doing anything about changing that, then I'm just part of the problem. *I* need to be looked at.'

I like grassroots organizing. I mean, it appeals to me. Politically, I believe that organizers must relate to politicians if they see themselves doing anything. They've got to. I am not a purist. I don't believe that because politics are 'dirty' you should ignore them. You can't ignore the process. Because you're always in the position to deliver something to people who don't see themselves as having any power.

The variation is Louis Farrakhan and [his self-determination] thing. It's the next day right now, and what's new? The Crips are still shooting the Bloods and vice versa, and we're all on empty because our only solution is to run away from the problem or to call for the one and only workable remedy — law enforcement. And here's what's heavy — we don't have enough law enforcement to deal with these problems.

Law enforcement is not all that it's cracked up to be in terms of any remedy, and that's where community organizing becomes an important variable that has rarely been supported. I think that it hasn't been supported because it's subversive. Politicians want to control you. Educators want to control you. It's turf. It means a collective effort. Not just law and order. Not just the church. We have to really come together and implement a plan of action.

In the alley behind the Community Consortium's office on Western Avenue, neighborhood regulars pause to shoot up amid the rusting refuse bins — a concrete needle park. They drop the syringes on the asphalt near, but seldom in, the dumpsters. When the Consortium set out to offer an AIDS-awareness program, Levi asked around about the location of the city's high-risk areas. He was told, in an LAPD letter, that he sat dead center.

When Levi and I arrive, there are no loiterers propped against the retaining walls. 'Almost like they knew it was going to rain', he says, putting on his fedora and scanning the lot. A small barber shop, a 'family stylist', and shoe repair store — all by appointment only — share space in this building as well. Levi stops by most days to pick up messages from the phone machine and to gather the mail that has begun to collect beneath the door. Today he comes to field questions, do a little investigative work of his own. He's somewhat puzzled by an anonymous message left at HIC, he tells me, about an obviously ill 'phantom man'.

Simmons the cobbler has his tiny shop directly beneath Levi's office. The junkies don't bother Simmons, Levi tells me. They respect him and often bend his ear late into the afternoon. Simmons steps outside with awl in hand, his faded blue smock spattered with black, brown and white polish. He speaks at a rapid but, to me, familiar Louisiana clip. 'You just missed him, not a half-hour ago, Levi', says Simmons, whose eyes travel to me. He tells me about the suit-and-tie from the Health Department who made his rounds down here a few weeks ago, and again today, flashing a photo and asking tenants earnest questions. Simmons says he recognized the face in the photograph as one of the young men who frequently collect outside his store. 'I've got some phone numbers for you, Levi.' Simmons disappears inside, then returns with a scrap of paper with notations made in black ink from a health-care official.

I follow Levi toward the C&F Variety Store, where they sell single cigarettes for fifteen cents and chili is served and sold in small takeout portions from a crock pot on the front counter. Eva, the woman behind the register, reveals that she left the 'phantom man' message at HIC for Levi. He was the first and only person she thought to call.

'Does anybody know *what's* wrong with him?' Levi asks.

'He was in here today', Eva explains. 'I just feel like his health is a hazard to society. He didn't do anything, just looked at the [video] machines and left.'

'But nobody knows what it is?' Levi asks again. Eva shakes her head.

Eva says that sometimes women from a local clinic stop in and stack AIDS materials along the counter: flyers, cards, phone numbers, maybe a newsletter. Some people just read them while they're standing at the counter to escape the bad weather. Others fold them into small squares and slip them into breast pockets. An AIDS hotline poster hangs in front of the counter, faded from the sun and torn and curled at the edges. Eva says she doesn't know much about it – about AIDS. Whatever this man has, she tells me, makes her uncomfortable. But she doesn't want to ask him to leave: 'He's a person, too.' As I listen to Eva, Levi is explaining to a group of teens clustered around a refrigerator case how AIDS is contracted – not by shaking hands, passing dollar bills, or taking in air.

Someone outside spots him, the 'phantom man', and as bodies spill out onto the sidewalk, onlookers from the alley and nearby bus benches cluster around the corner as well. By now it's begun to rain. First occasional drops that cover the sidewalk in brown dime-sized spots, then slanting, steady showers.

The man, in a brown baseball cap, sits on a concrete ledge in front of the doors of a fast-food restaurant just 100 feet from where we stand. Head down, he sways first left to right, then back and forth. The cycle begins again. 'This is a goddamn comedy,' Levi shakes his head. Eyes volley from Levi to the concrete ledge where the young man rests. He looks at me and laughs. 'What do they want me to do? Tackle him?' Instead, after a moment, he pushes his way back through the crowd and heads to his office with the numbers Simmons passed on to him. Over the phone he carefully reconstructs the scene to a health official: 'What we have here on the corner now is a lot of panic. . . . I can be reached here *any*time. Doesn't matter.'

'The essence of Levi, when it comes right down to it, is that he'll put bread on your table and he won't have any', says Henry Marin, the brains and bare hands behind the Pico-Union Development Project. 'Levi is constant that way.' This constancy has meant more than being an inexorable voice for a community. It's meant more than setting up community services – the multicultural Artsfest festival and youth, child-care, AIDS-awareness and minority entrepreneurship programs. It's required serving as eyes, legs and hands. It's meant roles that shift as community needs present themselves: psychologist, father, friend, patron, doctor, confidant, they've become second nature. It's meant being a fixture at City Hall; Santa-in-a-pinch at Christmas time; the resolute force holding the not-so-gentle giant USC at bay. It's meant quelling worry and panic. It's meant being on call 24/7. It is what Levi Kingston does best.

'We figure at the street level, at the true community outreach level, through network contacts Levi has already established, is how we can reach the user', says Adrienne Duar, project director of the Consortium's Community AIDS Awareness Project since 1987. 'You have to be out there in order to be trusted in the first place. Trust is foremost, and it continues to be a major community organizing principle that must be upheld.'

The Consortium's CAAP received its first bit of funding ($70,000) in 1988 from the Department of Health Services State Office of AIDS. Since then the project has coordinated counseling, bilingual education and a community youth advisory board. They're looking to add mobile 'guerrilla' street theater, a newsletter, videos, conferences, but problems have arisen early. There won't be money after June 30. This year, their request for funding was denied.

Part of our goal in general is to improve the quality of life in these neighborhoods. Without a question, you've got to have a concept of what your goal is. I think you have to determine what your boundaries are. And I am a stickler for that. You have to work in an area that's manageable.

A lot of people working in the community are frustrated because one of the major businesses is drugs. So if you're talking about all of these things — economic development, education, psychological well-being, like, 'Don't have a low self-esteem, have a high self-esteem' — you're competing with the pusherman.

*The [church-based] South Central Organizing Committee was organizing around
the contention that crime and liquor stores went hand-in-glove, but to me it smacked of
more like a temperance movement as opposed to recognizing fundamental issues like the
fact that there is no economic base in all of South Central and that economics, education,
psychology, politics are all interrelated and all have an impact on individuals, organizations, institutions. So to focus on the fact that too many liquor stores are in South Central
is one thing, but that certainly isn't all of it. It's an easy one.*

Outside one of the USC lots, students clog intersections with ten-speed
bicycles and white VW convertibles. Sprawling inconspicuously across the
street is University Gardens, a low- and moderate-income housing project
whose 112 units – singles, one- and two-bedroom apartments – constitute a
nondescript two-story complex painted somber shades of institutional beige
and brown. As Levi and I head across the empty basketball courts, blistering
rap blares from a set of tinny speakers. The bass is too dense to make out any
particulars. Levi speaks to one of the teens reclining on a lawn-chair in the sun.
He grunts back, barely moving his lips, averting his eyes.

Many residents here are strung out or afraid. People here won't knock on
doors, won't enlist in neighborhood anti-drug campaigns, even though they
persistently complain that the atmosphere leaves them prisoners in their own
homes. 'They're afraid of being moved on by the people who perpetuate the
problem', Levi explains. 'The dealers.' But working here, he says, you have to
be sensitive to everybody – including the dealers. 'Some of whom you don't
know, some of them you do, 'cause they were children when you first started
working. And now you're threatening their money.'

From an open window, a woman shouts an invitation. I follow Levi down
a set of cement stairs toward the sound. Mildred Tobin says that she used to
work with the Consortium a few years back, when Levi still felt that monthly
meetings were useful, when he could still gather glimmers of enthusiasm and
occasional support and reinforcement. Since then, Mildred says, she has to hunt
around for block club meetings, for interested neighbors to attend with her in
the evenings. She says she wants to tell people about the situation.

'Tell her what the situation is, Mildred, in one word', Levi says.

'Dope. Dope, dope, dope. And it's worse in here. Some of them won't
even go to school. Fourteen and fifteen years old and nobody's gonna do anything about it. A long time ago truant officers would get 'em. A lot of these

older people are scared to get out. Things are so bad up in here, if you tried to have stuff, they scared to come out. They scared that they dopin'. . . .'

Surfacing from Mildred Tobin's tiny apartment, I was struck most by what I didn't see in her face or hear in her voice. At some point acute despair (or frustration) turns barely perceptible. Over the last few weeks, I've seen different methods of battling it. Some fall back on mordant jests and gallows humor, others unleash raw and random shows of vigilante anger turned violence. But what is most prevalent, and most disheartening, is the apathy borne of a wilting spirit. The giving up and giving in.

'People in the community are frustrated', Levi insists. 'The major business here is drugs. And it's something only a collective community effort will cure. Back in the sixties you had the smokestack syndrome, you had the steel and the other types of things, but it was all compounded by the fact that you had racist employment [practices] and the lack of any kind of viable economic floor. In my opinion, there hasn't been much change. Yeah, people keep talking about change. But where, where is it? I think the community had a good chance, back in the sixties. They had a good chance back when they were fighting.'

I do believe that drugs and drug addiction are a health problem. I don't think it's appropriate to deal with it strictly through law enforcement. I support those people who talk about the legalization of drugs. I think it's ludicrous and absurd for somebody like Chief Gates, for example, to condemn people who entertain the question of legalization. He said people who entertain the notion that drugs should be legalized are treasonous. I think about what I'm dealing with as an organizer — how can he sit in an office and talk about all that shit? The victims are community people. It's so obvious. When ordinary people can't just maintain their lives without being fucked around by a dealer, it is a problem. Do I think that the situation calls for a show of force? I think if that's the only option that you give somebody, it's ludicrous.

DeShawn slips a large, square wooden block down the back of his shirt, takes a six-inch-long block in hand-pistol-style, then shouts 'Ghostbusters!' as he zigzags across the sunny classroom. Teacher Sylvia Spiller shushes him from her place across the room. She is sitting at a low table with six children holding fat markers poised carefully above white paper, instructing them in penmanship – 'Hold your paper, Rasheeda! . . . I'll help you with the "s", Carolyn, I know that some letters are hard. . . .' Outside, a smaller group plays in the sand, shimmies up monkey bars, sways quietly in the swings. Inside, boys and girls construct freeways out of blocks, roll heavy wooden automobiles and trucks along their mini version of a four-level.

Levi keeps a small, cluttered office just within the lee of the entrance way of the Hoover Intergenerational Care Center. He is not your typical executive director. His business style is folksy and comfortable, as is his attire, seldom more formal than a sports coat and bolo tie. Though he works out of two offices, he's rarely found behind the desk of either. (Nor does he draw a salary from either HIC or the Consortium; he lives on stipends provided through the program's funding.) At the Center, he's usually spread out in the multipurpose room beneath the skylight reading the Los Angeles or New York *Times* or clipping articles from *The Los Angeles Sentinel* and *The Wave*.

Friday afternoon, just a quarter after 12, I arrive at Sid's. Levi's bent over the jukebox in shorts and newsboy cap, feeding quarters. A worn and muzzy recording of Ashford and Simpson's 'Solid as a Rock' struggles its way out of the speakers. Despite the warning that his quarters are no good here, he continues to feed silver into the slot. He will play this particular selection at least three more times before we leave. I seat myself at the table with the crackers. Levi has already ordered his bowl of gumbo and is asking the waitress for the little container of filé on the side. Henry Marin, Levi's Friday-afternoon lunch partner for years, has ordered red beans and rice. Levi tells me that Jase is cooking today. I bypass my usual oyster po' boy to try it out.

This afternoon there are a pair of USC coeds in Sid's – white-powder pale, lips lined in deep reds. In a booth close by two old men quietly read the *Louisiana Weekly* in the sun. Every Friday, at about noon, Levi and Henry indulge themselves: a leisurely two-hour feast, a carafe-and-a-half of chilled rosé, and some spirited conversation that steadily becomes labyrinthine as afternoon eases toward evening. They run it down: world, state, local events, Consortium projects, funding, city politics. Henry assists with strategy, provides a carefully measured (though unsolicited) amount of chastising as well. 'We sit and chat', Henry tells me, 'because we love the game.'

Since Levi rarely speaks of frustration, it is from Henry that I gather a more vivid idea of the struggle, the dry years, the dead ends. I begin to see how work like this can slowly eat away at a spirit; I again wonder why it has yet to feed upon Levi's. Henry is not a stranger to the challenge. He built a community park (Pico-Union Park) and one of the first low- and moderate-income housing projects ever erected by a community in the United States. He hung on for ten long years, but had to stop. He admits matter-of-factly, 'It kicked my ass.' But for Levi, Henry says, community work is his whole life. 'You're not talkin' a poverty pimp. You're not talkin' a fly-by-night. This dude is there all the time for anyone. And it makes life difficult for him. I know that for a fact. But he survives it and continues. . . . He gets what he needs. Except for dollars. Levi doesn't make a dime. And he doesn't care. Well', Henry amends, 'I don't know about "caring", because he won't cop to me. We're that tight, but he doesn't cop to me. Now that's the kind of commitment. It was over in the sixties and he's a holdover from a bygone era.'

Levi, as another friend pointed out, 'is one of the few people who can still dream and make others believe in it.' But what does he dream of? Henry Marin leans into a big laugh. 'Decency for every human being that exists on the planet. He doesn't want much.'

April 1990

CHAPTER 6

GOING BETWEEN

On a recent Tuesday morning when Halford Fairchild answered the door of his West Adams craftsman, he wore a distracted, somewhat downcast expression. 'I thought you might be someone else', he explains, smoothing his tie-dye T-shirt emblazoned with the silhouette of Africa. 'Last night, my car was stolen, from right outside the house.' He motions toward the window, the space out front, the size of a midsize sedan. 'I didn't get a good look at the person stealing the car, but it's almost a sure thing that the person was black or brown. *And* it's almost a sure thing that the person knew that *I* was black or brown. We have black people preying on other African people because of the terrible economic hardship that they're in. So while I am really pissed off at who are probably brothers who stole my car, I'm even more pissed off at the economic situation that really leaves these brothers very little choice of what they can do. I'm mad at the politicians who have created an economic structure that feeds the rich at the expense of the poor.'

Fairchild is a psychologist, an educator and an activist who has lectured and written about race and intolerance and the increasingly virulent conflicts that grow out of them. An L.A. native, he grew up not very far from where we sit now. Fairchild explains that the cast of his eyes and coarse wave of his hair have always made race a salient and unavoidable issue. 'If you look at me you can see that I'm part Asian. My mother is Japanese-American. Growing up in black community all my life, I've been subjected to a lot of biases and prejudices and discrimination. I have a strong black identity, but I have developed pride in my Asian heritage as well. Because of my multiracial background, the whole issue of race has been a lifelong commitment for me – both in terms of grappling with some challenges that I've had as a biracial person in a very racially conscious society, but also because of my commitment to our American ideal of freedom and justice for all.'

Signposts of this peculiar brand of 'justice' remain, some erected in the not-so-distant past. Fairchild relates his history of this community, of the very house in which we're seated. He rattles off the strict stipulations within the city's restrictive covenants that, until the fifties, ensured that the occupants of these elegant craftmans were all white. The complexion of these neighborhoods remained this way as a 'result of social, political and legal design: the legacy of legally mandated discrimination is de facto segregation', explains Fairchild. Now, one look at the faces – mostly black or brown (save for the enterprising white gentrifier) – proves that much of this early legal handiwork remains firmly intact. Much of South L.A.'s tension grows from old wounds, needs that were never properly addressed, and that may never be met. Shifting demographics have left residents – African-American, Korean-American, Latino – scrambling for pieces of scant space. 'There is a great deal of tension, a great deal of rivalry, a great deal of racial animosity between African-Americans and Latinos. The difference [between the tension with Korean-Americans] primarily is that Latinos are not merchant class. They are not capitalist class; they are consumer class as are African-Americans. African-Americans and Latinos find themselves competing for jobs, for housing, for space, and I think for dignity; and frequently find themselves using each other as scapegoats for each other's frustration.'

Too much of the growing anti-Asian, anti-black, anti-Latino biases have to do with the media's perpetuation of stereotypes, says Fairchild. 'The reinforcement of stereotypes serves to dehumanize African-Americans, and Asian-Americans as well. I think that there is a *very* deep current of anti-black and anti-Asian bias in American society. The Korean-American community has grown almost astronomically in the last ten years or so. The Latino presence in South Central L.A., likewise. That, coupled with the ignorance that the groups have of each other.' When misunderstandings turn to conflicts and there is no more room to store the rage, the fear and anger can manifest in these ways: a Latasha Harlins raising her voice and fists; a Soon Ja Du keeping and ultimately firing a gun. 'When you're talking about the roots [of rifts], you're talking about origins. A lot of it begins with the dehumanization and exploitation of African people. African-American people remain in economic slavery, or certainly in a state of economic dependency. The terrible peril of African people places us in a position of having to do whatever we can do to survive, and a lot of times that means to steal', says Fairchild, reflecting on his own circumstances. 'We have an interesting situation, where Korean-Americans are coming in as capitalists, as merchants, as individuals who are selling goods for a profit in convenience stores and liquor stores, and I'm sure they experience theft on a regular basis. People steal because they don't have the money to buy.'

Most times it takes a cataclysmic event to spark community action, inspire a sense of unity. For some time the county Human Relations Commission had been quietly dousing hot spots and working toward ethnic conciliation in South Central L.A., but it took the murders of four Korean shopkeepers in four weeks in April 1986 to solidify the Black Korean Alliance (BKA) – an organization whose wide membership includes local merchants, city officials, community-based organizations, media and clergy.

'Overall, the mission was to improve relations between the two groups and to increase the dialogue between merchants and residents in the greater South Central L.A. area', says Human Relations commissioner and BKA member Larry Aubry. Much of their work is about wading through elaborate myths that have become city lore, 'about how Korean immigrants get their money, that they qualify for special loans.' There's not a lot in place, says Aubry, to alleviate tensions in the community. 'South Central is a worst-case scenario. In a lot of ways, the community is worse off than it was twenty-five years ago. There's not a public policy that has been developed to handle the problems, which makes for a lot of tensions across class lines.'

Jai Lee Wong of the BKA and Human Relations Commission agrees, having watched tension in the community rise as language, custom and cultural differences mount like steel barricades. In the last few months a great deal of attention has been riveted on the grisly particulars of the black–Korean conflict, Wong observes, rather than on bettering community relations. 'The media overdid it with the Pearl Harbor coverage. All of it breeds a tremendous amount of fear and confusion', says Wong, who is also distressed about conflict in the once harmonious Japanese-American/African-American community in

HALFORD FAIRCHILD   DENNIS WESTBROOK

Ladera Heights and the nearby Crenshaw strip. 'I have a friend', says Wong, who's been in the black community for twenty-five years. 'Never had a problem. Last weekend she was walking across the parking lot at Target and someone shouted, "Slant eyes! Go back where you came from!" An Asian woman in Compton was stopped by two black youths while waiting at a traffic light. They asked her if she was Korean. Before she could respond, they took out two baseball bats and proceeded to smash the windshield, and then turned to her. Things have become explosive. L.A. has become a very international city. Change was bound to happen. They knew it was coming. But policymakers didn't plan for it.'

The downtown L.A.–based Asian Pacific American Dispute Resolution Center and its South Central counterpart, the Martin Luther King Dispute Resolution Center, were both started in 1989 with funding from the 1987 Dispute Resolution Act. They have served to alleviate the bottleneck of small-claims cases in the court system. They can also work to assuage the frustration and powerlessness that people feel when butting up against the system.

The most common disputes these centers arbitrate are straight landlord–tenant issues or unfair employment practices. Domestic disputes and clashes with neighbors also place high. The Martin Luther King Center (sponsored through the Southern Christian Leadership Conference) receives about seventy-five calls a month; services are rendered on a sliding scale. About half of those cases result in an 'open case' (when both parties agree to sit down). The high-profile cases make up a smaller proportion of the case load. 'The consumer–merchant disputes', says MLK project director Dennis Westbrook, 'account for maybe twenty to twenty-five percent of our caseload and perhaps half of that might involve a cross-cultural kind of dispute – either between African-Americans and Koreans, or African-Americans and Latinos, or Latinos and Koreans. But at this point only a small percentage of consumer–merchant disputes are actually black- and Korean-related issues.'

The center maintains a roster of twenty to thirty mediators, about half of whom can be called on at any time. 'We then have an active group of maybe fifteen to twenty people who do intake and case development', says Westbrook. 'Those who have not completed their training wouldn't be called to mediate, but are available to do outreach and presentations to community groups and block clubs.' Westbrook has noticed that when cross-cultural conflict arises, people still run to the tried and true channels – long-standing, venerable community-based organizations like the NAACP and the Urban League. Though, he says, they've tried everything from TV and radio public service announcements and talk shows to flyers and doorhangers, 'Many people who find themselves in the throes of those disputes don't know that there is a dispute resolution center here and that there are other centers throughout the county. So they may not know how to gain entree to the system that can help them.' Since the Harlins/Du episode in March 1991, however, Westbrook has noted an increase in the number of cross-cultural conflict cases – indicating that there are scores more that go unreported and remain unresolved. They fear, as he puts it, an 'inappropriate response to the conflict' – another Harlins/Du incident.

'It's a mood of increasing intolerance on both sides. I think that it's fueled by some of the personal experiences that many people have in the community. The intensity of their conflict, or dispute, may not be the same, but a lot of people have had similar experiences with merchants in their communities. On the other hand, because of the difficulty of doing business in an urban community, many of the merchants – not only Korean merchants but African-American merchants and Latino merchants as well – feel like they are continually under siege from those who don't come into their establishment to

JAN SUNOO   MARCIA CHOO

buy goods. Merchants are becoming less tolerant and more suspicious and fear-
ful of the people who are the lifeblood of their businesses.'

Westbrook quotes a national statistic when he says that 85 to 90 percent of
those who agree to arbitration will come away from the table with a resolution
of the dispute. But the process isn't easy. It's often emotional and sometimes
the grudge just can't be shaken in the typical three-hour session. At other moments, Westbrook says, he is surprised that once the anger subsides and the real
issues are unearthed, the forum becomes a place 'merely to tell the truth about
what happened. To get an apology.'

Marcia Choo, project director of the Asian Pacific American Dispute Resolution Center has, like Westbrook, seen an increase in cross-cultural conflict
cases reported after the Harlins/Du media blitz. However, she cautions residents and outsiders against lumping all South Central community conflicts
into racial categories. 'A lot of people make references to this being "another
Black–Korean incident". On the one hand, I'm glad people are calling us and
are thinking to solve the problem through this avenue. . . . On the other hand,
sometimes it worries me that race gets called into issue every time there

happens to be some sort of disagreement or dispute. Sometimes it will be a straightforward "landlord wants to evict because the rent wasn't paid." But it gets translated into a potential race issue.' The city's shifting demographics – which has seen the percentage of the African-American population decline, Latinos become a plurality, the rapid economic rise of Koreans – has left its non-white residents scrambling.

What has proved the most effective (and borrows essential elements from the mediation process) is the current push to keep dialogue fluid. It is one of the main goals of organizations like the Black Korean Alliance, of which both Choo and Westbrook are key members. 'Right after Latasha Harlins was killed, BKA was very effective in pulling together a community forum in the local churches, bringing both communities together. Some of it was very angry. People yelled and screamed and they let out their anger and frustration, but I think that it was helpful. We allowed people to vent their emotions in a non-destructive way. We were able to channel that anger and energy and to identify some issue areas. Community contribution, community involvement – all of this was happening, but not everybody knew about it There are a lot of good things that happen, but what you get on the news is always the negative stuff – the violence and the blood and the gore. That's where people's orientations are right now, unfortunately.'

Recent meetings held in church sanctuaries or over business breakfasts, and those that took place long before the Harlins shooting, have outlined a framework for joint mediation projects, on-site mediation services and other concrete plans to keep community peace. Choo's mediation center has worked to mend rifts at San Gabriel High between Latino and Chinese students. 'We went in to mediate with the Community Relations Service and the Justice Department. Now these parents have formed a multiethnic coalition.' Another case in Compton earlier this year, involving a police shooting of two Samoan brothers, resulted in a series of meetings and mediations between the Compton city manager's office and Samoan community leaders. 'I think we've done some ground-breaking work. I think it's one of the first times the Samoan community really felt like they were heard. I want people to know that there are partnerships between African-Americans and Korean-Americans and Asian communities, across the board', says Choo. 'People don't see this enough. I don't mean to suggest that this is going to solve all the problems, but people really need to see that not everybody is at war and there's not *just* tension. It's not like we're all scrambling around trying to address that issue for the first time. We have our relationships. We have built our bridges.'

'The tension has to do with class and discrimination', says Jan Sunoo, a mediator with the Federal Mediation and Conciliation Service, and an L.A. City Human Relations Commissioner. 'I don't think you see Korean merchants shooting blacks in middle-class neighborhoods. You don't see them shooting Latinos in middle-class neighborhoods. I think what we're seeing is a very specific problem that happens in poverty.'

Sunoo has an impressive vita for bridging cross-cultural conflicts. He trains hopefuls in the fine art of arbitration, who are then fed into Dennis Westbrook and Marcia Choo's programs. Born in San Francisco of Korean immigrant parents, Sunoo has spent most of his life gathering and sifting through cultural specifics. Leaving San Francisco, Sunoo traveled to Germany as an exchange student. 'That', he says, 'gave me new eyes.' His first job out of school was with the Watts Health Center as a psychologist, a couple years after the uprisings. He followed that with a four-year teaching stint at New York's City College in Harlem. A job with UPS and a position as a Teamsters shop steward and representative, became his entree into the world of labor negotiation.

As a federal mediator, Sunoo says that you can't get involved with labor relations in Los Angeles without disparate cultures coming into play. 'At the bargaining table, you might have a Japanese businessman and his American attorney, and a Teamster business agent who may be a militant, head-knockin' Jewish radical and who represents Spanish-speaking immigrants. That's how my interests were piqued in the cross-cultural aspects of mediation.'

As for community tensions, 'Koreans', Sunoo explains, 'are ill-equipped to understand African-American culture. They come from a country that is monolingual and monocultural and has been for thousands of years. They're like babes in the woods when it comes to trying to deal with this multiethnic society that we just take for granted. In some instances, they don't know how to give respect to African-Americans – or to Americans in general. To some extent they are captives of their own prejudices because of their narrow exposure to African-American culture and lifestyles. They get it the same way the majority of Americans get it – from movies. So what do they see portrayed there? There are no respectful images.'

Over the years, Sunoo has collected an ever-lengthening list of complaints from ad hoc roundtables and his community of friends: 'That Koreans are rude, seem suspicious, sometimes they're abrupt and they don't smile. They throw the change on the table', he says. But Korean shopkeepers are not overly solicitous – Koreans consider it phony to smile too much. In terms of throwing money on the table instead of your hand, Koreans consider physical contact between strangers of different sexes improper.

'I think the other part of the problem is that some African-Americans are so frustrated by an economic situation that has not improved since the Civil Rights movement, has not improved since my days in Watts. In fact, it's gotten worse. The violence has gotten worse. I think that they are scapegoating these Korean grocers, who are not really the major problem. It's very hard to attack the establishment, or to attack the educational system, or to change the political economic structure, for someone on the street. So he'll say, "Well, maybe I can't change the world, but at least I can get this damn grocer to respect me."'

Education is just one part of a larger plan for primary prevention. The Black Korean Alliance has assembled a code of ethics – a set of posters to be displayed in all South Central convenience markets that will present a list of principles (merchandise clearly tagged, refund policies, a customer/shopkeeper respect statement and dispute-resolution hotline numbers) with which both merchant and consumer agree to comply. A video training project aimed at Korean merchants is in the works as well, which will brief Korean store owners about American business customs as well as give some history of African-American achievements. But projects like these don't and won't happen without funding. Support for the code of ethics project evolved relatively quickly, but funds for the video project have yet to be secured. And drumming up interest for it has been, curiously, difficult.

Still, mediators like Maria Choo – sometimes to their own surprise – hold on to optimism. 'I think oftentimes a lot of people, particularly in the mainstream culture, want pat little answers for what they can use when they deal with somebody of a different ethnicity', she says. 'None of us can know all things about another person's culture. You learn with your increased contact. You learn from experience and from your actions. And if you make that conscious effort to be more aware and to make yourself *be* sensitive – then you'll do just fine.'

January 1992

CHAPTER 7

SET THIS TANGLE STRAIGHT:
A PORTRAIT OF BLACK
INDEPENDENT SCHOOLS

YOU CAN GET LOST OUT THERE

As a public lecturer I endeavor to help to educate the public. . . . I do not
speak carelessly or recklessly but with a definite object of helping the people,
especially those of my race, to know, to understand, to realize themselves.
Marcus Garvey, 1937

'Clear your desk, brother', Vanessa Beverly commands in her chilly, eyes-in-
the-back-of-her-head voice. Backs stiffen, hands quickly fold, then rest on
smooth desktops. Striding toward the classroom's rear corner, she doesn't
bother to hold the guilty party in her stare, but you can pick him out easily
enough – astonished eyes, the slow incline of the head. The others know better: Don't dare work her nerves. A tall, regal beauty, Ms Beverly flows by in
layers of black, accented only with a brilliant *Kente* sash. Today she has her
long braids tied back with a thin piece of gold cord; Africa, in two tiny brass
silhouettes, dangles from her lobes.

'Let's drill.' Sister Beverly selects a leader. As he rises, a sudden draft
causes the classroom's African flag to skitter to the floor. Some students barely
suppress their giggles. 'Don't laugh', reprimands Donnie, a new fifth-grader
seated front-row. He retrieves the fallen flag, dusts it off, and ceremoniously
restores it to its proper place.

Jacques positions himself at the front of the classroom before a large relief map of Africa. Nearby, a print of Universal Negro Improvement Association founder Marcus Garvey in full regalia – bushy gold epaulets and plumed purple commodore's hat – keeps a close eye on his studious progeny. Grouped around the room there are other signs that remind 'There's a Great Future in Your Past' or 'Support Black Education' – or simply implore the students to 'TRY.'

They'll need this encouragement to tackle fourth- and fifth-grade vocabulary. Vanessa Beverly, like many other Marcus Garvey School instructors, works hard to ensure that her kids will not make careless mistakes. They cannot afford to. 'I like to get them when they're full of energy and alert. I've got to get them while I can.' Today's words include *hemotoxic, pachyderm, electrocardiograph, osteodentin*, but Jacques looks confident as he calls out random samples to which his classmates respond in spirited cadence: 'Neurotic', he announces. The class repeats it. 'Spell it!' he commands. They do so in unison. 'Define it!' 'A nervous disorder caused by or having to do with phobia.'

'Can you give me an example?' Sister Beverly breaks in from her corner perch. A hand shoots up at the back: 'If your partner got shot and there's helicopters and more shooting and stuff, after a while you're scared to go outside. That's a kind of neurosis.'

'Thank you, brother', says Sister Beverly with a stoic nod. 'Let's move on.'

Since 1975, lawyers, waitresses, insurance agents, public-school teachers, doctors, department-store clerks and real estate brokers have been bundling up their babies and sending them to Dr Anyim Palmer and his 'miracle school'. Jazz musician George Bohannon did. So did Stevie Wonder. Grandmothers Maxine Waters and Myrlie Evers were comforted to find that their children's children would be culturally grounded. Not, as wide rumor has it, a Muslim school or a secret outpost of the Garveyite cause, the Marcus Garvey School is the largest (400 students, preschool through ninth grade), most established (its budget last year was approximately $300,000) and third oldest of Los Angeles's four black private independent schools.

Along with the others – Omowale Ujamaa, Winnie and Nelson Mandela Educational Institute, and Uhuru Schule, all founded in the seventies as well – Marcus Garvey has provided black families with a way to bypass the deteriorating Los Angeles public-school system. 'Before I moved here from Missouri I heard about the crowded classrooms', says Marian Penny, whose two children

'BECAUSE TODAY IS BUILT ON YESTERDAY': MARCUS GARVEY SCHOOL

attend Marcus Garvey. 'I'd heard stories that if you went to school in one of *our* neighborhoods that you weren't necessarily going to get a good education. I grew up going to all-black schools with small classes and teachers who cared. I wanted my children to have that experience as well.' For an increasing number of African-American families, waiting for the public-school system to improve is a defeatist's answer, so parents like Marian Penny have voted with their feet. And what they have turned to is a pedagogical tradition that goes back almost 200 years – the freedom school.

The freedom school, or elements of it, has appeared in various guises over the years – as church- or community-sponsored rites-of-passage programs, Saturday schools and immersion programs. But what they all have in common is a strong, Afrocentric-based curriculum, which many educators hope will provide long-elusive answers to African-American students' declining achievement. Black independent schools like Marcus Garvey, Roots Activity Learning Center in Washington, D.C. (founded in 1977), St Francis Academy in Baltimore (1828), and a host of others have achieved such success that they are now serving as models for public-school programs throughout the country. Portland, Oregon's Boise-Eliot Elementary School was the first to implement an Afrocentric curriculum, in 1989; variations on it have sprung up in Milwaukee, Detroit, Atlanta, Pittsburgh, Washington, D.C., and New Orleans. Although Afrocentric public-school programs have their share of critics – conservatives suspicious of anything that smacks of 'multiculturalism', liberals (both black and white) suspicious of anything that smacks of separate but equal – there are just as many who see them as one answer to a generation at risk. 'I'm optimistic. I have to be', says teacher and educational consultant Itihari Toure. 'Working in a [black] private school, we serve such a small percentage of the community. These kids leave these schools and go back into the community school, get no reinforcement, feel isolated, run into the same problems. Curriculum is something that has to be looked at. Changes in the public-school system are going to *have* to be made. Students are so mediocre that it's getting to the point that they will try anything. Not because there is a tremendous sensitivity. Not because African-American children are in crisis. But because it's more cost-effective to keep them in school.'

The Marcus Garvey School stands at the corner of Seventh and Slauson avenues, just a few blocks away from the Crenshaw strip. Friday and Saturday nights, Crenshaw and Dorsey high school students 'roll the 'shaw'. It's black L.A.'s version of Hollywood Boulevard kicks, or the Valley's Ventura Boulevard's neon strip of malt shops and fortress malls. But only a few blocks east, the landscape alters drastically. Residents have given up whitewashing the walls. Warring gangs have left their marks in indelible inks and paint on the modest stucco homes that bank the railroad tracks near the corner of Slauson and Vermont avenues. It's hard to say when the homeowners gave up. For a long time they were stubborn – proud and boastful about their neatly clipped lawns and sculptured shrubs. But now even the neighbor ladies who murmured as they worked about those 'bad little boys' have saddened their bright bungalows into deterrent shades of olive, mustard and industrial gray.

South on Vermont, the stylized tags are the least of residents' day-to-day worries. Past the charred shambles of anonymous storefronts, past kids conducting loud and complex business at corner pay phones, an Asian herb specialist, and the One Stop Cafe scenting the air with a narcotic mix of tamales and collard greens, KCBS newlywed nighttime anchors Jim and Bree feign thoughtfulness from a remote billboard ('More Than Profiles, the Whole Story'). It's difficult to conceive that between coy smiles and smarmy domestic talk they could really flesh out this picture when longtime neighbors barely can.

'We worry about the little kids who walk from Gage to school, who pass those joints [bars, liquor stores] on their way', says Barbara Rickett, assistant principal at another neighborhood campus – John Muir Junior High on Vermont – a five-minute drive from Marcus Garvey. Rickett has been in the district for twenty-one years, at Muir for four. She has monitored startling demographic changes – from predominantly black to largely Latino – as well. And she's had reason to worry. In the first quarter of this year, according to the LAPD, there have been twenty-one street robberies, twenty-eight auto thefts, forty-four aggravated assaults, three rapes and one murder in the two-square-mile area bounded by Slauson, Budlong Avenue, 62nd Street and the Harbor Freeway.

Kids quickly accustom themselves to traumas, responding in unspoken ways – with poor attendance or short attention spans, sometimes a slow and inexorable retreat into an interior world. Pushed to verbalize, their dreams are often prefaced with ifs not whens. 'Gang activity doesn't come into the school overtly, but we deal with the psychological effects', Rickett explains. 'There is the here today, gone tomorrow [aspect]. We try our best to address the psychological effects of that.'

'Cougars, Believe You Can and You Will' encourages a black-and-white banner draped just yards away from John Muir's front entrance. Nearby an aide seated behind a portable table watches as a stream of students flash white passes before they move toward the one open door. On a wall next to the main office door hangs a modest-size oil portrait; an official-looking man in suit and tie – former principal Samuel Harper – smiles at passers-by. 'He died at his desk', the woman at the table says flatly, not taking her eyes off the steady flow before her. 'There was another principal here who died. He was driving to school and had a heart attack too. Tried to drive himself to the hospital. . . .' her voice trails. 'I heard they asked his wife if she would like a portrait of her husband as well. But I don't think she wanted [one].'

The school now has a hard-to-shake nickname – 'killer Muir' – but its academic statistics sketch an even grimmer picture. With an enrollment of a little more than 1,500 – 48 percent African-American, 52 percent Latino (a significant portion of whom speak little or no English) – Muir's dropout rate is 25 percent: the second highest in its part of the district. Twenty-four percent of the student body is absent daily, while approximately 5 percent is written up daily for disciplinary reasons. The monthly suspension rate averages about 20 percent. And out of the 450 ninth-grade students at Muir this year, some 350 will enter high school with at least two fails in required classes. Muir is ranked among the state's lowest in reading and math achievement scores.

Staff statistics look no better. Out of the seventy-nine full-time employees – including teachers, counselors, support staff, resource and magnet teachers – an average of six are absent daily. Over the last three years, there's been a 50 percent teacher turnover, and, to fill those quickly vacated spaces, 25 percent of the staffers have emergency credentials, are nonpermanent teachers or are long-term substitutes with minimal experience and training.

In district parlance, Muir is a 'school in crisis'.

It hasn't always been this way. Longtime teachers remember when the campus was considered one of the top inner-city schools in the district, boasting a congenial atmosphere and a dedicated faculty. 'Changes come gradually', recalls one 34-year veteran teacher (now retired) who wishes to remain anonymous. 'You barely notice that it happens. Then one day you look up and say, "Can this really be the same school?"' In some courses, class size has slowly increased to as many as forty. 'When you get too many, no matter how good they are, you can't teach. You expect to accomplish the same that you always have, but you can't.' At the same time, says the teacher, parental support dramatically declined: 'They didn't seem to know what to do with their kids. You tell them that you have a problem and they say; "I know what you're going through." It's here you can best see the breakdown of the family structure.'

Principal Ellen Zimet, walking these grounds for less than half a year, says it will take a sweeping effort to reconstruct the school. Their plans are eleventh-hour drastic, and will radically redesign classroom structure. The Muir Model would carve the school into three 'houses' that would provide smaller groups, intensive instruction and a more multicultural curriculum. But since the Los Angeles Unified School District (LAUSD) cut $241 million from its 1991/92 budget, Muir faces an even shakier future. 'It *will* affect the quality of the program', says Barbara Rickett. 'We're going to lose some very good teachers, and administrators just can't do it all.'

Working with what little is available, the school has launched an aggressive test-taking program to raise the student body's plummeting CTBS standardized test scores. Rickett and Zimet hope to keep other support programs going, including the College Readiness partnership with Cal State Dominguez Hills and the Adopt-a-School program with the local Boys Market. And, despite the coming year's bleak prognosis, they still have hopes of attracting more bilingual teachers through the Urban Classroom Teacher Program.

'With the cuts it's just been difficult to plan', says Rickett. 'People are so demoralized. We don't have as much campus security. They're cutting health support services and not all schools have the same personality. Schools need to have a say-so. But we're trying to be optimistic. We have to. We've got to get back to the business of education.'

For African-American parents ridding themselves of their own John Muirs, the Marcus Garvey School is one of the alternatives. Known for its strictness as much as for its academics (and where Tom Thumb kindergartners struggle with the weight but not the content of a fifth- or sixth-grade English text), the Marcus Garvey School has been the target of frequent speculation. For those in the traditional educational community who believe that programs like these offer no more than heavy doses of Afrocentric indoctrination, fears produce visions of an outraged generation harboring hostile, separatist notions.

For Shirley Woods, finding a place for her son, Donnie, in Vanessa Beverly's fourth- and fifth-grade classroom was a last resort. To keep him in his

Chatsworth elementary school, she was told that she had to feed him Ritalin and pin his spirit down. She received constant reports about his wild behavior, his smart mouth, inability to sit still. Teachers and administrators speculated about his background – that he was bused in from some inner-city inferno, or lived close by but under nightmarish conditions – and the staff treated him 'accordingly'. Any time a rock was thrown, dirt clods sprayed the street or a watch turned up missing, eyes would focus on the Woods household. 'If I didn't know any better', says Shirley, [I'd believe that] 'they were slowly killing my son.'

An LAUSD math teacher herself, Shirley was confounded by her son's situation – it didn't correspond to her daughter's experience in public school – and she was even more upset by her inability to help. 'When he came home from school, he always had something negative to say. He was sad. I didn't realize how unhappy. I was so wrapped up in work. I was angry with him because he could not just go to school and not get in trouble. I was so frustrated that I started blaming him.'

Shirley found out about Marcus Garvey while teaching summers in the city. She had to locate a place to stow the kids mornings and afternoons, and she had one requirement: that it was in an environment that bolstered their self-esteem. 'You can get lost out there living with all these white people', she explains. 'That's why I wanted my son back at Garvey, because he needed his self-confidence back.'

Since October, Donnie has risen bleary, some mornings as early as 5:30, to ride the thirty miles to school. His father, Donnie, Sr drops him off on his way to work – the hot-dog stand (Donnie's Dog House) he owns and runs on Florence – just a few blocks away. What makes it all worth while, Shirley says, are the after-school hours – the dinnertime quotes echoing Amiri Baraka, Malcolm X and the poetry of Paul Laurence Dunbar. His grades have improved, his confidence has soared. Shirley sees it in his penmanship, which has struggled out of tight little sketches into bold, declarative lines.

'It's all because they teach them the truth', says Shirley. 'They deal with more real-life situations for our black kids than white schools do. The white schools don't have the resources and they don't have the know-how to teach black kids who come from a different environment, different upbringing, a different vocabulary. I think all young black kids need to have a black awareness in order to make it in this society – if they don't have confidence in themselves and know who they are, they'll never be able to survive. Donnie's found out there's something about being black. There's strength and knowledge there. He has a lot to gain from that. I'm so happy that he realized that.'

Sometimes Donnie still gets a little out of hand (he was suspended recently for spinning on his head in an impromptu play-yard show-and-tell), but Vanessa Beverly says he's doing just fine. In six months his report card went from a collection of low C's, D's and F's to only a couple of C's, B's and even one A. 'When he came in he was restless. He didn't like to work', she recalls. 'I had to threaten him to get him to get things done.' A smaller classroom environment and individualized instruction both helped, but a lot of it, she believes, was peer pressure. 'He saw other students striving, trying to make good grades. He wanted to do that, too.'

'They wrote that I was retarded', Donnie explains after class, 'but I know I'm good inside.' Here at Marcus Garvey, Donnie says, he likes to learn his history and his math, but most of all he's here to make his mother proud. He wants to be a black leader, like his hero Malcolm X. 'I feel that he's in my blood telling me to do good. He's on top trying to help me pass through this world.'

THE FIRST DEGREE

Brother Reginald X likes to put his children through changes. You can see it in downcast eyes, in the strain clouding bright faces. But, as Brother Reginald figures, life outside will take them through much more. His stern approach isn't about breaking spirits, he says – it's about buttressing the weaker ones, or recovering others long lost.

'Reason you can't keep up, all that smoking and drinking makes you too tired to run.' Brother Reginald's voice booms and cracks like a hectoring drill sergeant's. He doesn't smile. In a steam-pressed, steel-gray suit and crimson tie, and a two-inch part carved into the side of his close-cropped fade, Brother Reginald keeps a steady eye on his junior high school class lumbering halfheartedly in imperfect circles around Marcus Garvey's dusty grounds.

The playground doubles as a parking lot, forcing students to weave in and out among Toyota Camrys and VW vans. Here at Marcus Garvey, you won't get tetherball or handball or tennis or basketball. It's pretty much make-do. Which means toiling through the familiar obstacle course before embarking on basic calisthenics – jumping jacks and toe-touches. Kids here at Marcus Garvey get as much physical education as the state requires. Not a second more.

In response to the rigorous routine, some students have been known to mutter 'Marcus Garvey Prison'. They sit through long classroom days with short breaks in the sun. Some extol the luxuries and free time of their previous schools, conjuring up visions of rolling green lawns and Olympic-size swimming pools. But Anyim Palmer feels that play is largely unimportant, that too much free time has played a large part in keeping the race behind. As one parent told me, 'We don't want to do anything serious. We want to jump up and down all day long. We don't even want to sit still in church. We need to sit still and listen, learn, read – educate ourselves and our kids.'

'A lot of you don't eat right', Brother Reginald barks at the laggers, preaching the evils of sugar and salt. One complains about a pain in his chest, another coughs and wheezes as he clutches his side. Brother Reginald's face doesn't crack. Those who have finished stand in a silent line in front of the school's front doors, waiting impatiently for the rest to fall in place. Once the rest of the class retreats inside, one lone student continues breathlessly, tracing the maze of the loop.

It's in junior high, Marcus Garvey director Linda Sanders says, when teaching the history becomes difficult, the content much more demanding, when the students are no longer shielded from slavery. Nearly three-quarters of Brother Reginald's thirty-eight pupils are first-time Marcus Garvey students, and their notion of American history rests almost exclusively on the achievements of the Vikings, Christopher Columbus, George Washington and Abraham Lincoln. New to the Garvey school himself, Brother Reginald relishes the challenge of breaking myths and opening new worlds to his students. Some arrive hostile, some bored; some don't give a damn and will let you know it. But none of this is allowed in Brother Reginald's room: you take that noise outside.

'I don't want anybody to sleep in class. Everybody stand up and get the Z monster off us', Brother Reginald commands, pointer in hand. The class stands and takes deep stretches. Then, facing front, he leads them through a booming afternoon chant.

'I will.'

I will

'Work on myself.'

Work on myself

'I will spend time.'

I will spend time

'Every day.'

Every day

'Working on my mind.'

Working on my mind

'Turn to the brother or sister next to you and tell them, "You got what it takes."'

Affirmations are tacked hastily to walls and bulletin boards, others emblazoned on T-shirts or bumper stickers: 'I Want an Education for My People That Will Elevate Them', 'Knowledge Overcomes Fear'. Today's history message elucidates this aphorism: 'Liberation Through Education'.

'After *Brown* versus *Board of Education*', says Brother Reginald, 'we spent too much time and money trying to assimilate students, and the last twenty years have been a total failure. I couldn't present history from a Eurocentric perspective. I couldn't teach African-American history watered down and condensed. I'm a firm believer that Europeans have no reason teaching our young kids. A European person won't teach you right. Same man who enslaved is the instructor?' he asks with a cynical laugh. 'It's nothing beyond that.'

Brother Reginald begins with a beautiful vision of the past. Not full of slave ships, sharecropping, and whips and chains, but of grand Egyptian kingdoms and universities (like the Grand Lodge of Luxor at Kemit or the University of Sankore at Timbuktu) filled with vast libraries and peopled by unheralded thinkers. These lectures reverberate like Sunday sermons. Traveling over broad and arduous ground, his words at certain points seem stream-of-consciousness, presenting an overwhelming sweep of information that spans continents and epochs. Students scribble madly in loose-leaf notebooks, flip pages quickly to keep up with his breakneck pace. Some, slouching into fitful catnaps, seem hopelessly lost, staring into space.

'Now, brothers and sisters, if we are ever to eradicate and uplift our condition spiritually, socially, economically and politically, we must go back and get that first degree. And that's a knowledge of self', says Brother Reginald, his voice booming. 'Any time you ride through South Central L.A. and a disproportionate [number of] the youth drive by in their 5.0s and their Nissan trucks and their sidekick Jeeps with names on the back – 'Sweet and Low', 'Easy Rider', 'Night Hawk', 'Professor X' – and on the back of the Jeep there's a 200- or 300-watt sound system blowing four or five blocks away. That's a people that have been robbed of a knowledge of self. That's a person crying out: "Please notice me", "Show me I am somebody", "I want you to know that I own this", "Please see me." Look at the people now. Understand the dynamic and all that you see.'

For many of these children, finding answers in the nonsensical and the horrific – friends clipped in drive-bys, others lost in the monstrous half-dream of crack – is the largest leap of faith of all. Building on the foundation that Dr Palmer has carefully laid out, Brother Reginald requires that students confront the pain of a troubled past and present. 'Brothers and sisters', he declares, 'there is not a more awesome incident to ever happen in the world than a people uprooted, torn, colonized, exploited and made slaves in this hemisphere. Brothers and sisters, what about your holocaust?'

'When you leave here today', he continues, 'when you run into the gang members, into prostitutes, into the drug dealers, the drunks, they are not our problems. They are a result of our problem. They are a victim of a bigger criminal. Remember, if you don't know what happened yesterday, you're not able and prepared to deal with today. Because today is built on yesterday.'

Here Africa gloriously resides as the cultural hearth – documented in the works of black historians like G. M. James in *Stolen Legacy, The Destruction of Black Civilization* by Chancellor Williams, and John Jackson's *Introduction to African Civilization*. In these volumes, they learn the essence of *education*. 'Educo', as student Brother Louis recites, 'means to be brought out of the darkness and into the light.'

It's taken some time for students to get over the shock of Brother Reginald. One look at the suit and tie and shadow of hair bespoke the worst. Before, many knew little more about the Nation of Islam than the silent security force that imposed order over rap shows or the erect figures hawking pink boxes with bean pies at the corner of Vernon Avenue and Martin Luther King, Jr Boulevard. But now they stop by after class and ask for advice. They try out Kiswahili phrases and shoot in between classes to offer Brother Reginald a sincere 'Peace be unto you.'

'They saw me as being real strict and overbearing', he recalls. 'We don't tolerate a whole lot of nonsense. We don't tolerate discipline problems. A lot of parents still walk in and say, "Man! You got one of those Muslims teaching – *and* he calls himself Brother X." They worried about how I dressed and what I'd say.'

Knowing how to be hard, but more important, knowing when to back down, is largely the secret to success in a classroom, as most teachers will tell you. And Brother Reginald has achieved classroom success in subtle ways: not stumbling around street slang, coloring his lectures with a catch phrase from the latest rap, speaking on the level about sex, drugs or gangs. 'Once they develop a trust, it's better. You have to show students – especially in the inner city – love.'

In June, Brother Reginald became a consultant at Garvey, and opened In Touch Books and Tapes in Long Beach. With briefcase and 9-to-5, he is a foreign symbol, a figure that some of these students have never seen before. If they would ask, Brother Reginald would tell them how he grew up in Florida as Reginald Shorter. How he spent his early years learning the 'three R's' in predominantly black classrooms, until his parents (his mother an assistant principal, his father a community college professor) were lured by the split-level houses, tennis clubs and golf courses of Florida's mostly moneyed and entirely white Lakewood Estates. Reginald had a difficult time in the classroom, trying to adjust to his new environment and the 'different social dynamic' that went along with it. Unable to shake the feeling that he just didn't fit in, he decided to attend a black university so he could return to an atmosphere where he would once again be pushed to succeed.

At Wilberforce, the oldest black university in the country, Reginald majored in political science, minored in pre-law, and put in time with the Army ROTC. After an abortive stint with a San Francisco law firm as a paralegal, he wandered from wardrobe consultant to residential counselor at the L.A. Job Corps vocational training center. Yet, he says, he felt aimless and empty, perpetually searching for something more. Finding his way into the Nation of Islam, he decided that it was the only black organization that could truly effect change. Through enthusiastic reports from Muslim parents who sent their children there, he heard about the Marcus Garvey School and applied for a teaching position.

Every week, Brother Reginald changes from his necktie to the familiar, more formal bow, and travels to local housing projects. He and other members of the Fruit of Islam set up tables in community centers or makeshift rumpus rooms, loading them down with leaflets, newsletters, newspapers. They sometimes screen videos that show that there is more to life than dealing drugs or finding sanctuary in flashing cryptic hand signs. 'Going in there, your walk has to be firm, confident', Brother Reginald says. 'I don't go in like I'm timid or afraid. I show the strength.'

AN EDUCATION TO SURVIVE

Talk to the generation of African-Americans who grew up with *Tarzan*. Ask them about their memories of Saturday matinees featuring pop-eyed, grunting natives stumbling with spears through rubber trees and swaying vines. They waited for an implacable, fearless, white Tarzan to lead them out of danger, to show them the light. These bewildered visions of slapstick primitives are what many thought (and often still believe) Mother Africa was all about.

For my generation it was television: a new, in-living-color *Tarzan*, paired with *Daktari*, the saga of a white doctor's struggle on the uncertain African savannas. Even worse was the cartoon world of *George of the Jungle*. (I bore an unfortunate surname, which only added to already well-stocked play-yard munitions.) Africa looked large, hot and empty.

In some ways little has changed. The mystery of the Dark Continent is still largely unsolved, a picture hastily, if at all, drawn. For many black children, Africa remains little more than a theme park. They don't know that Egypt fills out its northwestern tip; that Africans wore crowns and drifted in pleasure cruises down majestic rivers; designed temples, tombs and pyramids. They are too often oblivious to the Africans' glorious past of a productive era before the horrors of capture, the Middle Passage and slavery. They're unaware that their heritage boasts something grand. Something to be proud of.

A black child's education begins here. It starts with re-imagining Africa. 'We have a very strong African/African-American history program here, which is something that many of our brothers and sisters miss in public school', says Linda Sanders. 'The students coming from some public schools have missed out on their heritage. Their parents bring them here to find it.'

On the grounds of the Marcus Garvey School you can see the celebration of heritage everywhere. Though little black girls still play elaborate patty-cake games and chant familiar rhymes about 'Mary Mack', the ends of their thick pigtails are secured with red, black and green ribbons or tiny swatches of *kente* cloth exploding like festive excelsior. You hear it in the spirit of a two-year-old's voice shouting the word *negra* during a color drill in Spanish; in the rousing recitation of the morning motivational 'Ode to the Ancestors' that echoes James Weldon Johnson's Black National Anthem as well as Jesse Jackson's 1988 Democratic Convention speech. It's in the four-year-olds' cadence as they recite lines from Langston Hughes:

> The night is beautiful,
> And so the faces of my people.
>
> The stars are beautiful,
> So the eyes of my people.
>
> Beautiful, also is the sun.
> Beautiful also, are the souls of my people.

Here daily lessons revolve around the allegedly silent continent: Africa is the source. Traditional subjects like English, world history, or geography, are explored in part by changing the complexion of the central characters, or shifting the focus from Europe and North America to Africa and the African diaspora. The study of American literature might include the Harlem Renaissance poetry and prose of Countee Cullen, Claude McKay, Jean Toomer and Zora Neale Hurston instead of Hemingway's and Fitzgerald's remote worlds.

But while making history or literature Afrocentric might mean trading one subject (Spain's King Ferdinand, Thomas Edison) for another (Songhay's King Askia, Garrett A. Morgan), revamping courses like math and science is a more challenging project. At Garvey these subjects are taught as they might be in a public school, but their African roots are simultaneously examined. Though Garvey doesn't go so far as to teach children hieroglyphics before they learn Roman numerals, as some Afrocentric programs do, other adjustments are made. In Garvey's classrooms, Imhotep, a chief physician at the court of Egyptian King Zoser (who reigned some 3,500 years before Christ), is elevated to the position of father of medicine, dislodging Hippocrates. And Greek philosopher Pythagoras is said to have obtained the basis for his theorem while studying at the African Mystery School in Egypt.

Acquiring materials to pass along to students has always been tough. In the beginning, Linda Sanders recalls, Garvey students learned from used books. 'The Afrocentric material is not that easy to put your hands on', says Sanders, 'particularly for your primary-level children.' Sanders peruses local black bookstores like Nealy's or Eso Won looking for supplementary material; Garvey's teachers keep files stocked with articles clipped from various periodicals and make frequent trips to the library to photocopy readings.

Jawanza Kunjufu is familiar with this struggle to provide. When he graduated from Illinois State University in 1974, he knew he wanted to teach black students. But in the Chicago classrooms that he first entered, neighborhood kids were under the sway of street gangs, and many didn't seem to care about learning. Kunjufu knew that it was going to take more than readings in African achievements to hold their attention.

For Kunjufu, the best hope is a program that provides for black children – and most of all, young black males – the nurturing and role-model guidance that doesn't always exist at home. 'In 1910, 90 percent of our children had their fathers at home', he says. 'In 1960, 80 percent. In 1990, 38 percent. That's a big issue. We have to help teachers understand boys' learning styles. Even white boys go to special ed more than white girls.'

Now an educational consultant, Kunjufu's textbooks and curriculum guidelines, which cover language, arts and social science, have found their way into the hands of students in independent and public classrooms nationwide. Marcus Garvey School teachers lead their younger pupils through excerpts from his *Lessons in History: A Celebration of Blackness*, in which students are expected to do more than rattle off names and dates. They instead must understand the achievements as well as the mistakes, concepts as well as cultural strengths. These lessons end with earnest homilies explaining the significance of each major achievement. 'Most schools', explains Kunjufu, 'teach about Dr King between 1929 and 1968, and yet we need to be able to teach our children in 1991 how they can resolve conflict through nonviolence – what King stood for. The whole concept of his philosophy needs to be applied today – especially if homicide is the leading killer of black males between sixteen and thirty-five.'

Where an education starts, some teachers are now arguing, plays a large part in where a child ends up. 'Most of our children were being taught that their history began in 1619. If that's the case, that means they start on the plantation and they'll end up in the ghetto, but if you start them 4 thousand years ago, they start on a pyramid, and they'll end up being free.'

His curriculum lights a fire under students, molds pupils into active community participants. They learn to look at their surroundings with a keen and critical eye. As well as including units on Egypt and African tribes, broad lesson plans examine current issues and more immediate concerns like drugs, values, advertising and adulthood's rites of passage.

Kunjufu shares with Linda Sanders the belief that self-esteem lies at the heart of any successful educational program – private or public. There are children who may know their history, he asserts, but still use catch phrases like 'good hair' and 'pretty eyes' to acknowledge attributes based on a white ideal. Equally chilling is the assumption that being smart means being white. 'If you're on the honor roll, you're acting white. If you speak proper English, you're acting white. They will tease and call one another nerds. And if that's what our children think', says Kunjufu, 'then what does being black mean?'

Despite Garvey's successes, there are educators who believe that Kunjufu and instructors in independent institutions like Marcus Garvey are filling students' heads with empty slogans and flash braggadocio about as enduring as the latest consciousness-raising rap. The criticisms run from charges of breeding 'racial antagonism' to concerns that instructors aren't really teaching history but works of fiction, leaving children to later feel cheated and 'conned by Afrocentrists'.

Former L.A. Unified School District school board member and 9th District Councilwoman Rita Walters considers her words carefully, and thoughtfully conveys her reservations. 'There is nothing wrong with private education if parents want to afford that for their children. But I believe in the public school experience. It provides a broader range for learning, for developing self-esteem, human relations, and giving students an opportunity to learn about their culture. We should see history reflected as it occurred, not sterilized as we see it in some textbooks – contributions ignored, factual data being misconstrued or overlooked entirely.

'Texts should embody cultures as reflected in the school system. Texts used to be Eurocentric, and for African-American students, for example, their history wasn't discussed until Black History Month or Martin Luther King Day. We want them to know that their history didn't occur in a vacuum. 'Not just African-American children, but *all* children, need to be able to look around and see racial diversity. Anglo children need to hear it as much as African-American children do, and African-American children need to be in the classroom when Anglo children hear it.'

Nona Smith, director of education with the New York state NAACP, has spoken out against New York City's plans to fund a separate public school for

Latino and African-American boys. She supports instead the state's proposed 'Curriculum of Inclusion'. 'It's not about separating at all', says Smith. 'It doesn't mean taking away European achievements. It means expanding curriculum to be more inclusive of other cultural groups. Our children have to reach all requirements in all subject matter to get ahead. They have to know Shakespeare, and they should have knowledge of contemporary writers – be they Asian, African-American or Latino. They haven't gotten rid of the SAT. It's not healthy to focus on the achievement of solely one group. It doesn't promote harmony. We have to educate children for the international marketplace.'

For generations, African-American children, along with their Native American, Asian-American and Latino counterparts, have waded through elaborate inventions and half-truths. They've tried to locate bits and pieces of their history within cavernous holes. It's hard to know where to stand – with those who tell us Columbus discovered America, or alongside those who insist that Western philosophy is 'vomit'.

Anyone with a child must try to decide. Packing a lunch and chauffeuring a student to and from the school's front door is often not enough. Guardians are encouraged to do their part at home, to keep up to date with teachers and content. The answer for these children isn't to obliterate the contributions of other races – to retaliate by reversing the methods we've grown up with. As one Marcus Garvey parent explains, 'If you're sending your child here, hopefully that parent is teaching their kids what to do with that information. Marcus Garvey is letting them know how white people really are. The children are going to handle it when they get out because they know what it's all about. They learn awareness.'

Linda Sanders calls it an education to survive. 'Our material is not racist. It is *documented*. Those who are extremely capable in teaching it know that they cannot put facts out there that are not documented. Some people may view it another way, because they're not familiar with a certain segment of history. But the bottom line is the children, and the best reward is seeing their confidence and watching them get ahead in the world.'

Sanders and others at Garvey would like to see these children return and give back to their communities. Says Jawanza Kunjufu, 'In America we have more blacks with degrees than anywhere else in the world – about 1.2 million. But very few are dedicated to the liberation of their people. That's why we're in the state we're in. What good is it to have a B.A. or M.A. or a Ph.D. and no commitment to the race?'

A PLACE OF UNDERSTANDING

Listen long enough and you'll hear the stories. Some about one-room school-houses in Southern hamlets where children first learned to sound their way through a reader. Others about teachers who lived just a few doors away and volunteered their after-supper hours to help with arithmetic.

'There's been almost a total disillusionment in the public system. It is very difficult for parents to come to the realization that the schools are really a detriment to many of our youngsters', says Joan Davis Ratteray of Washington, D.C.'s Institute for Independent Education. 'Public education wasn't designed for students of color, especially it wasn't designed for African-American youngsters. It was designed to develop a consensus, a social contract where the plight of African-American children has never been at the top of the agenda. Some children are going to make it anyway, but that's a few. The majority of our African-American youngsters have to be in a setting that's going to cater to their needs.'

Since 1984, from her inner-city office, Ratteray has put independent schools in contact with one another, raised funds for them and charted their growth. With a budget of $248,000 (coming from foundations, individuals and schools), she provides technical assistance and teacher and administrative training. Ratteray publishes a comprehensive directory of independent institutions. She counts on parents and teachers all over the country to be her eyes and ears, to spot schools that grow out of storefronts or backyards. According to the Institute, there are some 284 independent schools serving about 52,000 African-American youngsters.

Though many connect the rise of the black independent school to the rush and tenor of the black-pride movement of the late sixties and early seventies, Ratteray traces these schools as far back as the eighteenth century. In the late eighteenth century, Richard Allen, the founder of the African Methodist Episcopal Church, provided a day school for children and night instruction for the adults in his flock at Bethel AME in Philadelphia. In Baltimore, St Frances-Charles Hall (now St Frances Academy) was started by a group of black nuns in

1828 and still stands as an inspiring example. In the early twentieth century, black leaders and educators like Booker T. Washington and Mary McLeod Bethune were proponents of an independent education.

Just as it's important for black children to understand their culture's history, it's important for those starting schools to know about the legacy of such institutions. To learn from an obscured past, students and teachers have to reconstruct it. Ratteray wants to connect modern institutions with their history, and with each other. 'Many of these schools didn't even know that there was another school around the corner. They don't have the time. There are people all across this country who have their own vision of education. They are part of the educational mosaic.'

Naima Olugbala hasn't purchased a new car in thirteen years, driving her temperamental Datsun to and from school each day. Since 1971, Olugbala has helped to run Omowale Ujamaa – the oldest black independent school in Los Angeles County – out of a storefront, various homes, a garage and, since 1986, from a converted electrical substation that she leases from the city of Pasadena. Approximately seventy students, in kindergarten through eighth grade, are taught by Olugbala with the help of five full-time staffers and two part-timers. Her son, Karume, has been groomed to take over when Naima is ready to retire.

Mornings serving meals for the East Bay Black Panther Party's free breakfast program in the late sixties, as well as teaching in a small village in Tanzania, inspired her community activism. When it came time to educate her own children, Olugbala wanted a place that would immerse them in their culture as well as offer a challenging academic environment. Lacking suitable options, she decided to do it herself. What began as a day-care/after-school service over the years became a full-time academic program.

Omowale Ujamaa ('returning home to familyhood' in Kiswahili) gets most of its money from tuition ($1,500 a year per child), the rest trickling in through everything from candy sales to children's performances. Olugbala admits she's felt disenchanted about the black community's indifference. She says she's gotten lots of claps on the back, curious phone calls, even some press. 'But it's hard to get black people to support. And if they don't, who else will?'

Despite financial woes, for the last twenty years Olugbala has been trying to 'take these children to a place of understanding'. Her program isn't as strict as the Marcus Garvey School's. But though students have more freedom – both on the playground and in the classroom – just as much is expected of them academically. And it's not just black students: Latino children read Nigerian author Chinua Achebe; a blond-haired, blue-eyed preschooler raises her arm in a black-power salute and recites the principles of *Nguzo Saba* – values and traditions of the African-American cultural experience.

'I try very hard not to put the brunt of problems on the public schools', Olugbala says. Teachers are doing the best they can, she adds; yet looking at the results, at the condition of urban classrooms and the dispirited children who exit them, she wonders. 'How successful has integration been? It was a good plan, but it hasn't worked. We just want something that works. If integration isn't working we need to see what does.'

'I know I never wanted to teach in public school', says Mwalimu Evans, founder of the Mandela Institute. Started in Long Beach in 1974, and in Compton since 1978, the school is run from Evans's home. 'I've always wondered, for many years, "Why do public schools do so poorly?" And they *do* do poorly.' Growing up in South Central, Evans says, 'I didn't hear anything that prepared me to deal with my surroundings. African children are not taught to see themselves in the system, and I think that's the only way children can learn. Once they see themselves in the system and see what their relationship is to the world, then they can begin to see that this is why they *have* to make a contribution.'

In the classroom, Evans teaches them to use the voice's quieter registers, not fists, to solve problems. Getting children to *think*, to gather empirical data and strengthen their problem-solving skills, is her goal. She has them write letters to Martin Luther King, Jr identifying problems in their community and suggesting solutions. She takes classes on field trips to Compton City Council meetings and to community colleges, where they can see black leaders and educators speak. They integrate those words and symbols, then use them as paradigms for their own lives.

'My two daughters *hate* Compton', Evans explains. 'But I will always live in an African area. I don't want to leave my community, even though there are periods where there are shootings and you might have to fall on the floor. I feel that it's important for us to stay here and set an example for our community. You just can't run all the time.'

There are many others who believe that pulling out of the system is just another way of running from problems. Since so few children are served by independent schools, abandoning public classrooms is as destructive as turning one's back on the whole community. What about the thousands of black children who struggle daily through public schools?

Black independent schools are 'one avenue', says Ted Alexander, an assistant superintendent for the LAUSD. 'But all teachers and . . . institutions should be trained to teach African-American males. Right now [in public schools] it's not the case. African-American male students have been educated in the past in segregated schools in the South. There's no reason why it shouldn't work in integrated schools right here.'

Gail Greer, who heads LAUSD's Black Education Commission, one of six community-based advisory commissions serving minority communities, is helping to develop an elective studies course for tenth graders. 'I believe in public education and that children need to have a good knowledge of self', she says. 'I'm into promoting academic excellence.' Greer helped to forge a contract that would require Houghton Mifflin to prepare a supplemental history textbook including the accomplishments of an assortment of ethnic groups. If the publisher doesn't incorporate the supplement into future editions, L.A. will not buy their books. 'We're sick of textbooks that start out with 1619 slavery business or the Reconstruction and don't include information about black doctors or explorers or inventors. We also need to know that African-Americans invented the stoplight and the gas mask as well. It's been a long process but I know it can be done.'

There have recently been even more ambitious efforts, in places like New York, Milwaukee and Atlanta, to bring an Afrocentric curriculum into the public schools. In Los Angeles, the school district has embarked on smaller-scale projects like the elementary school–level 10-Schools Program (which provides an alternative classroom structure and curriculum), and the county has started the Male Black Student Task Force. But Joan Ratteray of the Institute for Independent Education feels public school efforts will always fall short. 'You're putting black children back in a system that systematically destroys them', she says. For Ratteray and others in the independent school movement, removing black children from public schools amounts to self-defense. 'Parents have to rethink how they want their tax dollars spent. I think we as parent-educators need to sit down and say what it is going to be.'

'We've always struggled with the public education system', explains local teacher and educational consultant Itihari Toure, 'because it was never set up to provide quality education for poor people.' In the seventies she was part of the staff that built up the Pomona Day School, one of the first large-scale black independent programs in the L.A. area. Run mostly by volunteer college students who served as academic tutors, the Pomona Day School stressed political and cultural issues that affected black youngsters. Many of the schools and Afrocentric programs that exist today – like Omowale Ujamaa, Mandela Institute, Uhuru Shule and the New Afrikan Scouts – incorporated bits and pieces of the Pomona Day School model. Toure spends much of her time these days passing on the latest in teaching techniques and curricula to community classrooms, then bringing the quandaries faced by teachers and administrators to the attention of organizations that assist independent schools.

'These teachers are dealing with a set of problems different from what we dealt with in the seventies. It's not as simple a thing as teaching "black love". You're dealing with victims in a very real sense. We had a police officer come in and talk to the kinds about how to remove themselves from an area so they won't be a victim of an accidental shooting. Two students walked out in hysteria. Crying because it was real. The pressures are a lot different.' What leads parents and children to these schools, says Toure, is the threat of drug and gang involvement. 'It's too bad that it's taken such a tragedy in our community to get us to start dealing with ourselves.'

Independent schools won't be able to reach any of their goals if capricious funding and tenuous budgets persist. Toure says that fish fries and bake sales take care of only short-term needs, like keeping the lights on for another month. What must replace them are grants and endowments, money that will last lifetimes. Mwalimu Shujaa, national executive officer of the Council of Independent Black Institutions, a Buffalo-based organization for black independent schools, agrees: 'These schools run into the same problems businesses do. They go under before they've had a chance to really prove themselves. We're looking at the numbers each year. Numbers of graduates who haven't attained the minimal education requirements. They've become a tremendous weight for the African-American community to carry. It's a community problem.

'We have to and are beginning to assert ourselves. As African-American people, our adult responsibility demands the nurturing of our youth. The real world is not the model cultural society that many imagine. What we've been saddled with is a system where European culture is center and dominant. Others have been subordinated, not placed alongside. But no more.'

A CONTRIBUTION OF VALUE

It happened so quickly and so long ago that Elaine Parker-Gills can't understand why the image still stays with her: Little black boys and girls from a local Muslim school in crisp uniforms, strolling home alongside the remains of Central Avenue's nightlife. They met the gaze of passers-by. Offered earnest 'hellos' or 'good days'. 'They felt safe in their environment', Parker-Gills recalls. 'It seemed like they loved one another. It wasn't until years later that I felt the same way.'

For a little while she lived the dream.

From 1979 to 1985, at 54th Street and Fifth Avenue, children uniformed in red sweaters and blue skirts or slacks learned about Nelson Mandela's South Africa long before it was fashionable. They sang 'Lift Ev'ry Voice and Sing' and ran through rigorous Kiswahili drills. 'We always made sure that they were carrying themselves in a way that showed that they were proud', says Parker-Gills. 'It was how they were to live the rest of their lives.'

The W. E. B. Du Bois Academic Institute was Parker-Gills's attempt to provide an alternative to public schools. An inner-city private school that at its peak was teaching 130 children in preschool through eighth grades, Du Bois faced twin problems that many independent schools struggle with: a lack of steady funding and tenuous community support. When Du Bois closed its doors for good in 1985, it wasn't any one thing – not an electrical bill, not the cost of a new shipment of textbooks – that did the school in. Parker-Gills had run out of moneymaking schemes. She'd given up on miracles.

Like many others in the field, Parker-Gills will tell you that her child inspired her to explore the possibilities of independent education. Her oldest son, Dedan, was enrolled in Marcus Garvey School's kindergarten program, but Parker-Gills, an active Garvey parent, harbored concerns. She worried that the curriculum might be too narrow, that community involvement wasn't stressed enough, that children weren't releasing enough energy on the playground. Since she'd heard many prognoses about the school district's decline, sending her first-born to public school seemed too risky a gamble. She wanted to ensure that he would enter his adult years with 'his spirit intact'. She'd already explored other options – there was Omowale Ujamaa in Pasadena and Compton's Mandela Institute – but Parker-Gills wanted her child closer to home.

'Sometimes the [black] nationalistic view can be a little limiting. You also have to learn to deal with, as King would say, your "white brother". Our kids were exposed to not just African-Americans, but they were exposed to everyone – because *this* is our society. They needed a broader, more inclusive curriculum, more community service and involvement than Garvey would provide.'

With the money she received from a job-discrimination suit settlement, Parker-Gills had the collateral to move beyond a daydream. She bought a building for $75,000 and budgeted $110,000 to run the school in its first year, 1979. A business degree and experience in the corporate sector as an employee-benefits and -relations manager for a major bottled-water company helped her during strategy sessions. She knew up front what questions to ask, what false leads to avoid. 'I knew that you not only had to have a strong comprehensive curriculum, but you had to have a strong and viable board of directors and corporate structure.'

Embarking on this project as she would any business venture, Parker-Gills did market research, canvassing her community and passing out questionnaires. Unlike the founders of some other independent schools, Parker-Gills spent hours preparing a prospectus and screening her staff. She stubbornly sought what she knew was a rarity: people who came armed with both a strong academic background and social consciousness, and who wouldn't mind working for low pay.

Developing the curriculum took about a year. Though rooted in Afrocentric ideology, the course of study Parker-Gills envisioned incorporated traditional subjects – math, reading, history – and balanced the basics with liberal doses of African and African-American history and literature. 'Everything was integrated. Literature wasn't all African-American. We read *The Old Man and the Sea* and *The Souls of Black Folk, The Wall Street Journal* as well as *Amsterdam News*. Kids got into jazz – from Bessie to Billie. They knew who Adam Clayton Powell was. While King was studied, so was Malcolm. Jesse Jackson as well as Daddy Grace.' With a staff of five, Du Bois opened its doors to 60 students (some crossed the street from Garvey, others left surrounding public schools), but before it was all said and done, six years later, a couple hundred had caught 'the spirit of Du Bois'.

Du Bois and Parker-Gills became known for an astute business savvy, a high and often glamorous profile. Though Parker-Gills found moral support from other independent schools, and worked out student exchanges with Garvey as well as neighboring public institutions, Du Bois was different from other independents – those that remained far from the media's eye. Parker-Gills learned not only how to work with the media, but how to work the media machine. Elegant in her close-cropped Afro, tailored suits and heavy earrings, she appeared on news-magazine shows like *Today* and *Tony Brown's Journal*, even braved the phones and studio-audience questions on daytime chat shows. 'Other independent schools never went on *Donohue*, never *wished* to go on it, maybe felt a little uncomfortable about it – "That's kinda getting out of our realm." But I had no intention of just sitting there. I wanted other people to understand and help support. It was in all of our interests to reach out.'

Du Bois was not immediately accepted by those in the independent movement. With her business background, Parker-Gills just wasn't a part of the circle. Some felt that Du Bois was catering to the middle class and labeled it 'the Hollywood School' or 'the Bourgie School'. But the media exposure led to more funding. Parker-Gills was finding what had been, for independent schools, uncharted sources – making stock investments in the school's name, securing money from such corporations as Xerox and ARCO (which also donated office furniture and equipment). She also wasn't shy about hitting up the upwardly mobile ranks of black Hollywood.

One afternoon, Parker-Gills dispatched a half-dozen children to a Crenshaw barbershop where Richard Pryor was settling in for a trim. They carried with them a packet outlining the history and goals of the school. An amused Pryor fired a few questions; the articulate responses piqued his interest enough to inspire a visit to the school grounds the same afternoon. The following day, Pryor sent a check for $10,000 and later chaired the Friends of Du Bois Society, whose membership also included actors Robert Hooks and Glenn Tyrman.

Parker-Gills didn't encourage parental input, she demanded it. 'There's a myth about African-American and Hispanic parents that they don't have the same interest in their children's development. Well, we, as well as all the other independent schools, proved that was wrong. We found that historically in some of the schools, particularly public schools in the inner city, parents were made to feel that their contributions weren't of value.'

Parker-Gills soon discovered how difficult it was to please everyone. Parents, teachers, administrators and board members had very different notions about what constituted a vital education for young black children. 'We had parents who were very nationalistic. We had parents who were not. Some teachers wore African garb, some people said we were not nationalistic enough. Not everybody was satisfied.'

Ideological battles momentarily quelled, Parker-Gills would move on to the nuts and bolts of the operation. Du Bois spent thousands meeting Building and Safety specifications after the agency threatened to close down operations. When a company told Parker-Gills it would cost $30,000 to make the school earthquake-proof, parents volunteered and the job was done for $15,000. There were six teacher salaries at about $800 a month and the monthly mortgage of $454, as well as utilities, study materials and food for the younger students. 'I don't know how many times', recalls Parker-Gills, 'that I wished I had taken that money and opened a travel agency. I couldn't do it anymore. If we had taken a traditional approach, maybe it could have lasted.'

For many who worked hard to keep Du Bois afloat, its end, though always lurking right around the corner, was still a surprise. 'It's disappointing to see any endeavor like this fail. You lose an important chapter', says William Holland, manager of human resources at ARCO. 'The commitment to have something special was there. There was a sense of unity. No-nonsense instruction – the students were challenged academically. She was in trouble financially, but stood steadfastly for what she wanted. I tried to do what I could, to get her some money out of my budget to help out.'

'It takes consistency. It takes a high level of energy and motivation, and it just got to be too much. You cannot exist on shoestrings', says Parker-Gills. 'My hat is off to the people who run these schools. The fact that they are functioning says a lot. You need to know that the time and effort made a difference. Since it certainly wasn't because you thought, "Oh, I can make some big bucks now." What it takes for independent schools – Anyim Palmer at Marcus Garvey could tell you, because he's been around a long time – is a very distinct approach and philosophy. I may not agree with him on all the areas, but I can *never* question his commitment and dedication.'

Even though Parker-Gills is currently immersed in the City in Schools Program, a national organization devoted to education and dropout prevention, she still finds herself replaying those final Du Bois days, each time arriving at the same conclusion. 'I didn't have the resources or the commitment from parents. The long range wasn't happening', says Parker-Gills, who is now planning a Saturday school modeled after Du Bois. 'You have to have a constant web of support, and it's hard to get that in our community.

'Black people aren't used to having to pay for education. Since *Brown* v. *Board of Education*, they felt that they should be able to get a quality education in the public school. But that hasn't been the case. I did some battles with parents. Some didn't help out, not because they didn't want to, but because they couldn't afford to. Then there were others – those who wouldn't keep their commitment with the tuition plan. They'd say, "Sure, you turned my kid around, but *shouldn't* you do that because I'm black?" The consistent support just wasn't there. I always needed more.'

When Dedan Gills and his cousin Ché Parker come back on spring and summer breaks from Clark-Atlanta University, they take sentimental drives down 54th Street. What was once W. E. B. Du Bois Academic Institute is now the Unlimited Power House of God. Anonymous detritus, an overflowing refuse bin and a tree grown wild obscure the building's former identity – but only partially. Next door sprouts the chaos of a body shop, where husks of old American cars rust in the sun.

Dedan and his Du Bois classmates have gone far. Beneath African ankhs and other cultural icons, they sport sweatshirts with collegiate seals from schools like Berkeley, Howard, UNLV, Xavier, Vanderbilt, Hampton, Morris-Brown and UCLA. After leaving Du Bois at thirteen, Dedan had his first real test: moving from an entirely black environment into an exclusive, mostly white one – the Westside's Crossroads School. 'It was a big transition', he admits. 'Going from learning [black] nationalistic slogans to being at Crossroads. There weren't really ever any confrontations, though I could talk about Farrakhan and Malcolm X and people would label me nationalist. But since I had so much knowledge of self, of black culture, I was able to respect myself, and they were able to respect me.'

Staci Thornton, who also started out at Garvey but graduated from Du Bois, didn't find the transition into Pilgrim School on Sixth and Commonwealth as easy. 'It was a difficult period. In my class there were only six black people, and they didn't know who Medgar Evers was, or George Washington Carver. I came from a place where I thought every black kid knew those things.' She says that staff and students pegged her early as the wild little girl who couldn't sit still and just do her work. 'The teachers were giving me work, especially math, that I had already done at Du Bois. Or I'd pick up a history book and there would only be two pages of black history, and that would be the slavery part. That was kinda frustrating. Pilgrim was used to quiet and sedate kids who would come in and go to class, and I wasn't like that. People thought that I was bright, but that I talked too much. But I always had been encouraged to speak out.'

Thornton credits her Du Bois education, as do other alumni, with making the difference. 'When my friends Talib and Brooklyn and I get together, we talk about how lucky we were to learn about Malcolm X, King, Garvey, at such a young age', says Dedan Gills. 'We remember when we ran into kids from around the neighborhood there'd be a lot of jokes – Africa this, Africa that – they'd say, "Why do you go to that African school?" But 1987–88, when Public Enemy got popular, *they* were wearing Africa T-shirts, talking about Egypt, and asking *us* about Malcolm X and Farrakhan. They were only just discovering them.' And if they're lucky, both Dedan and his mother can only hope, with a little help they might be on the right road to discovering themselves.

A PEOPLE WITH KNOWLEDGE

'You're not Mr Garvey, are you?' asks the young woman standing just outside the office threshold. Removing her sunglasses, she takes in the clutter – overflowing bookshelves, chairs stacked with papers, a disorderly desk. Before he can respond, Dr Anyim Palmer's ringing phone interrupts. 'Garvey School, Anyim. . . .', he answers, as he motions for his visitor to venture farther. 'How old are your babies? . . . No, we don't have openings in the fall, but you can enroll your child right now. . . . No, that *is* the best that I can do. We want your baby here. Only problem is, there might not be any room.'

This is the message Palmer has politely relayed all morning. Resting the receiver on the cradle, he shifts his attention back to the woman, who remains standing. 'I'm janitor, lackey, yard boy. . . .' Palmer rattles off only a fraction of his numerous roles, still forgetting to introduce himself. The woman looks perplexed. He doesn't bother to explain further that, depending on the crisis of the moment, he is whatever the school demands. This hour he's answering phones, as he takes a break from painting the school's exterior – methodically covering the weathered coat of gray with an attention-getting chartreuse. Dressed in a faded blue sweater riddled with moth holes and splattered with paint, Palmer presents an enigmatic figure to prospective Garvey parents – eccentric uncle, maybe vagabond sage. Certainly not the founder of the fastest-growing black independent school in Los Angeles.

When Anyim Palmer set about building the Marcus Garvey School, he says, he was subconsciously influenced by a single model: the crowded one-room schoolhouse in which he spent the early days of his Fort Worth, Texas youth. He tells the story with the same elevated melodrama as a parent passing down a twenty-miles-to-school-in-gale-storms-and-snow tale, but with a shade of sincerity and earnestness absent from those family boasts. For him the word *segregation* does not suggest inequality or inadequacy. In his experience, the converse has proved true.

'I was very fortunate to have gone to the old-type segregated schools', says Palmer. 'My teachers loved me. They saw me as an extension of themselves, and they probably would have committed mass suicide had I graduated from school not being able to read or write. But I hear that is the norm now.' At the Marcus Garvey School, Palmer has been working since 1975 to change that norm dramatically. Destroying myths about lagging achievement, he's attempted to alter expectations that society holds about black youngsters and their learning abilities, while at the same time correcting the perceptions that black children have of themselves.

When Palmer left Texas in the fifties and migrated to Los Angeles, he had no intention of shepherding classrooms full of inner-city adolescents. Enrolling in classes at City College, he was on the road to becoming a lawyer. But as Palmer was soon to learn, Southern California's version of equal opportunity in education was worse than the model he had left back at home. He realized he would be more useful in a classroom than in a courtroom.

Working with incarcerated youngsters at the Youth Training Center, Palmer witnessed black children's struggle through the public-school system. 'I was shocked that young people couldn't read their own names. I had never experienced that. When I saw what was happening to the young people in the schools, I felt that I could be of more service in that area.' Palmer refers to this period as his 'transformation'. In 1966 he spent his first year in the public schools, teaching social science and English at Pasadena's McKinley Junior High. Believing that adroitness and sensitivity could keep restless pupils from becoming unruly assemblies, he didn't mind large classes. What did trouble him were deplorable study skills and low grades.

While working in Downey in another youth program, called Los Padrinos, Palmer was confronted with more young men in trouble. 'I had never seen youngsters like this. In the South I had been exposed to an entirely different system.' One of the counselors took Palmer aside to explain his own reading of the problem: lack of role models, the absence of authority figures who cared. The counselor's point was that these were smart kids who had never been challenged. To illustrate, he handed Palmer and a struggling student a football playbook. He instructed them both to commit the contents to memory. In about a month the teenager had learned the intricate formations, cover to cover. 'And I haven't learned it to this day', admits Palmer.

But teaching, he almost immediately realized, didn't give him enough room to experiment. Within the confines of the school district's highly regimented system, Palmer found that there was little room for innovation. 'It was a very frustrating experience. I'd get them going, then I'd see them the following year and they'd be right back where they were before.' Seeing students backslide made him reassess his own abilities. 'I was a teetotaler until I started teaching. That was the first time I'd ever had a drink of alcohol.'

Confounded as an instructor, Palmer moved from behind the lectern to counseling to being an assistant principal and, finally, to university-level work. 'But wherever I took my wares, I found it was very difficult. Not because of the children, but because no one seemed to care about them. Many people didn't feel that they were capable of being educated. After years of frustration and inner turmoil and wrestling with my conscience and the feasibility of my mission, I decided to open a school that would be dedicated to the education of the young people of our community. And we've done rather well.'

Started in 1975 with Palmer's tiny life savings, five ex-students who had been groomed to be instructors and only seven students, the Marcus Garvey School grew to seventy pupils in its first year – solely through word of mouth. In 1985, the school moved from its small 54th Street storefront to a larger two-building operation that Palmer plotted from the blueprint stage.

Palmer likes to take skeptics on tours. He beams as fourth graders work confidently through chalkboard calculus equations, showers teachers with praise as a student who was once considered a public school 'problem child' studies from a college-level literature text. He's adamant that these are not 'gifted' children, just students who'd long been given up on. Parents, says Palmer, are attracted to the school's curriculum. Although it's strict and regimented, the children seem to bloom academically as well as spiritually. But it's more than just the Afrocentric framework that draws them in. 'Primarily they come because of the academics. It's great to know that "black is beautiful", but if you can't read it, so what? They learn that, but a great deal more as well.'

Palmer admits to a strain of jealousy, to imagining fantastic incarnations of the Marcus Garvey School with public funds at his disposal. 'They have millions of dollars and are failing, and we have to be out selling tickets to dances. It's very, very imbalanced. But we're determined. If the public schools get all the money, I guess that's their reward for destroying our communities.' Palmer has seen children arrive mute and hostile, common symptoms of a debased self-image. There are fifth graders who can't read or write their own names, seventh graders who clumsily wend their way through elementary multiplication tables. 'They pass them on and on', he says. 'As one parent observed, if they would retain the children who failed in our communities, the entire ghetto would be one great kindergarten class.'

The Marcus Garvey School is not without its detractors. Reservations are wide-ranging, including charges that its staff of uncredentialed teachers are unfit to teach, that its strict Afrocentric framework doesn't prepare students for life outside Garvey.

Palmer dismisses the objections. 'Wouldn't you expect there to be [critics] when you're successfully educating the young people who were said to be ineducable? Look what Eurocentric education has done to our children. In L.A. it's a miracle if a kid comes out and can read.'

Palmer and his staff have fashioned small miracles out of loose ends, scholars out of cast-asides. But without more resources, tracing students after they leave Garvey is almost impossible. 'We don't know how successful we've been', he explains, 'unless parents write.'

Palmer will root through his cardboard banker's boxes to assemble some semblance of a school history for those who require one – prospective parents, probing journalists, dubious educators. It is here that he stows the thank-you notes, photocopied commendations, letters about a child's restless transition back into the public system, and enrollment applications that have yellowed and frayed with time. The average stay at Garvey is just three years. Only two students, Palmer believes, have gone the full distance from preschool to eighth grade. Just skimming the brief information accompanying the applications reveals dramatic stories: lengthy commutes from Fullerton and Diamond Bar; parents at their wits' end with the public system, with only enough funds to place their child for a short period; the welfare mother who alternated her children's years of enrollment because she couldn't afford to send them all at the same time.

In light of the downward spiral of public classrooms and the chaos of life outside them, parents are looking for effective alternatives. 'Sometimes they say, "I can only afford to send one child." But somehow they'll get them all here', says Palmer. 'It's so unfair that parents in this community have to pay for their children's education. But they know that if they send their children to public school, they are sending them to their destruction.'

Lately Anyim Palmer has been a little more encouraged by what he reads, what he sees behind the headlines. He's impressed by the conscientious drift of black educators nationwide, who are responding to the crisis in black education with bold and often controversial solutions. The new models are frequently quite similar to Palmer's sixteen-year-old program. Across the country, immersion programs proliferate, as do much-contested bids for separate urban public schools; across town, Saturday schools and culture-based rites-of-passage programs (for both black boys and black girls) are emerging as alternatives. L.A.'s largest black church congregation, First AME, recently broke ground for a church-sponsored private school that will serve students from kindergarten through high school.

Palmer is girding up for big changes at Garvey as well: science and computer-lab additions, a second library, and structural expansions that will allow the school to accommodate tenth through twelfth grades. As such schools move out of the awkwardness of early adolescence, Garvey, and all independents, have to grow more sophisticated, the funding sources more stable. Curricula and techniques are now only tentatively shared among such schools, and the lines of communication need to be opened up. The dream is to touch many more lives. The growth and endurance of black independent schools helps to combat a condition that United Negro Improvement Association founder Marcus Garvey often warned against: 'A people without knowledge is like a tree without roots.'

'I want to tell *our* story', Anyim Palmer explains. 'We already know *his*story. It's time we wrote our own.'

August–September 1991

CHAPTER 8

AFRICAN-AMERICAN ME:
OUT OF AFRICA AND INTO THE MIX

T'was mercy brought me from my *Pagan* land
Taught my benighted soul to understand
That there's a God, that there's a *Savior* too:
Once I redemption neither sought nor knew.
Some view our sable race with scornful eye,
'Their color is a diabolic dye.'
Remember, Christians, Negroes, black as Cain,
May be refined and join th' angelic train.

Phillis Wheatley, 1773
'On Being Brought from Africa to America'

Poor Phillis Wheatley. Forgive her for she knew not what she set the precedent to do. Most certainly she wasn't the first African transplant to wrestle intellectually with, then attempt to reconcile, two disparate worlds: the dense shadow of the old, the complex uncertainty of the new. Yet in the rhyming couplets of her single-stanza 'On Being Brought From Africa to America,' the much-lauded freewoman Negro poet earned the dubious distinction of quite publicly, though ever eloquently, condemning her African past. With a few pen strokes, she flaunted her new 'refinement' and sought complete absolution for her 'pagan' ways.

I remember briefly studying Phillis Wheatley's charmed life and poetry during a Black History Week unit somewhere at the beginning of my teens.

Only recently did I rediscover the poem. I'd lost it amid the jumble of required texts and dates and exams. Confronted by Wheatley's antiquated voice once again, I found that the same vague emotion resurfaced – something wedged snugly between frustration and pity. In her report from the field, Africa's landscape was an indistinct netherworld, every remnant of its essence scrubbed free from her memory.

Though these lines were published in 1773, 1992 doesn't always bear much more evidence of authentic cultural awareness, let alone a significant sense of enlightenment. African culture is still too often blurred, if not completely obscured, in America's vision, either by the high-gloss myopia of *National Geographic*, the persistent vision of TV's midcentury *Wild Kingdom*, or a quick laugh at the expense of Hugh Masekela as noble savage in gray flannels and briefcase accessorized with spear and zebra. But across the expanse of land and ocean, Africa sometimes regards the perceived path of the misguided not-quite-African in America – the *Time* magazine crack babies abandoned by their gangbanging daddies – with the same tentativeness and the same disdain.

Language, blood bonds, rhythms and the liturgy of ritual lost in the journey, once 'Americanized' these new 'Negroes' found it difficult to mine for common bonds. Because of the way America skewed the vision of the African continent, of its history and culture, generations of African-Americans looked back with a sense of empty detachment, sometimes freighted with embarrassment and, like Phillis Wheatley, not often with pride. Despite the current thrust to shake the family tree – Afrocentric education, message raps, fashion's brilliant Kufi hats and Berber beads, taking up Ethiopian or South African political causes – African-Americans, like offspring separated from parents by a chasm of years, miles and/or mishap, still find themselves attempting an awkward embrace.

A Negro is dumber than two dead police dogs buried in
somebody's backyard. *Jelly Roll Morton*

In New Orleans they call it *passe blanc*. My grandfather could detect crafty insurgents stationed behind the fragrance counters at Maison Blanche department store on Canal Street. Though certainly black blood flowed through his veins, Jelly Roll Morton, the self-proclaimed progenitor of hot jazz, claimed Creole heritage and washed his hands of the darker hues. In old issues of *Jet* magazine, 'passing for white' found commercial viability: smelly pomades and 'fade creams'. Malcolm X, before he embarked on the road to Islam, scorched his scalp with lye attempting the perfect conk à la Nat Cole. Sammy Davis, Jr's hair became a covert cultural barometer for middle-of-the-road self-esteem as it evolved from processed, to modest Black Power afro, and then returned in later years to patent-leather sheen.

The pomades and skin bleach have been replaced this generation by the eerie countenance of Michael Jackson, whose iridescent skin and nose jobs conjure neither Africa nor America but some galaxy far, far away. But Jackson has become an easy target; there are more clandestine ways of moving away from one's roots. The specter of multiculturalism has given people license to reach back and peruse their 'colorful' accoutrements, adorn that 'prosaic' black heritage with some peppering of the exotic other, to reach back for various streams of the bloodlines that flow through one's veins – the 'one-eighth Cherokees', 'one-sixteenth Blackfeet'. These claims to Native American as well as Turkish, Spanish or East Indian blood wouldn't be a point of contention if African heritage didn't suffer in the hierarchy or arrive in that lengthy list as a mumbled afterthought. James Baldwin wrote of it in a heavy sigh:

> Self-hatred is so common and takes so many forms: it is not a local or a racial or a regional matter . . . the nation, [is] full of people who *look* White and *are* Black: some claim their ancestry and some seal it off with a change of address; nor are their new neighbors likely to challenge their identity.

I've often wondered what Africans make of this curious obsession. What do they see when they look at Oprah's green eyes (*hers* 'cause she paid for them) or Prince's powdered *faux*-Porcelana skin? What do they make of African-Americans wandering around lost, caught in the sticky web of superficial pluralism?

I got a good idea when I was traveling through London. I met two women from West Africa at an open-air market, who, after quizzing me about movie stars and the frequency of drive-by shootings, asked about my family's origins. 'Pennsylvania and Louisiana', I replied, to which I received only an exasperated look and weighted silence. Only then did I understand that they meant where *originally*, where on the continent of Africa. I didn't know. It wasn't that I didn't care, I attempted to explain, just that I'd only been able to get back so far. Overwhelmed by the task, I found myself pulled into the romance of stories about my uncle's Pullman-porter youth or lunch-counter tales of a Philadelphia uncle's American-dream enterprise, George's Bright Spot. The sisters shook their heads, made pity sounds, tongues to teeth, then carefully examined the arrangement of my facial bones, the cast of my eyes, like a flesh-and-blood topographical map, in a goodwill attempt to usher me home.

Journeys back, whether spiritual or physical, are nothing new. Marcus Garvey, of West Indian heritage, in plumed commodore hat, tried to orchestrate a mass exodus in the twenties. Pre–civil rights Southern freedom fighters, attacked by German shepherds during marches or bitten by bedbugs while seated in 'colored only' theater balconies, drew strength from their own personal notion of heritage when inspired to search for something more. In the seventies, Alex Haley's *Roots* became a handy how-to for tracking down one's own personal Kunta Kinte.

The eighties and nineties have offered their own flashy paradigms. New-jack nationalism feels good on the lips. It billows and crests and is highly infectious. Rap has offered a bodacious way to explore and celebrate the culture. Many of these gestures, well-intentioned and commendable, suggest a sincere effort to set out and explore a labyrinthian past, but the problem is that the back-to-Africa rhetoric is all too often oversimplified or, worse, ill-informed. The cultural faux pas serve to exacerbate an already volatile situation.

'If African-Americans want to cling to the history, they have to understand that culture is ongoing,' says Meri Nana-Ama Danquah, a local poet of Ghanaian descent. Sometimes, as Danquah explains, a respectful nod to the heritage can be as simple as the correct drape and placement of the *kente* cloth. 'It is a cloth of royalty. You're not supposed to cut it up, wear it as patches on your jeans. I was watching an episode of *The Cosby Show* and Cosby was out barbecuing with a piece of *kente* around his neck. He looked good, but I was enraged. It was highly disrespectful.'

Danquah grew up in Washington, D.C., and considers herself a cultural chameleon who quite easily traverses two worlds; firsthand knowledge of both has aided her in helping others to make the transition as well. The PC multicultural dictum that seeks to fit all those of African descent neatly under too broad (or, depending on how you look at it, too narrow) an aegis doesn't consider the vital differences in environment and individual experience. Danquah hears the rumblings on both sides – African-Americans who misinterpret African aloofness as arrogance, Africans who view African-Americans as those 'who bring

'THE CULTURE IS ONGOING': MERI NANA-AMA DANQUAH

trouble'. 'There is a term used in Ghana, a Yoruban word originally, meant for African-Americans: *akata*. Literally it means 'one who picks cotton'. *Akata-akata*', Danquah explains, 'is someone or something that is trouble. For example, "Don't bring your *akata-akata* here".'

On Zimbabwean soil, trouble made itself known a little too close to home when brothers Akim and Dumi Ndlovu pumped up fly canned beats and hard rhymes for family and friends. 'What do you want to do?' appalled relations responded. 'Be *American*?!' When Dumi and Akim ventured over to the United States a couple of years ago to give their crew, Zimbabwe Legit, a go on American stages and airwaves, they were warned, 'Don't lose the culture. Don't become one of them.' That was far from the intention. The brothers promise to do much more than put a new spin on rap. They have grand plans for this American music form that has distinct and firm roots in African terra firma. 'We've come', explains Dumi, 'to legitimize rap.' The slogan is less empty boast than loaded challenge. 'Not [all rappers] are aware of the substance behind what they're saying', says Akim. 'They talk about Africa as if it is heaven. Africa isn't just a trend. To dress African isn't just a trend. As soon as the medallions went out of style, they took them off. End of fad.'

Inspired in spirit by American hip-hop heroes BDP, Public Enemy, and Eric B. and Rakim ('Because', says Akim, 'they talk about *us*. They talk about Africa'), their beats and rhymes are a slow-roast dark blend, a cross-cultural hybrid, offering up something new and confrontational. The music moves beyond African-American culture specifics – in this soundscape African drums meet samples from Steely Dan, lending the Ndebele rhymes a PC 'multicultural', 'we are the world' aspect. African languages, Dumi explains, are intrinsically musical: 'The words tend to rhyme. African people have always told stories in song.'

The stories they want to tell might help stimulate the dialogue, a colorful, listener-friendly primer to a new and not-often-glimpsed Africa. They discovered through questions asked and assumptions made about the continent – stitched together from Tarzan movies with 'chiefs wearing skins, and uncivilized jungles' – that some sort of clarification was needed about things as complex as a labyrinthine political system or as simple as winter climate and variations in terrain. They hope for in-concert colloquies, a forum for point-counterpoint. 'When you leave your family, you represent them out in the world. When you leave your country', Akim has come to realize, 'you become a dignitary. But we've come to learn as well as to share.' The process moves well beyond an elementary-school-style show-and-tell: 'Anyone with African blood needs to wake up and keep waking others up. Stop talking about revolution and *do* something. Telling me how great the black man is, isn't much of anything. These are superficial things. And we don't seem to be in a hurry to connect.'

The bond that connects these cultures is at the surface enigmatic. The methodical journey toward it is like glimpsing the features of a stranger and finding startling aspects that mirror your own. UCLA linguist Mazisi Kunene agrees that because the strongest connections between Africans and African-Americans are often abstract, they are difficult for most to discern. The bonds are subliminal, sometimes coded, messages. They are deeply embedded cultural links that have connected the two cultures over miles and centuries and despite misconceptions fed by spurious information. 'It is a lesson the people here must understand they are teaching. They have preserved the African traditions under incredible conditions. It is incredible because every method was tried to sterilize Africans of their old ways. We admire the African-American struggle. They derived alternative methods of communicating the sacred word among themselves. The sacred word is crucial for a society. We need to combine [African/African-American] skills and history and not exclude others. It is dangerous to be the only one.'

Born in South Africa, Kunene has become expert at picking out traces of the newly transformed 'sacred word': in the emergence of rap; under the roofs of venerable inner-city churches (in both its oratory and sacred song); even in the modes of dance that stress staying close to the earth, keeping one's feet planted firmly on the ground. 'Otherwise', as Kunene explains, 'you will not be able to express all the multiple rhythms and movements which are sacred and very important to our tradition. "Get down" – what does it mean? It actually means making a relationship with the earth.'

The physical journey of the African who has been separated from the homeland parallels the development and metamorphosis of the 'sacred word'. This journey away and the awaited reunion of the 'new African' with the homeland becomes a metaphor: 'The world is both banal and sacred', Kunene explains. 'The physical and the spiritual move together, and sometimes they integrate. Sometimes they temporarily separate, like the African from Africa.

'IN SEARCH OF THE SACRED WORD': MAZISI KUNENE

When they integrate again, each will be enriched by the other.'

The distance in both years and geography has created (in America) a more expansive and inclusive vision of what it means to claim African blood — through a language and style and aesthetic that builds on a sturdy foundation that has refused to submit to either the violence of slavery or the whitewash of assimilation. What will make this extended community stronger is a push to integrate *within* the culture. A true form of multiculturalism should force us, as Africans/African-Americans to find a functional cultural hermeneutic, a definition that joins us together beyond the shade of skin. A meaning that we assign, not one that is fashioned for us. This form of multiculturalism would require this new emboldened race to attempt not meltdown assimilation but an understanding of the past and present, the painful struggle as well as the accomplishments. The onus is on both cultures to establish give-and-take and dialogue.

What will also help, Kunene believes, is a commitment by African émigrés: 'We too must be part of [solving] the problems. The African presence in America is meaningless unless you are committed and concerned with the racism that hounds the African people in America. I think in some ways it's worse than South Africa, because here in America the Africans are a minority. I am part of this community, this community is [now] my community. I have to help. [I have] to empower them.'

Kunene stresses that the Western world still has much to absorb from a culture incorrectly believed to be backward and/or provincial. 'Americans have a great deal to learn from African socialization. Even Africans have to relearn the elements. Sometimes these elements are called superstitions, but they are not superstitions. They are actually formulas used to reinforce the social code. It is our tradition to learn from other people as long as we don't sterilize our own.

'It is not necessary to be without your *own* meaning. Your meaning is the most important one. It is the primary one. You cannot say to a black American, "You are American." He has his own meaning, his own essence, his own perspective that makes him, him. Everybody, of course, comes with his own baggage, but it's how you modify your baggage in such a way that the baggage is not lost.'

June 1992

CHAPTER 9

ONE MAN'S FAMILY

Myrlie Evers has been learning to sit. For this unprecedented occasion, she's accustoming herself to informal attire – soft blue jeans, a loose-fitting chemise, comfortable rubber-soled shoes. But a simple chignon undermines her efforts. This transformation, she will tell you, has been far from easy, and as her family will quickly amend, it's been anything but silent

Since taking a fall on the job as an L.A. Board of Public Works commissioner, Myrlie's been favoring her back. The injury – a herniated disc – has triggered sudden, phantom pains, so, rather reluctantly, she's taken to swimming for therapy. Her youngest son, Van, she says, 'pulls a Myrlie' on her, delivering stern, unblinking orders. Ignoring the grumbles and mock threats that inevitably follow, he packs her into the car then heads out to a heated indoor pool on L.A.'s Westside. Once there, she shivers with the rest of her timid classmates, waiting to dive in and take her prescribed strokes. Myrlie says that she prefers to begin at the deep end so that if she runs out of steam she'll be in safer territory.

She recalls the first time she slid into a large body of water, on a Chicago vacation with her first husband. 'Medgar took me out to Lake Michigan. He always pushed me to go beyond what I thought I could do. He told me to come out a little farther . . . farther . . . a little farther. "I'm right here with you,"' until suddenly her foot slipped away from sand into uncertain space; panicked, she drew in great gasps of water thinking that it was air. 'It frightened me to death', she says with a laugh that softens her formal countenance. 'But I went. I went out of faith and love.'

'The sin is to do nothing', Medgar Evers would always say. His words, unceasing reminders, travel a familiar route in Myrlie's thoughts. In the middle of this century, escaping the mouth of a headstrong black man, these were charged, fighting words, equivalent to meeting a white man's cool or inquisitive stare with hard, defiant eyes. When Medgar Evers returned from the Second World War to the strife of the Jim Crow South, he'd long since tired of the deferential posture expected of blacks. In 1954, as field secretary for the Jackson, Mississippi chapter of the National Association for the Advancement of Colored People, Evers launched a no-holds-barred attack against segregation in the city, organizing a series of militant boycotts and demonstrations. He encouraged black voter registration, decried and publicized the lynching of fourteen-year-old Emmett Till and became Mayor Allan Thompson's constant, noisy nemesis – his name quickly shooting to the top of Mississippi's infamous nine-man death list.

Medgar would tell Myrlie and others of a series of angry phantom eyes watching him, attempting to memorize his often irregular routine. The presences were so constant and tangible that a new household procedure demanded that family members hit the floor and crawl for cover if anything resembling the crack of gunfire cut the night. On June 12, 1963, an apparition finally found form as Evers returned home from an NAACP strategy session and stood in the driveway, unloading a box of sweatshirts that demanded 'Jim Crow Must Go'. Myrlie and the children – Darrell, nine, Reena, eight, and James Van Dyke, three – who had earlier that night heard President Kennedy acknowledge on television the 'great change at hand', stood by watching as a single shot knocked Medgar Evers off his feet, stunning then slowly stilling him.

Myrlie Evers precisely recalls the bullet's hot flight, its unerring path, as well as its long-lingering physical remains: a shattered window; a ruptured wall; a dented refrigerator. She retains the impossible-to-erase mental scars: the sound of his angry shouts, the local news reports that followed, callously highlighting the bullet's resting place: 'on the counter, under a watermelon'. 'For me it was a nightmare', she says in an even voice. 'You relived those scenes as though they were constantly happening before your eyes. Every time you walked out of that front door you could see the body there, you could see the blood. I was never able to get the blood stains up off the concrete.'

Myrlie didn't kid herself about the system, the well-oiled good ol' boy network. In the beginning, she preferred to invest little time in empty optimism. Instead, she spent the months that followed in a daze, mechanically complying with authorities and caring for her family. 'It was the first time', Myrlie remembers realizing, 'that I was ever alone.'

Yet people reached out to her. Letters of support arrived daily from concerned Mississippians, black *and* white, and from sympathizers the world over. Ralph Bunche, Helen Gurley Brown, Thurgood Marshall and President Kennedy all found time to commit their condolences to paper. Former associates ('people who had moved away from Medgar, as far as they could, who would cross the street because of the danger of the association') arrived to offer sympathy and claim 'best-friend' status. A fair amount of hate mail and ill-tidings arrived at the Evers home as well — scribbled notes that spat 'I'm glad he's gone . . . ' and reports of local teachers who led their classes in noisy cheers at the news of Medgar's passing.

When ardent segregationist Byron De La Beckwith was arraigned for the murder, Myrlie was caught off-guard. 'It was a shock that they apprehended someone. A miracle that there was a trial.' But any real hope for justice was quashed early on. District Attorney William Waller felt it necessary to advise Myrlie on 'dress and behavior' in the courtroom ('As though I didn't know how to act') and stubbornly refused to address her as 'Mrs Evers' during the proceedings — indeed, she says, he addressed her by no name at all. And to ensure that no one misunderstood the state's position on the trial, Governor Ross Barnett strolled in during Myrlie's testimony, glared in her direction, then gave the accused a hearty clap on the back.

So it wasn't surprising when, despite strong circumstantial evidence against him, including his fingerprints on the murder weapon, Beckwith was set free in 1964 after two successive all-white juries deadlocked. What does seem remarkable is that last December, Beckwith, now seventy-one, was roused from retirement in Chattanooga, Tennessee to face a third indictment; the case is expected to go again to trial in Jackson early this fall.

The first push to reopen the case followed a series of 1989 articles appearing in the *Jackson Clarion-Ledger*. They revealed the interference of the Mississippi Sovereignty Commission (a now-defunct state agency formed in the fifties to preserve segregation) in the selection of the jury for the second trial of Byron De La Beckwith. Myrlie went to Jackson to meet with Hinds County D.A. Ed

Peters, who told her that the case could not be reopened. For one thing, the murder weapon and court records were missing. But public demand grew for a reindictment. Assistant D.A. Bobby DeLaughter was assigned to look into it and showed surprising energy on the job.

Soon the murder weapon, a military rifle 'lost' since the second trial, materialized in the closet of a former judge – ironically, DeLaughter's father-in-law. A team from 'Prime Time Live' came to town and found witnesses to place Beckwith in Jackson the night of the murder. (Two white policemen had testified at the original trials to having seen him half an hour after the shooting, nearly 100 miles away.) And Myrlie hand-delivered her own trump card: a transcript of the first trial she obtained twenty-seven years ago.

But by far the most dramatic event was the chance discovery of a passage in a sixteen-year-old book written by a member of the John Birch Society, William H. McIllhany II, entitled *Klandestine* – the story of Delmar Dennis, a former member of the Ku Klux Klan who became an FBI informant. Dennis claimed to have heard Beckwith confess to the murder at a Klan meeting. 'Killing that nigger gave me no more inner discomfort than our wives endure when they give birth to our children.'

For Myrlie Evers those tenebrous words presented the first glimmer of real hope in almost three decades. She knew a little something about Southern justice and had kept up her own discreet, small-scale investigation into the case, maintaining contact with old friends and associates back home who might have access to new leads. And as the case gathered steam, Myrlie worked extensively with Jackson officials, preparing for the coming summer and by far her most important journey home.

The South holds a complex of memories: the soft curve of a familiar road; a fragrant honeysuckle thicket wherein an assailant lay in wait; her husband's bountiful plum tree in full and vibrant bloom. Some things, Myrlie admits, were harder to leave than others. 'Sometimes I would go in the closet and just bury my head in his clothes and smell what was left of him.' One year, one month and ten days after the shooting, when it became more difficult to live with those reminders than without them, Myrlie picked up and moved her family out of the house on Guynes Street into a modest wood-and-stucco home in Claremont, California.

Myrlie knew little about Southern California's Inland Empire. What she did know was that she much preferred the small-town atmosphere of Claremont to the L.A.'s imposing, rapidly metamorphosing grid. Plotting her move, she struggled not to soften under the persistent attempts by her grandmother and aunt to tempt her back to Vicksburg. Myrlie harbored fears that she would wilt in the shade of the two strongest female figures in her life. 'I was determined to grow. Medgar would have expected that. Everything I did during that period in my life was based on what I thought Medgar would have approved of.' California was one of his unrealized dreams, and like other displaced hopefuls, the family headed west from the humid and unhurried conditions of the South in search of a second chance.

Rolling through grassy, tree-lined neighborhoods that reminded her of Jackson, Myrlie never stopped to consider the racial makeup of her new home, or even the possibility of conflict, 'because as we drove I saw a number of my own people.' She shakes her head at the memory, marveling at her wide-eyed naïveté – 'only to find out that we had been driving through *Pomona*.' It wasn't until later that she learned of indignant white neighbors who, having caught a glimpse of her, quickly packed and fled, and of town meetings at which a nervous community gathered to sort out its fears in advance of the Evers's imminent arrival. More immediately, she understood the challenging stares, the indifferent glances that at once acknowledged and coolly dismissed.

Yet Myrlie descended upon the community as only a veteran freedom fighter would. Like the Southern students who sat hours-into-days at drugstore luncheonettes, waiting for the intangible, Myrlie marched front and center – thinking someone might try to stop her – looking for a fight, she now admits, when sometimes none was to be found. 'I was very angry, very hurt', she explains. 'And though I'm not proud of it, I think for the first year I kept going only because I was full of hatred.'

It took time for those feelings to subside, for Myrlie to fully adjust to living in an essentially white community. The family endured the familiar: shouted racial epithets, as well as the disapproval that simple silence sometimes implies. But at least they didn't live in constant dread; they no longer feared for their lives. 'I think that people truly meant well. That they did not want any trouble. I think there were those who really did want us to be able to make a smooth transition here.'

While Myrlie went back to the books, working toward a degree in sociology at Pomona College, the NAACP did what it could to help support the family financially. Myrlie took odd administrative jobs on campus and hit the lecture circuit with the dual purpose of keeping Medgar's memory alive and helping to make ends meet. When there wasn't a sitter, the children were trusted to fend for themselves. Grabbing a few hours before the first of three alarm clocks rang, Myrlie studied until it was time to get the kids up and ready for school. Her grades suffered, as did her spirit. She worried about Darrell's silences and vanished appetite, Reena's nighttime tears, and how to begin to explain his father's work to young and inquisitive Van.

During those years, the family avoided discussing the particulars of the summer of 1963. At home, within the children's earshot, Myrlie felt uncomfortable articulating her loneliness and grief. 'I tended to be overprotective, and they have been protective of me. And when I wanted to throw up my hands and say "stop the world", I'd look at them and realize that I couldn't, because they were looking to *me*.'

The family merged into a tight support system. Friends and concerned outsiders marveled at their inner strength, their endurance, and above all at Myrlie's ability to appear so candid and coolly philosophical about so devastating a tragedy. She earned her degree in 1968, went to work as director of planning and development at Claremont College, ran for public office twice, and in the mid-1970s became ARCO's national director of consumer affairs. Mayor Tom Bradley appointed her to the Board of Public Works in 1987. In 1976, she married Walter Williams, a longshoreman and organizer.

Over the years, sharing her story, whether in print or in lecture halls, has allowed Myrlie to vent her pain and helped her to reorder her life. But the children, she worries, haven't had such an outlet. Despite their successes (Darrell is an artist, Reena a representative for United Airlines, and Van a professional photographer), Myrlie sometimes wonders about what her children *haven't* shared with her, what questions they haven't found the courage to ask. 'I think this [forthcoming Beckwith] trial, this whole process, is helping us fight the ghosts and goblins. It has already helped us to open up feelings that we tiptoed around. We've been very open. I think that it's helped us to focus more on our personal relationships. Now my adult children understand that their mother was not a person made out of iron, that I had some horrendous emotional problems, but I was always strong. I knew what I had to do and kept going, fighting not to lose my sanity. It was a difficult time, making those adjustments.' But she adds with a small reflective smile, 'In many ways I think the children did it much easier than I.'

Across town, Darrell Evers wanders the perimeter of his sunny Leimert Park studio looking for an unoccupied electrical socket. He has a recent piece of work to share. No matter the intended destination, a first-time visitor to Degnan Boulevard – a strip of galleries, artists' studios, boutiques and performance spaces in L.A.'s Crenshaw district – will be steered directly to Soupbone Arts's white-and-red facade, the Brockman Gallery space that Darrell has occupied since 1983. Dionne Warwick, Brock Peters and Vidal Sassoon have all paid visits. Henry Luce III proudly departed with his own Evers original.

The news of his celebrity would make Darrell blush. It is the awesome weight and pull that his surname carries. As eldest son, Darrell is used to eloquently parrying inquiries about his own political plans. Though he remains committed to grassroots, community projects, his passions take a more creative turn: But his own commitment to the community is limited to hands-on artistic activities: unifying local black artists, lecturing about art in local classrooms, helping neighborhood museums with fund-raising events. 'Painting is the closest thing to my soul', he explains, readjusting floor-to-ceiling canvases struck in ominous tones of brown and gray. 'They are not pretty things. Some are spiritual. Some are political. But mostly they're something to stimulate your brain.'

Having found the socket, he watches as *Brillo* shimmers to life. One of a series of 'conceptual miniatures', this hardwood-floor replica blasts blue-hued static through a tiny 'window' carved into its lower corner. Next to the window rests a Barbie-doll-size box of Brillo pads. The window (a Sony Watchman screen) is shaded with a half-dozen different grades of African-American hair – from pressing-comb straight to fresh-from-the-shower kinky. After collecting samples from a local barber, Darrell arranged them in wispy patterns echoing Van Gogh's *Starry Night*. It is, Darrell says, an answer, twenty years late, to his Claremont playmates, the ones who would shamble up to him and boldly ask to touch his hair. There are other works – painting, sculptures, sketches – inspired by this period, whose mere titles (*Oh My God They Moved Next Door, Cowboy Bob Meets the Flaming Baboon*) are imbued with bittersweet comic irony. Despite those occurrences, Darrell felt that he was fortunate to have been raised in two very different environments: 'Claremont gave us a balance of cultures. Though sometimes it kinda made you a little lonely.'

After receiving a B.A. in advertising and illustration at Pasadena's Art Center College of Design, Darrell worked under a master draftsman. From there his professional course took a dramatic and unexpected detour. Becoming more interested in his own spiritual development, Darrell switched to meditation in the mid-1970s, studying with Guru Maharah Ji in Denver before returning to L.A. in the early eighties, ready to embark on his career and start a family.

Darrell finds that his own childhood memories remain vague. He's given up trying to fit them together jigsaw-puzzle perfect. Visions of his father appear as bright flash vignettes: Medgar charging down a hill entertaining Darrell's laughing friends or the strong pull and warmth of his generous spirit as Medgar lay dying at his feet. Only with time has he been able to confront that past. His father plays a part in his work: not as a recognizable face or abstract form, but in its spirit and purpose. As he slowly gained an understanding of his father's struggle, Darrell was better able to confront his personal loss.

'We were in the middle of the hornet's nest. And if you're shaking nests . . . well . . . my father did what he had to do. He wasn't a separatist. He believed in people's true nature and that people could come and work together and make monumental things happen. He always stressed self-determination, self-esteem, and the importance of looking for truth.' These revelations, Darrell feels, pushed him to search for his own understanding of truth – his father's words, in subtle ways, the basic blueprint for his meditation years. 'Growing up I had to go to church. I believed in a Supreme Being, but looking around me in the South I saw a lot of contradictions. Even as a kid I was asking why. Why I couldn't see and touch God. But through the meditation it was revealed that truth was inside all along. Oh, I get it all the time: "That meditation stuff, man, that ain't black! You've been in Claremont too long",' he says with a laugh. 'But I know who and what I am. Beyond my race.'

The assassination of Medgar Evers came at a time when racial tensions had reached a violent apex, yet powerful numbers persisted. As Taylor Branch reported in *Parting the Waters*, his sweeping account of the early Civil Rights years, Evers's murder marked the midpoint of a ten-week period in which 758 racial demonstrations and 14,735 arrests occurred in 186 cities across the nation. Beckwith's third indictment and subsequent trial comes at a crucial time as well. When race-hate crimes claim frequent headlines. When more black men fill prisons than university lecture halls. When black infants have one of the highest mortality rates in the country. 'You want so badly for it not to happen. The anger and hostility', Myrlie Evers explains. 'Particularly when so many people have worked so hard and have given so much.'

Resolving the case would mean much more than a personal victory for the Evers family. It would do more to establish Medgar Evers as one of the freedom movement's trailblazers. In a time of vanished, tarnished or absent heroes, it would serve as well to revive the languishing notion that civil rights are universal and inalienable.

'When I left Mississippi I had such a struggle. Leaving Medgar and everything he fought for to come to California. Only to find out that California had its own problems. It's painful for me to see us as a people kill ourselves and each other. People eliminated through dope. A segment of our youth giving birth to babies on drugs. Do we end up with a lost generation?' asks Myrlie Evers, looking into the California sun with eyes that have had to confront too much. 'These things we as a people cannot afford.'

July 1991

PORTRAITS

CHAPTER 10

THE LONG-DISTANCE
RUNNER: CHARLES BURNETT'S
QUIET REVOLUTION

When the American Film Institute's Black Independent Cinema panel convened last spring, attendees with natty dreads and bulging Filofaxes scanned the room, hoping to catch a glimpse of the latest local son done good – Charles Burnett. They had their business cards at the ready, questions carefully rehearsed for Burnett, who had captured the attention of industry types, both here and abroad, with his stately portrayal of a black family in Los Angeles. *To Sleep with Anger*. Burnett's first major feature film (it received a Special Jury Prize at the US Sundance Film Festival in Park City, Utah), offers an exquisite, long-overdue cinematic look at working-class black life. Yet as African-American filmmakers, including Julie Dash (*Daughters of the Dust*), Keenen Ivory Wayans (*In Living Color, I'm Gonna Git You Sucka*), Wendell B. Harris, Jr. (*Chameleon Street*) and Warrington Hudlin (*House Party*), assembled on the dais to share horror stories, softened by sound advice, an empty seat awaited Burnett.

More than likely, Charles Burnett was taking his 'well-received' film around festivals in search of a distributor. 'Have you ever noticed that every time you see Charles he's out of breath?' a friend of his asked. The three times that Burnett and I meet, in fact, he's either running behind schedule or running hard – making up, one senses, for lost time. In the twenty-three years since he began film school, he has directed only five movies: two student projects and three independent features. His first feature, *Killer of Sheep*, won prizes at the Berlin International Film Festival and the US Festival. He's received Guggenheim, NEA and Rockefeller Foundation grants. Yet it was the MacArthur Foundation Fellowship in 1988 – the 'genius' grant that showered him with $275,000, no strings attached – that thrust him uncomfortably into the media spotlight. 'I remember that Charles was pleased', says Kenneth Hope, director of the MacArthur Fellows Grant program. 'But I don't think he was one of those people who went bouncing off the walls.'

Now *To Sleep with Anger* has a distributor and Charles Burnett has achieved recognition, but maybe for all the wrong reasons. It's troubling that so many people find the image of a unified black family unusual. Equally irksome is the media's nervously reverential treatment of a director as gifted as Burnett – who also happens to be black – as a shimmering piece of exotica.

Burnett gracefully deflects the inevitable comparisons with Spike Lee (Lee's work is labeled 'issue driven, confrontational'; Burnett's, 'subtle, textured and poetic'). The director prefers the low profile that has allowed him to traverse his neighborhood streets unnoticed. But lately, he finds it harder and harder to keep the business of The Business from distracting him. In the last two months, he's traveled to Cannes, Munich, Toronto and Spain. But if you 'take a meeting' with him on home ground, he'll suggest someplace low-key and convenient for both parties – Sizzler or I-Hop.

He arrives – out of breath – casually dressed in a fresh white T-shirt, the factory creases still at sharp points, a warm-up jacket and crisp blue jeans. Lowering himself into a booth, he politely requests coffee or a single glass of white wine that he'll nurse for three hours. The conversation winds through expansive terrain, from gruesome tales of hangings in German military prisons to the films of Vittorio De Sica to Ray Charles's proclivity for grabbing one's wrist on first acquaintance ('to gauge weight, height and carriage'). Burnett touches on his extensive research for projects that never saw the light, such as his hours taping ex-Black Panther Elmer 'Geronimo' Pratt in San Quentin. 'Make sure you have Charles tell you a story', an old school friend of his insists, '*any* story. Charlie tells a great story!' That's clear from his new film, which, like his conversation, is full of storytelling. Burnett tells stories with his hands, with dark, serious eyes, continually tempering and reshaping them. And the best ones always circle back home.

CHARLES BURNETT: STORIES IN SHADOW AND LIGHT

In Charles Burnett's neighborhood no one wanted to be a filmmaker. For his family, he remembers, 'it was sort of embarrassing in a way. That just wasn't one of the things that you considered as an option. It was something that you didn't want to tell anybody. After I'd been in it for a while it sort of dawned on them I was very serious. Then they were very supportive.' Burnett had moved with his working-class family from Vicksburg, Mississippi to Watts when he was three years old. 'I lived in a neighborhood where people looked out for one another and for one another's kids. We were very close-knit. It was the fifties, when a lot of the black middle class, among them carpenters and masons, still lived in South Central, before civil rights.'

Burnett recalls long, dusty afternoons playing on the undeveloped land where Los Angeles Southwest College now stands. 'Devil's Dip' offered a place where he and his friends could slide down untamed hills, tear clothing and break limbs. There was a golf course where they would take BB guns and bows and arrows for long afternoons of exploring. After the rains, Devil's Dip would become a muddy swamp where they'd collect tadpoles, or journey to its farthest extremities on homemade rafts that sometimes sprang leaks. Many of these details appear in *Killer of Sheep*. Sometimes he'd take his trumpet (which turns up in the hands of a small boy in *To Sleep with Anger*) and, if he could find another interested horn or two, assemble an impromptu jam session.

Burnett remembers his childhood as a 'sunny period', yet he doesn't ignore its darker aspects. 'I remember pressure from the police. They never let you forget who you were. Also the schools. I suppose there were some conscientious teachers out there, but at that time the school system was a mess. There was no justification for any of that. It was wrong, and you have to attack things that are wrong. Later, when I could, I felt obligated to do something about it.'

Burnett grew up an eager movie-goer, traveling to neighborhood drive-ins with family and friends to see Tom Mix and Buck Jones shoot-'em-ups, or moody *noir* films like *Double Indemnity*, or thrillers like *The Red House*. A high-school English teacher ran 16-mm reels in the classroom, but Burnett didn't look to film as a career. 'I would've liked to have taken a photography course', he recalls, 'but it wasn't the right environment.' He was headed the 'practical route'. After graduating from Fremont High School, he enrolled in classes at Los Angeles Community College and was working toward an A.A. degree in electronics – until a writing instructor inspired him by revealing the virtues of subtlety. 'There were no set rules', he began to understnad. 'She showed us a gentle way of arriving at what art is.'

At the time Burnett enrolled in UCLA's theater department with an emphasis in film, his classmates included directors/writers Penelope Spheeris (*The Decline of Western Civilization, Parts 1 and 2*) and Colin Higgins (*9 to 5* and *Harold and Maude*). 'I'd ask myself, "What if?" What if you weren't in a certain [affluent] socioeconomic bracket, had different opportunities, how would life be different?' recalls Burnett. 'I was trying to view the solutions. What I saw in mainstream films – portrayals of black life – had nothing to do with what I saw day to day. They didn't address realistic concerns.'

At UCLA, in the late sixties and early seventies, when the Black Muslims and Black Panthers were making their steely presence known on and around campus, Burnett became part of a small, tight group of black filmmakers – Haile Gerima, Ben Caldwell, Larry Clark, Jamaa Fanaka, Julie Dash and Billy Woodberry. They made films that followed neither the Hollywood 'black exploitation' strain, with its pimps in platform shoes, nor the static and airless educational reels that, if the filmmaker were lucky, made the rounds on the high-school circuit. What emerged instead were cinematic vignettes that reflected the spirit of the Civil Rights movement: from African wind goddesses to working-class women in Watts, these images of strength and resilience celebrated the race.

Burnett's thesis film *The Horse* (1973) was an 18-minute study of five young men's emotional reactions to the shooting of a sick horse. 'The studios were clamped so tight at the time that the only way to deal with the situation was to look at film as a hobby. You made films because you enjoyed making films. If you didn't make an educational film or a crime film, it was underground cinema, films at midnight. You just didn't get your films shown.'

Throughout school and afterward, Burnett juggled odd jobs as a clerk at the downtown library, a teacher's assistant and as a reader for a talent agency. To drum up minority-student interest in film, he also found time to teach a class in ethno-communications. All the while he continued to develop his own voice, making gritty films about black urban life. 'A filmmaker must have a background in making independent films outside of the Hollywood product; one gains experience by working and through dialogue. It's like long-distance runners who know how to pace themselves; they don't worry about who's ahead, they know the pace that's right for them.'

Burnett and his colleagues forged a strong alliance. They alerted one another to open slots at festivals; when funding was scarce they learned to apply for grants. As Billy Woodberry recalls, 'There was a tremendous cohesion among these people. Minority students at the school were a new thing. They were all young and excited and dynamic and getting their hands on this thing for the first time. There were different ideological tendencies; some of them were into Pan-Africanism, some of them were into Marxism. So you had to have a position about culture and film and politics. You had to earn their respect.'

Woodberry knew of Burnett long before he met him. Sometimes he would catch sight of him across campus, but more often heard stories that he haunted the upstairs editing rooms after dark. 'He was totally unassuming', says Woodberry. 'He looked younger, slightly built. You didn't know that he was in the school or was as far along as he was. It was his manner.'

Burnett's films are full of images and details that have appeared nowhere else. Woodberry remembers a collection of icons pulled from Burnett's neighborhood that quickly became trademarks: a butcher shop on 103rd Street that sold live chickens or the nearby neighbors who kept a handful of grazing horses that somehow remained oblivious to the urban noise. 'He was working in a way that was not exploitative or stereotypical. He had decided early on that those lives were epic in quality. The people who lived in the stories didn't realize it, but it was his job as an artist to give them form and shape.'

Beyond the boundaries of their small group, these filmmakers battled with the outside world. Skeptical police officers would stop and interrogate black film crews shooting on location in surrounding neighborhoods. On campus, they faced insidious, insulting images and stereotypes dreamt up by white (oftentimes well-meaning) colleagues. Tempers blazed at the screening of Steve (*Fritz the Cat*) Krantz's *Coal Black and the Seven Dwarfs*, which featured wraparound Cadillacs and black women with more-than-ample backsides swaying to Cab Calloway (the voice of Coal Black) singing 'Hi-De-Ho'.

The filmmaker, Caldwell recalls, saw the film as a tribute to black people. 'He thought we were being too sensitive. The professor agreed. One sister cried. I was angry and vocal. But afterwards I wasn't sure what difference it made. We were just beginning to realize the power of media, how this new art form could strengthen the movement. We all watched the film *Superfly* change black people's consciousness. We felt that we had to get out there and do something. Charles never really showed anger in a verbal way. He just did his work. He expressed his feelings that way.' Burnett's work tended to veer away from sharp political messages. He was influenced instead by the poets and essayists who emerged from the ashes of the 1965 Watts rebellion: 'It was that celebration of blackness more than anything else', says Burnett.

We are sitting in the Sizzler on Stocker Street, near the Crenshaw-Baldwin Hills Shopping Center. Dinner is long finished. Burnett glances up occasionally to wave a greeting to friends who wander by. He is talking about the more marginal films at this year's Sundance Festival that impressed him, *Rodrigo D.* (from Colombia) and *A Little Fish in Love* (from the USSR). What they have in common with his own movies is their love for stories – stories as history, stories as moral lessons.

In the African-American tradition, storytellers – be they as formal as the African *griot* (storybearer) or preacher, or simply a chatty great-aunt or mournful bluesman – provided a sense of history when there was nowhere else to go, thus preserving and strengthening the culture. Burnett points to the legacy of early black filmmakers – Oscar Micheaux or Spencer Williams. They too were storytellers who, in the twenties and thirties, were plagued by the same obstacles that Burnett butts up against today: tight budgets, short shooting schedules and limited distribution. Like them, he has learned to work with what's available. And he's discovered that there has always been something – or someone – to fall back on.

Killer of Sheep (1977), which was shot on weekends on a $10,000 shoestring budget with the help of close friends and family, springs from a story Burnett 'collected' during a cross-town bus ride. In this film, L.A. appears as a mirage, its palm trees mere silhouettes that shoot up behind the gray haze of smog; it's a smoky backdrop to the somber particulars of life among the black working class. Burnett fleshes out these sketches by setting rich moods with deep shadows and song – pulling from old blues, jazz, gospel and smoky torch songs. When pained lovers can no longer find adequate words to express their confusion and their despair, they sway in half-light to Dinah Washington's 'This Bitter Earth'. 'With that music', he explains, 'a voice singing with a band, you see everything that black people were dancing to. You see black culture.'

Burnett's camera examines the problems, and the deleterious conditions contributing to them, that with time can either destroy a spirit or make it stronger. There are no neat resolutions; he shuns sentimentality and, without heavy moralizing, celebrates the survival of the black family, even when the societal factors threatening to erode it often seem insurmountable. As with *Killer of Sheep*, both *My Brother's Wedding* and *Bless Their Little Hearts* (directed by Billy Woodberry and written and shot by Burnett) are firmly planted in the family. The unit threatens to crumble from within as unemployment, a sliding economy and the more immediate anxiety of too many mouths to feed work in concert to chip away at self-esteem. With ripe silences and long, probing glances, Burnett allows the atmosphere of this life to unfold leisurely.

A more interior film, *To Sleep with Anger* tackles the struggle between good and evil within a family. Dabbling in the talismans and charms of Southern folklore, Burnett makes the venerable customs of the oral tradition the centerpiece of his movie. As early morning tales are shared over a sunny kitchen table, Harry Mention (Danny Glover), an old acquaintance from 'down home' who's paying a visit to his friends in the big city, eases into the role of the classic trickster summoned up from African-American folklore. (Zora Neale Hurston collected oral histories and folk tales about a notorious apparition named 'Daddy Mention' who spent time in various Florida jails, prison camps and road farms, for her book *The Sanctified Church*.) Harry casts an ominous shadow over a splintering family whose father mysteriously falls ill. 'It's one of these stories that happens in the mind', explains Burnett. 'What becomes the battleground is Gideon's [the father's] body. They're fighting over the house inside, getting Harry out. And what's at stake here is the family. So it's more of an interior thing, with references to the past and future, set in a world that is neither real nor fantasy.'

Festivals aside, Burnett's been encouraged by the response from screenings in cities like Atlanta, whose black population, like others around the country, is starved for a film that reflects a familiar experience. 'Everyone was saying, "I'm going to bring my parents . . . because they can relate to it." [People] want to feel like they're part of this human community, and films, quite frankly, have really been disrespectful to black people.'

For too long, Hollywood films have defined African-Americans in Anglo terms. Charles Burnett has found himself in the formidable position of recasting the African-American experience on film, capturing a full range of black urban life from black class distinctions to the resonant and disparate cadences of black speech. 'Charles is very much steeped in our culture', says Carol Munday Lawrence, *To Sleep with Anger*'s post-production supervisor. 'Yet he taps into all of mankind. He really is a storyteller and we – black people – need to be allowed to tell human stories. This film is about people; what makes it black are the trappings, the approach, the layers *we* bring to it. He does such a beautiful job articulating particular black people. Charles recognizes that we are not monoliths.'

Though his current projects (a couple of documentaries and a film to be shot in Louisiana that will pair him once again with Billy Woodberry for *American Playhouse* production, *My Father's House*) will take him well into next year, the battle for finding distribution and cooperation is far from over. In many ways he's just begun scaling walls, working to demystify and humanize the black image on screen. Overseas he patiently explains to European audiences that African-Americans do indeed own washing machines, have father figures and functional families. Unwittingly, he's become a spokesman for the African-American experience. 'Even in this country, whites in some communities don't see black people', says Burnett. 'People don't interact. So they have that European mentality here; all they know is what they get from the media – that blacks are cheating each other or rioting.'

Berenice Reynaud, New York correspondent for *Cahiers du Cinema,* concurs, pointing out that *Killer of Sheep* was one of the first films in which European audiences saw a sensitive, uncondescending portrayal of a black family. 'There is a quality of generosity in the way he looks at his characters. There are two kinds of directors – one who loves his characters, and one who doesn't. Charles is the first kind. He is a great creator of images – a closeup of a face of a black woman goes into the soul of that person. The Renaissance painters like Leonardo inserted a glow – Charles Burnett does this when he looks at faces.'

Like the others who gathered on the dais at AFI, Burnett has horror stories of his own to share. After months of looking for a distributor, with plenty of curious nibbles but no takers (until the Samuel Goldwyn Company picked up the film), Burnett is now looking at the issue of marketing. Filmmakers and producers throw up their hands over how to mount a campaign to sell a black film that doesn't boast a 'slammin'' rap score or a familiar face plucked from pop culture. '*To Sleep with Anger* is a different kind of film. A lot of distributors were interested in it, but one guy came up to me and said, "Well, Charles, we like the film but there's no sex, no drugs, no violence, no car crashes or any of this, so how do you sell it?" Some of these distributors you talk to ask you, "What kind of movie are you going to make?" And I'll say, "I'm going to make one that's going to heal society." And they say, "Get this *mess* out of my office." But if you go in and tell them you want to make a cheap movie that's going to make $20 billion and it's gonna have rap in it, and we're going to sell the script for $3 million and we're going to have sex scenes from one end to the other – nonstop – and we're going to have 500 murders and we're going to have this guy rapping over this guy's dead body: "You wouldn't have died if you hadn't've dissed me." Then they say, "Oh my God! Just what we're looking for!" It's that sort of stuff.'

'This film is not for everybody', Burnett admits, 'and you don't want to compromise yourself to try and attract people. So you make choices. You have to expect that some people are not going to try and analyze things. The people who stand at the door and determine what people should see are very close-minded. They don't want diversity. They think that they can tell what reflects the marketplace by looking at either the Nielsens or trying to understand the mind of an eighteen-year-old white male. These people are irresponsible. They're not catering to intelligent people, and it's keeping the masses dumb. You have to have someone with a passion, who is committed to making sure that the people *you're* interested in get a voice. You have to be prepared, because you have to fight each step of the way.'

Early in the morning, when the crews were setting up, adjusting lights, clustering in small circles over morning coffee, lining up for the 'Andy Gumps', children began to explore the area cordoned off by heavy cable and wire. Local families residing on or about 20th Street near Adams Boulevard wandered over to see what all the trucks, food and noise were about. The two-story wood-frame bungalow upon which Harry Mention, hat in hand, would descend, became a community gathering place. Whispering residents waited on tiptoe, hoping to catch a glimpse of Danny Glover, Carl Lumbly or Sheryl Lee Ralph. Some carried scraps of paper to collect autographs, others simply stood at the sidelines watching the machinery at work, still others became extras. 'I didn't have a closed set', says Burnett. 'We had kids, people walked around and observed. It's like anything else: You're building a house and people look at it. Somebody on the crew looked around and said: "You oughta have a child-care center with all the kids around." It was no big deal.

No one disrupted anything. They just wanted to see what was going on. They don't often film in these neighborhoods, and when they do, they tell them to get back, saying "You don't know what you're looking at." It's the simplest thing, for example, to explain what a lens does. Kids understand it, and you never know, maybe they'll go out to be a filmmaker after that.'

October 1990

CHAPTER 11

THIS ONE'S FOR THE LADIES

Denise Wilson tends to the posse, in a sea-green jumpsuit and crowned by a shiny crop of brown cornrows anchored with a simple topknot. Denise counts heads before heading eight noisy little girls past security and into the Sports Arena backstage netherworld. No one dares stop her, or even bothers to glance at the VIP pass clipped to her belt. It's all in her assured, imperious air. 'We're looking for Yolanda Whitaker', she announces to the room, flashing perfect teeth, enunciating each syllable. 'For Yo-Yo. . . .'

Wedged in the middle of an endless Valentine's Day bill of women rappers, Yo-Yo makes those preceding her appear like one long opening act. Prowling in black leather walking shorts and a billowy silk blouse that looks like a Mondrian mosaic (no micro-minis or spandex allowed on this set), she's light on her feet, with the lyric grace of an NBA forward, but from the waist up it's a different story – arms flailing, hands in fierce little balls. Her blond braids, collected in the same topknot as mother Denise's, whip around in a blur as she voices her message to the ladies: 'I don't know any intelligent women who are bitches. Callin' yourself "Miss Bitch", "Tracy Bitch". . . .'

Yo-Yo is flanked by members of her crew, the Intelligent Black Women's Coalition, in black T-shirts emblazoned with Yo-Yo's woodcut visage as Lady Liberty. The girls stand rigid like Fruit of Islam sentinels, faces severe, shoulders squared. 'Brothers in the house, you hear what I'm saying'?' Up go some hands, then rise the voices as flygirls jostle their moody Valentines into response. In the front row, Denise and the girls are laughing and cheering. But in a far corner, on the second level, a teen in *Kente* and a small brass ankh trades a glance with an equally lit homey and shouts. 'Yo, bitch', he yells, breaking off into cascading laughter, 'get off the stage!'

In the late seventies and early eighties, rap was the voice – any MC would tell you. Although promising powerful words for a heretofore silent generation, rappers really spoke for African-American males. Somewhere in the mix, amid the crotch-grabbing and the calls to uplift the race, a large part of the demographic found themselves unceremoniously swept aside.

For black women, the revolution was yet to be vocalized. At peak drive-time, tuning in to any urban-contemporary or 24/7 rap station, you would be assaulted by a list of insults from 'tramp' on down. Why many women failed to embrace rap had little to do with the big beats and aggressive execution, as some suggested. Hands down, it was the message. Not until thirteen-year-old Roxanne Shanté got tired of hearing UTFO's misogynist 'Roxanne, Roxanne' and went lip-to-lip on her twelve-inch 'Roxanne's Revenge' did things start to get interesting. Roxanne Shanté paved the way for the New Jills: M. C. Lyte, Ms Melodie, Shazzy, Nefertiti, Queen Latifah, Ice Cream Tee, L. A. Star, Monie Love and many more. If Vanilla Ice doesn't take over rap, women will.

Now Yo-Yo has the mike. Her debut, *Make Way for the Motherlode,* is a collection of blistering womanist anthems, produced (in a move that seems more incomprehensible than incongruous) by Ice Cube, author of some of the most misogynistic raps in the business. But Cube wouldn't rap about sex and contraception ('Put a Lid on It'), smooth operators ('Tonight Is the Night'), pride and self-determination ('You Can't Play with My Yo-Yo'), or the 'Sisterland' like Yo-Yo does. This isn't 'Dear Yo-Yo' giving just-say-no advice to the lovelorn. These are fighting words. With the help of Cube, who drops steely beats and lends his backing crew the Lench Mob's ominous voices, Yo-Yo applies what she calls the 'lady's touch'. That means self-respect across the board, from her thundering delivery down to the samples from honorary Intelligent Black Women's Coalition members LaBelle, Sister Sledge and the Supremes.

Listening to Yo-Yo work is like kicking it with your ace-boom. Free of preachiness, of holier-than-thou homilies, she doesn't claim never to have been weak. 'I Got Played' plunges her into a classic girl-meets-boy dilemma – to give it up or not to give it up. Talking a lot of smack about the fine art of roping in a live one, she slips and takes a fall. 'It was directly to the ladies. Giving examples of how you can meet a guy and he has nice money and your girlfriends say, "Girl, go 'head and have sex with the boy. Give'em a whimper pill. Make'em squirm." Then you really give this guy your all and . . . well it's really just like Ice Cube's 'I'm Only Out for One Thing'. I'm just giving the other side. I let the ladies know about the guys, and the guys about the ladies. That it's time to get offa that tip. So that enough women really know what time it is.'

Ice Cube: 'When it comes to hip-hop/this is a man's world
Stay down and play/the playground, you little girl. . . .'

Yo-Yo: 'I make brothers like you play the backyard/
You used to flow with the title/But I took it/Bring home the bacon/
but find another ho' to cook it . . . ' *from 'It's a Man's World'*

Yo-Yo is settled behind a table at her manager's office on Victoria Avenue, trying to make sense of a suddenly prodigious schedule. An interview with *Rolling Stone,* a possible radio spot on KDAY, miscellaneous phone calls to return before she leaves town on the next leg of her tour. Last night she was recording a commercial for St Ides Malt Liquor, and it's left her already-throaty voice sandpaper-hoarse and at least a couple of shades deeper. She takes out a pen and autographs her publicity photo – Yo-Yo standing solemn, with both of her Doc Martens planted on the back of some insane brother who had the nerve to cross her.

'Some people say I take things to the extreme. Like when I'm in an argument with a guy or something and he says, "Yo-Yo, just leave it alone." But I want to let them know that I won't be disrespected. I always handle it in a ladylike manner. I believe in being sassy and classy and getting my point across. I might not use as vulgar a word as you may use, but I will get you back', she laughs. 'In a fair way. But you *will* know. What I say stands out. I always had something positive but strong to say. I wasn't an okeydoke person. I grew up in the hard part of the ghetto. To me, rap's the only way for a black teen. If you're not in a private school, if you're not a straight-A student, how else can you get out of the ghetto?'

And just when she was about to give up, along came Cube. As the story goes, he liked the seventeen-year-old's sass. The worldly, wise-ass, big voice

YO-YO AND MOM: MAKE WAY FOR THE MOTHERLODE

pelting hard words just before tossing off a haughty giggle. Ice Cube was look-ing for a woman with whom to go head-to-head: to be a South Central Bonnie to his Hub City Clyde. On his *AmeriKKKa's Most Wanted,* Cube took only a quick break from dogging women, whites and Arsenio to allow room for a little point/counterpoint. Yo-Yo's voice, like a glimmering scythe, slices through the white noise – a collage of venomous voices muttering the usuals – 'bitch', 'ho" . . . and sets the story straight.

While growing up, she was frequently the shoulder to lean on. Working through her own problems with an often absent father, Yo-Yo began peer-coun-seling at Washington High. And she's never really stopped: brainstorming with her manager, Yo-Yo came up with the Intelligent Black Women's Coalition, her chance to keep on top of what's ailing the sisters. 'I wanted to get something going where all the girls could meet up and be more positive, be stronger and stand together for what we believe. When you're growing up, people like to say that they're not competing, but [they] are. You want to wear the same thing that they wear. Just to be hip. I thought it was cool for guys to buy their girlfriends clothes for school, y'know. But my mom bought my clothes. . . . The [girls] that have all the trunk jewelry are the ones that drop out of school pregnant, on drugs – those are the ones I'm tryin' to reach.'

To enlist, new members write letters describing problems in their neigh-borhoods. The plan is to establish interracial IWBC locals of fifteen to twenty women, Yo-Yo presiding front and center when her tour stops in your town. 'I read a lot of my mail and people tell me that it's great to have a strong, black female who stands up. "You're out there making it possible for us to really stand out", they tell me, 'to let us know that we're not just for making beds and laying in them.'

> Trying to ignore me
> you playin' yourself
> because if it wasn't for woman
> you'd be layin' yourself
> Yo-Yo's a lady who's down for mine
> won't hesitate to put yourself in line
> If you ain't with me
> you're behind me
> think about it
> because I'm stompin' to the nineties.
> *from 'The IBWC National Anthem'*

Listening to the Isleys, Denise Wilson relaxes on a black leather couch. She flips through snapshots, pointing out pictures of Yolanda at a backyard birthday party posing in a blue, backless sun dress, her hand resting coyly on her hip. 'See, she was fast even then', Denise says, shaking her head. Yo-Yo rolls her eyes and sucks her teeth. She's busy in her kitchen, finishing up chicken wings and dip. With only a hint of lipstick and mascara, her hair styled in a short press-and-curl, she looks as if she could still lead cheers on the sidelines.

'I had to watch her', Denise explains, moving to the elementary-school shots. 'I was just the type of mother that stayed on her. Stayed on her butt. I wanted her to go off to college and take up nursing or study to be a doctor or something, but she just starts holing up in the bathroom. She used to stay in there all night writing. We had one bathroom. That was her little office.'

It took awhile for Denise to adjust to all the 'bumpin' and shoutin''. She prefers oldies, slow blue-lights-in-the-basement velvet vamps – Lou Rawls's 'Tobacco Road' was just about her perfect speed. 'I just couldn't get ready for rap until she was in a contest at World on Wheels with Young MC. I stayed in the car the whole time until she got ready to go onstage because I didn't want to hear the noise. When I went in all these kids were clapping for my daughter. I *missed* everything. So I thought I'd better start staying at these things.'

Once she got used to the idea of her daughter as an MC, getting other people involved was easy. Denise had a lot of practice: when Yolanda was still at Washington High, Mom took it upon herself to lead the 'Most Popular' campaign for her. She passed out suckers, posters and pins to Yolanda's classmates. When Yolanda busted rhymes at skating rinks and community centers around Los Angeles, it was Denise who canvassed the neighborhood with fliers, then loaded up her van (nicknamed 'The Battering Ram') to capacity the night of the gig. 'Mama, don't be givin' out fliers', Yolanda would wail. 'I don't want people seein' Yo-Yo's mama promotin' the show!'

But with or without help, Yolanda turned heads. When others were rapping about parties and passion in campus talent shows, her words carried documentary weight. Her first rhymes focused on drugs, gangs and teen pregnancies ('I was beginning to think that my school was turning into a pregnancy center').

Denise became proficient at spotting and bouncing bogus entrepreneurs ready to chart Yolanda's future – including one who, Denise recalls, even went so far as to pull up in front of their house 'in an old green Cadillac as long as

Broadway'. Contract in hand, he was also packing a crew of underage girls in back, drinking coolers and smoking weed. But it wasn't the business shysters who most worried Denise, it was the maneuvering men with romantic designs on her daughter. 'I didn't want her to get pregnant. I didn't want her to get hung out. I didn't want her to grow up wild. I wanted her to be someone.'

Before quite literally running into Ice Cube at a local swap meet, Yolanda had been getting her name out, headlining skating rinks, small clubs, correctional centers, schools – even the King-Drew Medical Center. She'd decided that if rap didn't take her anywhere right away, she'd pull out the contingency plan and seek a career in psychology. 'So when Cube told me that he wanted to work with me', Yolanda recalls, 'I thought it was just some old BS. He said, "Take down my number", and I was like, "Nah. You take down my number." Then he said, "I like your attitude."'

For Denise, Ice Cube posed a unique problem. She didn't know what to make of him pulling into the driveway in his black Jeep, waiting for Yolanda to slip out so they could work on their rhymes. All it took was a little asking around to place her immediately on tenterhooks. 'I had to work up my nerve', says Denise. 'I told him, "You know what, Cube? I hope you don't think Yolanda's a bitch. I don't want you to ever call Yolanda a bitch." Now he's cool. Just like my little son. Another baby in the family. I'm always adopting somebody.'

Nowadays, Yolanda lives by her mother's advice, but it's 'Yo-Yo' who's learned to work by Cube's. 'He taught me how to rock a venue, how to get the whole crowd's attention. What to look out for, how to prepare myself financially. He talks to me almost like a counselor. From me I think he's learned the other side of a woman.' Then she pauses with a smile. 'The back fires.'

March 1991

CHAPTER 12

JOHN CARTER
BLOWS HOT AND COOL

Worst of all, nobody understood our kind of music out on the Coast.
I can't begin to tell you how I yearned for New York. *Charlie Parker*

Before I knew John Carter, the avant-garde demigod whose mere name makes
my musician friends speak in tangled tongues, I knew Mr Carter – from
across the street. With clarinets tucked under his arm, he traveled to exotic
places when he'd finished teaching school for the semester. I knew the high,
raspy practice notes; fragments flavoring every telephone conversation I ever
had.

He wasn't the kind of jazz musician I'd read about or seen on the yellowing
covers of some of my mother's best session bids. Those men stared blankly out
at me. Hard, cold eyes, mean and lean. The music suggested the same. The jazz
cliché: a defeated soul, slipping toward rage or despair. Junk skinny. That
wasn't Mr Carter. He wasn't about sloe gin or smack. He was and is about the
straight and narrow. The centeredness that comes with aikido. Life and family.
He takes the kids to the Christmas Eve Music Festival at the Music Center
every year. Drove me to my first rock concert, pointing out old jazz clubs on
the way.

When you reach his office answering machine, Carter's whisper –
'patience' – fills the dead air between message and beep. You won't find
Carter's name in the weekend performance listings more than a few times a

year. His music, during the summer months, takes him east and into Europe. Playing solo at larger festivals or Greenwich Village clubs, he sometimes shares the stage with reedmen Jimmy Hamilton, David Murray and Alvin Batiste as part of eclectic ensembles like the Clarinet Summit.

Carter's jazz has been called cerebral by some, inaccessible by others. It can bang you over the head or slither just out of reach. It's playful. It's confrontational. It's from Los Angeles. And for a man whose mantle is serenity, his musical voice is a paradox, rife with raw anguish, but offering a settling calm as well. 'It sounds like the instruments are having an argument', his daughter told him when she was five. He laughed: 'Something like that', he said.

See him duke it out live at the Catalina with cornetist Bobby Bradford, the ex-Ornette sideman who is his most frequent collaborator. Listen as cornet and clarinet move from conversation to altercation. Roberto Miranda works the bass – a slender, dark lovely – swarming over the instrument with thousands of hands and fingers. William Jeffrey's urgent snare cracks; abrupt, shrill bleats make you wince and take notice. Carter favors the very top tones. Bradford's cornet gains frantic momentum, screams, then sighs.

For Carter, music was a gift from both sides of his family: a great-grandfather was a virtuoso fiddler; his mother danced at elegant fetes where Jimmie Lunceford, Cab Calloway and Duke Ellington lifted their batons. Influences? Old Bluebird 78s played on an RCA windup; Tommy Dorsey and Artie Shaw on the radio. 'I would lay by my window', he says when I catch up with him at the Wind College [a music school started by Carter and a collection of friends], 'and listen to that radio music night after night. You'd never hear black bands.' But Carter's roots lie more in gutsy Texas blues, the heavy, lusty music pumped out of pool hall jukes in his native Fort Worth, Texas. Arnett Cobb, David Newman, James Clay and T-Bone Walker came out of the Southwest scene. So did Ornette Coleman, Charlie Moffet and the great tenor-man Dewey Redman. Carter himself packed a tenor through most of the fifties and sixties. 'I'm a Texas blues person', he says, 'and I couldn't change that if I wanted to. I think some of what I write now, things that perhaps could be called avant-garde or very modern, is still grounded in that.'

When Carter first came to L.A. with a master's degree in the early sixties, he looked into Hollywood session work: onscreen glamour in dinner jacket and tie as part of a live television orchestra; offscreen, sleeves rolled up, working through motion-picture scores on a back lot. Mingus did it. So did Buddy Col-

JOHN CARTER'S WELL-TENDED SOUNDSCAPE

lette. 'It occurred to me finally that I had been a jazz player all my life', he says. 'Studio work involves a different process of making music. The creative aspects are totally different. I decided to look for a rhythm section and return to what I was supposed to be doing.'

He took a day job teaching music to grade-schoolers, and nosed around L.A.'s jazz community. Central Avenue's juke-joint heyday had begun to dissolve into memory, but a wide assortment of swank neighborhood clubs still dotted the South Central area, like Mart's and the Rubaiyat Room. The organ trio was in vogue. You could go to a show on Friday evening and not resurface until well into Sunday afternoon. But underground in the mid-to-late sixties, the Pan-Afrikan People's Arkestra was the thing: Horace Topscott's ensemble dedicated to jazz, 'African-American classical music'. Carter, Bradford and Arthur Blythe were among the featured players.

The music of bebop musicians like Bird and Diz had led Carter away from Texas blues as well as from the notion of playing bop himself: 'They had played most of the things that had to be played', he says. 'It had been done already. And the great social upheaval in the sixties had a lot to do with shaping my musical style. I just got caught up in that.' The choice of instruments was a little more difficult. But by the late seventies he decided to make the clarinet his sole voice: 'Personalities are given to certain kinds of instruments.' The clarinet, unusually expressive, whispers a melody as it swells from soft to loud, much like the human voice. 'Bottom line has to do with what you feel you can best express your musical thoughts.'

In the mid-seventies Carter's eldest son returned from a trip to Africa. Fascinated with his son's stories about the 'castles' of Ghana – the trading posts used to house Africans before they were sent to the Western Hemisphere – Carter wrote a suite inspired by the tales, *Dauwhe*, for an octet. 'I wanted to help make it known that the African that came here arrived not as an illiterate, but from a viable, productive society. The music of the African has in many ways formed the foundation of what has grown to be America's national music: the whole notion of making music, poetry, dance on the spot. Improvisation. That is the life-blood of jazz. That's what jazz is.'

The ensuing series of five album-length suites, *Roots and Folklore: Episodes in the Development of American Folk Music*, is Carter's idea turned obsession. It has absorbed him for more than a decade. The programmatic suites *(Dauwhe, Castles of Ghana, Dance of the Love Ghosts, Fields*, and the work-in-progress *Shadows on the Wall*), all octets, trace the metamorphosis and evolution of African music and culture from homeland to America.

So he's teaching kids about this, too. Not exactly: 'My idea is to prepare people to be fine musicians, not simply fine *jazz* musicians. But across the country kids are taught to listen to what are generally called "the classics", by which they mean Western European music: Bach, Beethoven, Tchaikovsky. There's nothing wrong with that. But that is not America's music; that's not what we're about as a people.' Carter's dream project is a grade-school program directing children toward an appreciation of American art, dance and music: 'To me that is primary. I don't think Mozart is more important than what's happening on Hollywood Boulevard or in Greenwich Village.'

Making money as a jazz musician in L.A. proves difficult for a number of reasons. But Carter, unlike Charlie Parker some forty years before him, doesn't really yearn for the caffeinated New York scene. He's amassed a wealth of richness in other ways: there are kids to teach, quartets and quintets to write, solos to conjure, ballads and blues old and new. Mr Carter from across the street prefers to landscape the hill, and tend the barbeque on summer afternoons.

John Carter died on March 31, 1991, at the age of sixty-two, of lung cancer. Leaving a wife, four children, seven grandchildren and a musical mosaic conceived in stolen moments between his 7-to-3 jobs and fathering duties. He fell into confident step alongside a family of dancers, preachers, poets and storytellers – a legacy of restless, creative souls who found second voice within his music. He reminded me that we, as African-Americans, come from a long line of people who historically seldom had time to pursue artistic endeavors. But as he and those before him proved, through those experiences and despite the constraints, 'The beautiful music has come.'

April 1989/1991

CHAPTER 13

PRECIOUS MEMORIES:
THE REVEREND JAMES CLEVELAND'S
JOURNEY HOME

'Reverend Cleveland must've had a pretty wealthy congregation', says the man with salt-and-pepper hair palming crisp tens and sticky ATM twenties. 'Nothin' but *big* bills from this group.' He waits for change, watching expectantly as a baby-blue stretch Caddy sweeps into this usually vacant lot. But the Cadillac brings in another $10. A BMW, $20. 'We just need a bigger lot', says a woman emerging from a Toyota with primer splashes. She passes him a crumpled mound of ones and struts out the alley toward Slauson. Curious neighbors stand close by on porches.

'Aretha's coming. He taught her, y'know?'

'You know she never leaves Detroit.'

'Nah, man, I heard she got on the train . . . '

Traffic along Western is at a crawl all the way back to the Snooty Fox Motor Inn at 41st. A woman in a black miniskirt carrying a baby makes her way to church, oblivious to the 'hey-babys' and the handmade placards along the sidewalk: REPENT / JESUS IS THE KEY.

At the corner of Western and Slauson, a red, white and blue fluorescent sign glows: 'The Cornerstone Institutional Baptist Church, Rev. James Cleveland, Pastor'. .It hangs above a structure that at one time most likely housed a Ralphs or a Safeway, before big chains abandoned South Central L.A. For seven years in this spot, fourteen in a smaller storefront, this institution has fed a community spiritually.

No cars fill the parking lot tonight. Instead, a couple of hundred folding chairs form a road crescent around three TVs. Their screens hold pictures of exotic sprays of flowers; of a teeming sanctuary, of a choir shrouded entirely in black. Most of the chairs outside remain empty while hundreds press against the only open door. 'You ain't all gonna get seats', reprimands the young man with a neat fade who stands at the gate. Only a bewildered handful – some homeless, some eyes blank with alcohol – sit in the folding chairs beneath the palms, enjoying the company, waiting for this walk-in movie to begin.

Inside, a red cross made of 800 floods on the ceiling emits a deep crimson glow, ignites the red carpet and the sanctuary's pews. Anthuriums flank the body. The Reverend James Cleveland wears a black suit and shiny, soft leather loafers, resting in state before the marble altar he'd had imported from Italy; before the pulpit where he preached comfort words on Sundays; before the vast choir he directed. The 'King of Gospel' lies calm, atop crushed red velvet quilting, his folded hands like earthen clay.

The Reverend James Cleveland – arranger, pianist, composer, teacher – moved to L.A. in 1964 at the urging of his friend and manager Annette May Thomas. When singing the Word wasn't enough, Cleveland turned to preaching it, and founded this church in 1970 with a flock of sixty. Cornerstone's current membership exceeds 7,000.

The SRO crowd is asked to remain flush against side walls as those outside are permitted to quickly view the body. As they file through, in Reeboks and two-tone patent leather pumps, sporting nascent dredlocks and snaky Senegalese braids, some try to blend in until church members unceremoniously shoo them away. Occupying the pews, women and men sit with tambourines and heavy leather Bibles. Pulling out Instamatics, they take occasional photographs of the altar. No one will tell them that the shots taken from the rear rows will not record an image. There's not enough light thrown from the flash to illuminate the subject. Photos will be a perfect square of near black, the space void, as if there were nothing there. As if they had photographed a ghost.

'Please don't talk', says Edna Tatum, the mistress of ceremonies. 'We're about dignity and sadness. You don't have to make noise to look at somebody.' The room's air thickens. The red tint seems to push the mercury higher; hot enough to sweat out a press, hot enough to be a humid summer Sunday, instead of a chilly Friday evening in February. It is hours before ushers pass out tattered Angelus Funeral Home fans. A woman in a nurse's cap makes her rounds with paper cups and towels.

Church choirs from all over California take turns – the Pentecostal Community Choir, Original Voices of Watts, Northern California Community Choir. The singing seems endless, yet the voices rise strong and tireless. They traverse Cleveland's career – 'Peace Be Still', 'No Ways Tired', 'I'll Do His Will', 'Lord Help Me to Hold Out', 'Jesus Is the Best Thing That Ever Happened to Me.'

All night, people have been telling miracle stories, about the voice the Reverend Cleveland miraculously found Sunday, February 3. How he hadn't sung for thirteen months and suddenly he lifted his voice, and then at a revival a few days later shouted, and then fell eternally silent on February 9.

'What's going to happen to traditional gospel music now that Reverend Cleveland is gone?' came the question from the pulpit. Bobby Jones, host of a gospel radio show in Tennessee, says he has no fear. 'As long as there is a turntable, Reverend James Cleveland will be in the hearts and minds of everyone.'

'But I just feel kind of empty', says Jeff Crawford, a Cornerstone choir member for five years. 'Like this space won't ever be filled. I'll miss hanging out with him, hearing him talk about old times. About being Mahalia Jackson's paper boy, about the Caravans. We don't have a leader. He was more than a pastor, he was a friend. We will always feel this loss.'

At the eleventh hour the next morning at the Shrine Auditorium, some come in marching, heads bobbing to the choir's thundering handclaps, their arms upraised, palms open acknowledge the Holy Spirit. White-gloved ushers from churches all over the city – Pilgrim Baptist, Second AME, Tear of Christ, West Angeles Church of God in Christ, Second Baptist – assist with crowd control. 'Those are some serious people out there', says Toni, one of the Shrine ushers who's been peering out the auditorium's glass doors all morning. Ted, who's working security, agrees. 'They told us to treat it like a concert. There isn't supposed to be flash photography, so we're supposed to be searching purses.'

A quick glance around the Shrine confirms that this is not a day of mourning. Many want to wish the reverend godspeed: Senator Diane Watson, Stevie Wonder, Andrae and Saundra Crouch, Stephanie Mills, Gladys Knight, Tremaine Hawkins. Considering James Cleveland, now laid out in white robe and sash at the foot of the stage, the Reverend Ike intones, 'This is not a funeral. This is a celebration of love of a great life, of a great gospel performer.'

People fight tears with spirit dances and jubilant song, but grief slips through, consumes some in tears and shouts. 'I'ma miss you, Reverend', wails a choir member from the stage, her body in violent tremors of grief. Two women in smart white suits and red pill-box hats stop their tears by placing a hand at each other's heart and sinking into private prayer.

The Reverend William Turner of Pasadena's New Revelation Baptist Church believes that Cleveland is getting ready to lead an angelic host. 'I stood on Thursday on Hollywood Boulevard, and there we memorialized James's name in the stars on the sidewalk. Last night we stood in the Cornerstone Church. There were young people, old people from across the country testifying that they got their start from James's spirit condescending to them.'

'A lot of singers didn't know they could sing before James Cleveland came along', recalls Shirley Caesar of the Caravans, her rich, throaty voice a bit unsure. 'He helped out little Cassietta, little Albertina. Hear those children singing today? James did that. I was explaining to my son, how we made it as a people. Especially in the South', says Mt Zion Baptist's E. V. Hill in his afternoon eulogy. 'We heard James's "Peace Be Still", Clara Ward's "Surely God Is Able", Mahalia Jackson's "Move On Up a Little Higher", Sister Rosetta Tharpe's "Strange Things Happen Every Day". . . .'

Outside people are humming: Their steps are still metered marches. The phantom signs have returned: REPENT / TURN TO JESUS; SEX KILLS 'OUTSIDE' MARRIAGE / ONE WIFE / ONE HUSBAND / JESUS SAVES FROM HELL! / AIDS / DIVORCE / ABUSE / IF YOU COME.

A young man in a dark polyester suit sells James Cleveland cassettes for $10, telling his customers he picked them up for $6. A woman asks for a senior citizen's discount; he asks her for proof of age. A few steps away, another man sells postcard shots of James Cleveland in cardboard frames: '$5 with, $2 without.' Farther down the street a smaller crowd gathers to wait for the 26-car procession to sweep down Shrine Place and head east toward Figueroa Street. The wind kicks up fiercely, not the balmy weekend the weatherman promised. A woman, absently fixing her mussed braids that from a distance form a silver nimbus, speaks outloud while watching the cars leave. 'We never know what we got', she says to no one in particular. 'Never know what we got till we lose it.'

February 1991

CHAPTER 14

FAMILY ALBUM

They bring them in elaborate leather scrapbooks sentimentally inscribed in chipped gold-leaf paint: 'Pleasant Memories from California'. They carry them tucked inside massive family Bibles, in calfskin-soft paper shopping bags from markets now long defunct. Yellowed and mildewed Kodak snapshots, Polaroids, curling tintypes that now seem to hold only an outline of a ghost have been stowed in hatboxes and manila folders bursting at the seams with the weight of years.

Community activist 'Sweet' Alice Harris, founder of Parents of Watts Working with Young Adults, has this bright Saturday afternoon brought a short stack of images to the Watts Towers Art Center on East 107th Street. Waiting to tell her story, she's picked out a few, but important, pieces: some yellowed newspapers, black-and-white 8-by-10s of women with elaborate bouffants, polyester flares and maxiskirts. They are members, she explains, of the Jordan High School P.T.A., who during the tense days following the Watts Rebellion in 1965 began the first of their troubleshooting sessions. They were in search of a community-based solution that would do more than put a cap on the violence, that would instead provide constructive outlets – youth programs, job training – to help the community begin to rebuild itself from the inside.

'This', says Alice nodding toward long folding tables filled with people digging through L.A.'s visually forgotten past, 'is like a reunion. A home-coming. I've seen people I thought were dead. I've seen the ones that kept *me* out of trouble. We're up in age and when we go, if we're not careful, the children will never know. When neighbors die the neighborhoods die right along with them.'

The Shades of L.A. project, sponsored by the L.A. Public Library, is in its own modest way reanimating historically neglected city pockets. Through the images a new take on local social history unfolds, one that now documented can live well past the lifespans of those who recorded and then diligently protected it. The project took on the ambitious task of collecting the lost histories of L.A.'s marginalized ethnic communities, beginning with African-Americans, by photographing important fragments drawn from memory books.

'I came to the center excited', says Sweet Alice. 'We're finally getting history about *us*. I hate that we didn't have this before – back then. Most of our children have something. We've done plenty, just that most of it's in the closet. And the problem is that if we didn't know it ourselves, we certainly didn't teach it.'

The fear of living without a clear sense of one's past is not unfounded. For ethnic communities, subsisting in urban centers across this country, the media have done an expert job of obliterating a cohesive past while at the same time stoking a sensationalized, nightmarish present. Electronic and print news sources have done the most damage – guilty as much for what is reported as for what remains ignored. In the case of the African-American community, the media, constructing a recorded legacy that generally ignores strength and resilience, has fabricated a backdrop that offers little else but crack-houses, tenements and penitentiaries populated by a cast of gangbangers, crack babies and pimps who appear nightly as a host of pariahs. These images occupy the worldview's center stage. And these skewed (and ultimately harmful) stereotypes do more than miseducate outside those in the community – they serve to trim the options and narrow the outlook for future generations.

This updated portfolio of Los Angeles's African-American community from 1860 to 1960, and the photographs to be gathered in the ensuing months, will chronicle the lives and environs of other ethnic communities in the L.A. basin. Families of darker hues also boast happy nuclear families – Ozzie and Harriet-style – with wide-eyed children mischievously mugging, a proud-to-bursting mother with her fresh-from-the-beautican coif, and a loving patriarch who provided handsomely for his family.

Black Angeleno lifestyles through the decades, like any other middle-class American enclave, ran from kitschy-lavish to the workaday mundane. Snapshots preserve these domestic scenes: Saturday croquet, boy scout meetings, back-yard weddings, Tijuana holidays, making ice cream or lounging by a heated kidney-shaped pool. The comings and goings and highs and lows of these quiet, often commonplace lives more than likely wouldn't arrest anyone's attention on the evening news.

In earlier decades, the Southland's African-American community at-tempted to work within the limits the city fathers ascribed – law and medical practices, 24-hour general stores, and restaurants thrived within city blocks that were decreed their own. These residents built their neighborhoods up from the inside out, long before, out of long-simmering frustration, they sought to tear them down. Restrictive covenants circumscribed the West's great possibilities; segregated beaches, social clubs, and musician's unions meant that Jim Crow's arms spread far enough to touch the Pacific as well. But despite the restrictions and bans, blacks met Hollywood's glamour eye-to-eye at the posh Dunbar Hotel and in clubs like the Paradise and the Alabam that lit up black L.A.'s main drag, Central Avenue.

Aspiring black starlets and beauty queens attempted to negotiate a chance at the Hollywood dream, but often were 'too dark' to pass or 'too light' to play the befuddled maid that the Hollywood machine allowed. If they didn't give up on the fancy, some of these ambitious women became floor models in trade shows or tried to find fame within their own communities.

There were others who managed to shine for a moment, like Joe Adams, handsome in the 'Dark Gable'-fashion, who occupied the best ringside tables at nightspots like the Club Pigale on Santa Barbara Boulevard (now King). A disc jockey, Adams occupied a local TV slot in addition to his radio duties, sat prominently as community emissary, then slipped off into city-lore oblivion.

During the project's first four Saturday sessions, Carolyn Kozo, who heads Shades of L.A. with the help of a roomful of trained volunteers and a mobile photo unit, assembled thousands of images that filled in the gaping holes in L.A.'s visual black history. With family snapshots in hand, and with vivid stories to share, residents fueled with chat, eagerly descended upon local libraries, museums, the Watts Towers Art Center, Crenshaw-Baldwin Hills

Plaza, not knowing what a valuable link their photos of a trip to Union Station or the alligator farm would turn out to be.

'For too long, people went along without a sense of their past', Cecil Ferguson, a Watts resident, recalls. Ferguson, who brought with him two hand-tinted family portraits framed behind dense glass, remembers when he would find himself in junk stores rescuing family photos of anonymous black families. For evidence, he explains, that there were strong and unified black family units. 'I hope this project will give people a sense of self-worth.'

'Social history of everyday man is priceless', says Carolyn Kozo, who launched Photo Friends of the Central Library, a nonprofit support group dedicated to ferreting out the library's missing cultural links. Over the years Kozo had been haunted by requests for the collection's omissions – inner-city high-schools whose reunion committee wanted vintage shots of sock hops and pep rallies, journalists searching for a piece of verisimilitude to authenticate a story – but, Kozo says, not being able to fill orders for photos of pre-1965 Watts for a project commemorating the twenty-fifth anniversary of the community's uprising was the proverbial last straw. 'We just had nothing. Nothing of Watts as a community. I just got tired of saying no.'

Kozo, curator of the Central Library's 2.5 million–image photo collection, can pretty easily explain the primary reasons for these gaps. Many of the photographs stowed in the library's collection prior to the project were commissioned decades ago by the Chamber of Commerce who dictated the city's look and painstakingly sculpted its public face. 'They *did* want to present L.A. as a culturally diverse city, but most often presented it in ethnic celebration – fiestas and the like.' The collection, admits Kozo, prior to Shades of L.A. outreach, contained only four images of black L.A. at work: record shots of black-owned businesses along the Central Avenue corridor. As well, public collections usually acquire the work of professional photographers weren't generally interested in ethnic communities. It became obvious to Kozo to pursue those who had lived in L.A.'s restricted and thus isolated communities – African-American, Latino, Asian – and were documenting their unique way of life.

With $40,000 donated by Security Pacific Corporation and another $25,000 by Sunlaw Cogeneration Partners-I (a privately owned energy corporation) Kozo was able to more comfortably plot the grand scheme: assemble and train a staff, then target and secure the best and most easily accessible sites to peruse and copy photographs. 'We looked for places in the communities in which people felt comfortable and thought of as theirs.'

Prior to each session, volunteers learn basics about the history of the ethnic group whose photographs they will be examining in a slide show and lecture presented by library historian, Kathy Kobyashi. 'We try to teach the volunteers about 4,000 polite ways to tell people that we can't use their portraits unless they have some sociological or historical significance.' While Kozo and her staff primarily look for technical, aesthetic and historical qualities, Kozo admits that there are other images that don't fit neatly into those categories but instead convey something else. 'Some photos', says Kozo, 'don't leave you alone.'

One donor Kozo recalls, shared what appeared to be standard sand-and-surf photos, small keepsakes from an afternoon in the sun. But it was more than just the elaborate bathing costumes that she and her beau featured that made the portrait notable. 'It's a wonderful photo', says Kozo, 'but the fact that it was a segregated beach makes it poignant.' The same pathos is mirrored in another image of a beach-bound family draped in street clothes, standing under the restricted sign at Bruce Beach. Instead of smiles, disappointment quietly inhabits their faces. 'A camera is usually used as a celebration of an experience. This obviously was used to record something quite to the contrary.'

'This project', Kozo now realizes, 'isn't something that you can just start and stop.' Its historical weight and scope have already eclipsed her usual routine at the downtown library's history desk. Presently she's working to secure funds to have a photographer on-site once a month to shoot the books and stray photos that arrive at the Spring Street library in the weeks after the formal collecting sessions. In the works as well are oral history and video projects, books, and traveling exhibits. People come into the library and wander toward the exhibit bearing the spoils of the project's first phase. They see a face, a cluster of buildings or a street that triggers a memory. They work to recreate what lies just outside the frame, ascribing their own story. Carolyn Kozo is usually standing by to receive it eagerly.

'I spoke to one woman who told me the story about buying her first house in a restricted neighborhood, and how she had to go through so much red tape to secure it – including finding a white person to buy it. That was the story behind her first house. It is very different from my story about my first house. You see, all the photographs are similar. The celebrations especially – baby's births, birthday parties, holidays, vacations, that first house – they all look the same, familiar. So you learn the most by comparing the details', says Kozo, 'It's when you start relating the differences. That's where the story begins.'

May 1992

CHAPTER 15

NOTES FROM A NATIVE SON

Sometimes Paris still beckons. Marc Anthony Thompson recalls longs strolls inspired by insomnolence, along the Rue de Lappe in 4 a.m. drenching rain. Plugged into a Walkman, muddying a fine pair of English workboots, he admired the view. 'Los Angeles', he confesses, 'hasn't been so kind. . . .'

Thompson has manipulated this city into his own version of a 1920s Left Bank – dark cafés, zinc bars, and smoky cellar haunts, like La Poubelle over on Franklin Avenue, where the owner brightly greets him with a quick kiss on each cheek, and a waiter serves his triple espresso in three dainty porcelain cups. Here, his carefully tended fantasy grows quietly and undisturbed, dead-center of a Hollywood at its most irresolute.

At his hilltop studio, 1 a.m., just up the street from the *parva sed apta* building where Nathaniel West sweated out *The Day of the Locust* some fifty years ago, the Capitol Records flashing red light confirms our true location, while Thompson pulls in found sounds from other lands, times and emotional landscapes. He rifles through cassettes, which fill in the narrative's gaps. The music is unwieldy, shakes the glass within the window frames; it snakes and slides, hides from definitions. His voice springs free of it, struts about, then suddenly recoils. 'Armageddon music', he explains with a smile.

Thompson writes songs that are long, fond letters to old friends. They are bits and pieces of a sonic diary that parallel his own intemperate and itinerant path; long afternoons surfing in Oceanside, painting grand homes in Montecito, playing hotel lounge–band saxophonist in the Bahamas, gigging in dark, unfriendly Southern redneck bars. It is peopled by the folks he has met or dreamt up along the way: junkies, dotty old sages, French bohemians. His pet media figures – Ricky Ricardo, Jimi Hendrix, ZaSu Pitts – file through, as does Paul Simon toting his 'masterpiece' *Graceland* as a sinister specter. Much of *Watts and Paris* saunters along like Thompson himself – the boulevardier of Franklin Avenue.

Born in Panama, Thompson moved to Los Angeles with his parents before he was quite a year old. They settled near Will Rogers Memorial at 103rd Street and Central Avenue in Watts. He describes his truck-driver father as a man of 'street knowledge', his mother a mathematician/teacher; both enthusiastically encouraged his many musical flirtations from voice to flute to piano. In high school you could find an assortment of vinyl on his turntable: Miles Davis, Eric Dolphy, Weather Report, James White and the Blacks, Frank Zappa, Iggy Pop. 'This is really weird to admit', says Thompson. 'In an age where Public Enemy is demanding, *"Be aware of your blackness! You're a black man! An Afro-American!"* I'm goin', "Damn, man, but that Bowie record really changed my life." *"But you're a black man!"* "But I'm a black man who likes David Bowie!" *Ziggy Stardust* – that record was an absolute turning point.'

Post-*Ziggy*, pre-*Lodger*, when Angelenos were making their first punk sightings in the aisles of Tower Records Sunset, Thompson was deep into Ornette Coleman and Rahsaan Roland Kirk, and paying Black Flag little mind. If punk made an impact, it wasn't a conscious one. He was busy sweating it out on the local club circuit – the Starwood, the Mask, the Blind Pig – in a garage band that changed tags on a whim (the Charles Laughton Band, 50/50, The Relievers). The music he describes as 'Steely Dan on acid'; the onstage antics ranged from acrobatic silliness to back-flips off the stage into a sea of befuddled faces to the stoicism of a junior-league Art Ensemble of Chicago. 'After the show, instead of a encore', he confesses, 'we came out and bowed, all holding hands. We were so cocky. We took ourselves very seriously.'

Nowadays, Thompson favors an understated flair for the dramatic. Dressed primarily in shades of navy and lace-up boots, he's easily lost within the folds of his natty wool overcoat. You'd overlook him in his tennis whites strolling the pasta aisle at Trader Joe's, but with little effort his smoky voice alone could

MARC ANTHONY THOMPSON

mesmerize a club. Unassuming to the point of invisibility, Thompson emerges as some sort of detached shadow man; a consummate voyeur, lighting everywhere yet settling nowhere in particular. One gets the feeling that maybe Thompson hasn't exactly found an 'image' (or non-image), for the business of show-biz.

In an industry that markets strict genres, Thompson has become something of a 'problem child'. If pressed to describe the music, he'll halfheartedly settle on something as innocuous as 'pop music with a real hard edge'. 'Musical chameleon', that pet seventies journalist's tag, which validated Daryl Hall and John Oates's vacillations between blue-eyed soul and lackluster pop, or sought to explain Joe Jackson's mild forays from new wave to jive to after-dinner 'jazz', doesn't exactly capture Thompson's slim oeuvre either. With two quirky/arty albums behind him, he finds himself precariously placed between rock and funk, kitsch and slick, Spartan and grandiose. He's also finding that crossover dreams for black artists remain just that, illusory meditations.

The recording and radio industries see rock and R&B as two distant worlds, with separate sets of symbols, icons and metaphors. What would be acceptable for one audience, they think, wouldn't be palpable to another. Some artists like Daryl Hall (who made a name – and a mint – by alternating stylistically between David Bowie and Al Green) come right out and say it: 'Even though our stuff is superficially R&B, we sing about what white people think about. Our songs have white images. Like in 'She's Gone', for example, take the lyric: 'Up in the morning, look in mirror/I'm worn as her toothbrush hanging in the stand.' It's a white image. That's why black people can't really cover our songs' [Rolling Stone, 1977]. Toothbrushes are 'white' images? At least that's what industry decision makers are quick to believe. It is why they have difficulty marketing black acts that bend the rules – Tracy Chapman, 24-7 Spyz, avant-guitarist Jean-Paul Bourelly, etc.

Thompson has seen both sides of it. Black audiences haven't been that much more receptive to new voices like Thompson's either. Neither blacks nor whites knew what to make of Prince losing his 'fro, donning fishnets and stilettos, and posing for an album cover shot with silver earrings dangling from his lobes. Black acts who aren't crooning love songs or embarking on deep bass dance orgies quite often aren't considered 'black enough'. The issue has picked up steam most recently with the success of Vernon Reid and Living Colour, who had radio programmers (black and white) hemming and hawing over 'suitable' classifications.

Watts and Paris was declared off-limits by black radio, but Warner Bros. had elaborate and expansive crossover plans. Thompson was given a sixteen-track studio, installed as project producer, and given free creative reign. Releasing his first album, *Marc Anthony Thompson,* Warner brass planned to play up the enigmatic angle and bank on word of mouth. 'They figured that the mystique would just build', explains Thompson, 'but unfortunately there is a really, really thin line between what's mystique and what's completely oblique – or who gives a shit. The record fell into the oblique part of the canyon.'

Thompson's predicament isn't all that novel. 'There is a precedent to Marc Anthony Thompson', says Steven Baker, Warner Bros. vice president of product management. 'An artist like Prince got away with changing styles. I think what Warner Brothers was most guilty of was not having more patience. [You] won't find anyone here who says that Marc isn't a multitalented guy who can play any type of music. We just weren't capable of sticking it out. It's a shame that we weren't able to market it.'

The dilemma, at the time, wasn't so much how to sell 'pop/poetic/obscure'; rather it was how to sell an avant-garde artist who also happened to be black. Marc Anthony Thompson takes this equation one step further: whereas Prince embarked on his stylistic metamorphosis gradually, from album to album, Thompson takes his great leaps from cut to cut. 'It was Tom Waits meets David Bowie meets Curtis Mayfield, and every member of the A&R department loved him . . . but Marc just wasn't your tried-and-true R&B artist', says former Warner Bros. director of A&R, Felix Chamberlain. The first album's single 'So Fine' was marketed as a pop-crossover black single (this time complete with video), and Warner, Chamberlain believes, gave it a fairly good shot. 'We thought it was a given single. But it didn't happen that way. There was no follow-up single; he should have been touring, playing in intimate settings.' Looking back, Chamberlain feels that there were several fundamental mistakes made by both Thompson and himself: more records should have been made between the first and second releases, promotion should have been more aggressive, the recordings themselves more focused.

In retrospect, what probably hurt Thompson the most were the three years he spent tinkering with his follow-up. In the time it took to hone *Watts and Paris,* Warner Bros. had almost doubled in size. Within that time as well, a new European strain of black acts (Soul II Soul and Terence Trent D'Arby) began to make indelible impressions on the international music scene both in sound and fashion.

In print, he's been handled gingerly, a curious study. And though many of the cuts would fit comfortably enough within urban contemporary/'Quiet Storm' formats or on public radio or college playlists, local radio, except for KCRW's Deirdre O'Donoghue, has all but abandoned him. What to make of a musician who seems as comfortable with shouting out vacuous technodance chants as with sharing seamy post-coital revelations? Darker and moodier selections ('Bird in Hand', 'Kate's Bush') display Thompson at his most indolent yet most enticing. An arcing voice, expanding into a full caress, pays homage to Bowie's golden years; as well it harbors Peter Gabriel's ambient emotion. But Thompson, flattered yet at the same time frustrated by the comparisons, begs to differ: 'They're all a paler version of me.'

African-American audiences are starved for images that better reflect the nuances within the black experience; we too should support those who present these new black perspectives. Listening to either album's more 'accessible' cuts ('Great Big Heat' from *Marc Anthony Thompson*; 'Perfect World' from *Watts and Paris*), it's nothing less than maddening that Thompson isn't riding a crest right about now. He knows what it takes to conjure shimmery, catchy pop tunes, but more importantly, he also knows how to conjure complex, resonant inner-worlds. The universe he carefully composes is neither solely black nor solely white. Thompson has found himself up against the same wall impeding many African-American artists of his generation. Be they writers like Trey Ellis who chronicle the life of middle-class buppies in fiction (*Platitudes*) or renegade directors like Spike Lee who capture the scope of African-American life, from bohemians to b-boys, they work in concert to obliterate the narrow parameters (stereotypes) that define 'blackness'. The other side of it, as Thompson points out in this age of renewed black awareness and pride, is that there is little tolerance for fence-sitting. The temper of the time stipulates that the race be celebrated, and if not celebrated at least prominently recognized.

Although allusions to Europe blossom in his work and though he's often nudged by friends and supporters who believe a simple change of scenery is the key to his elusive success, returning to Europe for any long stretch isn't an option for Thompson. Black artists for decades have been tempted by the fabled open-armed 'acceptance' that awaits on the other side of the ocean. But

Thompson chooses to hold his ground. 'It's like the James Baldwin syndrome. Paris is very easy in a lot of ways. They really have a high regard for black Americans, especially in the arts, but at the same time Parisians have this way of looking, this condescension you can almost taste on the Métro. When you see how they react to Africans you [realize that] if you weren't in this field [this is how] they'd be treating you. Then too, I'm an American, there's no way I'd want to leave the country now. . . . If there is something that I want to change, I'd just as soon stick here and fight. . . . It would be the easy way out. I want to conquer home.'

Between labels, he's writing, playing the infrequent live show, and spending time with his six-year-old daughter, Tessa. He picks up commercials and documentary scores and rents out his Hollywood studio space to local musicians. As for his next recording, despite the battles, he says, 'Maybe I'll make the songs of a larger piece, with a thematic center. Maybe I'll make it a little easier for people to find the personality.'

Or maybe he won't. Hard to say what to expect the next time around, or which way Thompson's head will turn – a nod to Public Enemy with deepest apologies to Lou Reed: 'I always thought Charlie Pride was kinda an oddity. The things he must go through. I'd love to live in his world for a day, and see. Be a black country singer. Cool.'

May 1990

CHAPTER 16

I HEARD IT THROUGH THE GRAPEVINE

It is amazing how much black people, in ritual settings such as barbershops
and pool halls, street corners and family reunions talk about talking. . . . They
do it to pass these rituals along from one generation to the next. They do it
to preserve the traditions of 'the race'.
Henry Louis Gates from The Signifying Monkey

They call themselves prophets. Poets. Ministers of information. Yet skeptics
poised on the sidelines see them as little more than angry ghetto noise. These
self-named 'lyrical terrorists' pass it down, spread urgent words across the
aisles of gymnasiums, arenas, halfway houses, a remote prison or two. Their
voices fan out over radio airwaves: with searing first-generation R&B beats
and sampled snatches of the gospel according to Martin, Malcolm and Minister Farakhan, rap – the medium and the message – is custom-tailored for the
ears of African-American youth.

Behind these street gospels and their Afrocentric rhymes are the spirit and
intent of an age-old oral tradition practised first by Africans in their homeland
and handed down in their new world. Rap rolls out as this decade's model, but
toasters, bandleaders (like Louis Jordan and Cab Calloway), Chicago bluesmen,
spit-shined railroad men, praise-singers, verse-spouting preachers and wizened
tribal *griots* paved the way for MCs as messengers of strength and hope and
standard-bearers of the gift of gab. Within the same ten-year span it took rap to
be accepted as a viable musical force, organizations and festivals such as the
Association of Black Storytellers and the 'In the Tradition . . . ' National Festival
of Black Storytelling have led a major resurgence in the oral tradition of
storytelling. Universities across the country offer folklore-based programs,
while more folklorists emerge in public-sector positions, studying ethnic diver-

sity and its effects on changing urban communities.

Committing the wealth of African-American folklore to the page has been an ambitious enterprise of black writers for decades. Immersing herself within some of the more secluded Southern hamlets of the US and later the Caribbean, Zora Neale Hurston spent the thirties and forties collecting oral histories, beliefs and superstitions, amassing an imposing cache that became the blueprint for a succession of folklore-inspired novels and monographs. Unheard of for a woman, inconceivable for a black woman, her achievements defied the obstacles of the day. Years at Barnard and later Columbia were spent under the tutelage of cultural anthropologist Franz Boas. Hurston's copious notes on culture and customs evolved into vivid lyrical fictions conveyed in black Southern vernacular, their roots sunk deep within African-American traditions. Within the decades bookended by the Harlem Renaissance and the Korean War, Hurston became the most prominent black woman writer in the nation. Her notoriety reached its apex in the early forties, her works curiously and suddenly abandoned by the public after the mid-fifties. She died in a Florida welfare home in 1960.

Langston Hughes and Arna Bontemps's *The Negro Folklore* (1958) provided an invaluable one-stop source, gathering tale-types ranging from slave testimonials to chronicles of the jazz life. The most recent addition to the literature, Linda Goss and Marian E. Barnes's *Talk That Talk: An Anthology of African-American Storytelling* (1990), assembles a new, wide-ranging collection of folktales and histories, celebrating a vibrant, enduring art that doesn't begin and end with the antebellum tales of Uncle Remus.

> I learned to talk in the street, not from reading about Dick and Jane going to
> the zoo and all that simple shit. . . . We exercised our minds by playin' the
> Dozens. . . . We played the Dozens like white folks play Scrabble.
> *H. Rap Brown*

In Africa, tales were told by elders in the wash of twilight, around an after-dinner fire, while women pounded yam and men set out to hunt. The *griot* (*gewel*) was entrusted with the task of reconstructing the precise history of his people. In a position acquired only through bloodline, this oral historian passed etiological tales that sought to answer the inexplicable – from summer rain to sudden death.

Tales metamorphosed on American soil. Uprooted unceremoniously from family, familiar terrain and mother tongue, Africans carried within their mind's eye fragments of their past. What survived the Middle Passage and what did not depended on usefulness – a sort of linguistic natural selection. Stories endured when African tongues or religious practices could not. Historical tales, more memorates, were more important than myths, as were stories featuring a 'trickster' figure – the weak outwitting the supposedly stronger foe. Though carefully disguised, the 'Br'er Rabbit' tales closely mirrored the master/slave relationship while at the same time fostering a spirit of solidarity. 'We brought a lot from Africa, it's just that much of it took a covert form', adds UCLA theater and folklore professor Beverly Robinson. 'It shows a cleverness of our ancestors. I think Zora said it best: "You may be able to read my letters, but you can't read my mind."'

Formal stories exchanged late at night in slave quarters or after Sunday meeting eased into various forms. The call-and-response of work songs eventually found its way into blues and jazz. Fragments surfaced in sermons as parables, as well as in casual testimonials that offered direction and inspiration. Quilting and weaving, hand-clap games, jump-rope rhymes also served as story-bearers. 'When we loaned our heads [for cornrowing], we loaned our ears and mouths as well; that's when all the good gossip came out', explains Dr Robinson. 'So who cares if you spend eight or ten hours getting your hair braided – you come out with at least five months of information. You've caught up with the latest T, as we call it – the gossip.'

> It seems to me that in a school that's ebony
> African history should be pumped up steadily
> But it's not and this has got to stop
> See Spot run; run get Spot
> Insulting
> To a black mentality
> *Boogie Down Productions*
> *from 'You Must Learn'*

Carving out time and place for storytelling today, in the face of grim headlines and even grimmer personal testimonies, might seem a naive proposition to a desperate and floundering generation. But storyteller Nailah Malik suggests

IN THE TRADITION

that, with the disintegration of the family unit, the rebirth in storytelling represents a return to tradition. 'A storyteller has to be aware of the conditions in his or her environment', Nailah explains. 'I tend to gravitate toward stories that I think can feed, that have some type of healing power. The gang problem, teenage pregnancies, low economic progress on the part of black people are at the heart to me.' Unlike many tellers, Malik's stories are seldom drawn from her own experience; she reaches for stories, quotes and proverbs from West Africa to help youth look inward for answers. As the 'Vela Storyteller' (*vela* means 'to rise and grow' in the language of the Xhose people), she travels to museums, libraries and cultural events resurrecting tales from books within the Los Angeles library system. 'In my work I'm also trying to combat illiteracy. I've taken the dust off a lot of these stories that have been put in the back; to me they are just jewels in the rough.'

'Storytellers today have a great opportunity to teach and expose others to various other cultures of the world', says Elaine Warren-Jacobs, a local storyteller born in Antigua. 'If we take this role seriously we can really bring to the lives of people other places, other people and their way of life.' Settling in the US in 1979 – 'donkey years ago' – she points out that her four children, though born here in California, know all about bush tea (for colds) and *fungi,* the cornmeal mush that is served with fish dishes. 'Story', she adds, 'is just a repository in a way. It's just a venue through which the culture passes.' Trading tales was an integral part of island life: calypso music, superstitions, beliefs and remedies carry bits and pieces of her history and culture. Her mother passed along old slave stories, remedies and Anancy-the-Spider tales, these informal sessions sparked by something as innocuous as a random image on the evening news.

Storytelling's importance, Warren-Jacobs worries, seems to be waning in the islands. As everywhere else, it battles with television for a child's attention. 'It threatens the culture. . . . I'm very much concerned because the people see some unrealistic things on TV and they begin to think, well, that's the way I should be. We need to get back close to [our culture] so that we can have a real sense of self. You need your family and you need people for the real richness in life. And that kind of thing can happen through being conscious of your culture and deliberately setting out to pass it on.'

A culture that is passed on is at the same time validated, Elaine Warren-Jacobs believes. Contemporary storytellers like Jacobs and Nailah Malik recognize and welcome the diverse mix of styles – from puppeteering to rap – that affirm African-American customs and traditions. Rap, in a broader sense, has the potential to do more than turn out bursting urban dance floors. This past decade rap hammered down hard; charged and raw, it promises to bellow full force into the next. As young black men and women find themselves too-swiftly-rendered police statistics – victims of crack wars, stray bullets, unemployment and anything else tense streets may breed – some of the more politically conscious rappers have taken hard looks at this ravaged terrain. Like the silhouette – arms folded, defiant – caught in the eye of the rifle sight on Public Enemy's logo, black youth are society's victims, but no longer silent.

These MCs aim their messages (albeit at times vague and underdefined) at uplifting and educating the race. Too often the rhymes project distorted images of misogyny, hate and city violence. 'But that', Nailah Malik concedes, 'is what we give them.' This inveterate oral tradition demands that rappers be responsible when preparing and conveying their messages. If traditional storytellers carefully fashion their presentations to address today's environment and lifestyles, the words from the mike should seek to stimulate black consciousness and build a sense of self-esteem, not encourage decimation of the race by way of counterproductive propaganda and ambiguous philosophies. With direction and purpose these can be the voices to safely usher youth out from the dark.

Beverly Robinson makes it simple: 'Rap is all part of the continuum. We are a verbal people. From the 'Signifying Monkey', Willie Dixon, Malcolm X, the Bodacious Bourgerillas, the Watts Prophets, the Last Poets, Gil Scott-Heron, Oscar Brown, Jr, Louis Jordan, Eddie Jefferson and other mastertellers, you can see that rap music doesn't start with Kurtis Blow. Rather Kurtis Blow, like Minister Farrakhan, is simply part of a continuum of black narrators.'

April 1990

CHAPTER 17

THE BLACK GALLERY

There are moments when . . . expression reaches a zenith, when it is so
real it becomes universal, it finds its stillness. If you don't capture it at that
moment, all you get is a transitory particular. When you find it at the right
moment, it is not only particular, it is universal. *Roy DeCarava*

Bob Douglas, cameras in tow, motors east towards Riverside. Riding shotgun,
Max Roach, bebop's heartbeat, hides his eyes behind a customary pair of Ray
Bans. Despite wildfire reports of Charlie Parker's 'precarious' emotional state,
his management has secured a plumb Southland gig. The tight ensemble boasts
tough, no-nonsense personnel including Shelley Manne on drums and Chet
Baker, a young, sloe-eyed trumpet player fresh from an impressive set of dates
at San Francisco's Bop City. Gliding in VIP-style, Douglas and Roach are
quickly ushered backstage and placed face-to-face with an anxious and somewhat distracted Bird.

'There was a bunch of kids just hanging around out back', Douglas recalls.
'Bird just opened the door and let them in. Management got mad at him and
he – well, he just left.' A makeshift search party is hastily assembled and assigned to comb the surrounding terrain. But after about an hour, without much
fuss, he's led back to the theater. Casually cradling his horn, he wanders on
stage, takes a breath, and then just blows. Roach is coaxed out of the audience
mindset to sit in. 'That's how Max got to play', smiles Douglas, '. . . and how I
got the shot.'

Bob Douglas, however, hasn't been as lucky as jazz chroniclers William
Claxton, William Gottlieb, or even right-place-at-the-right-time black photographer Chuck Stewart, whose works have graced album sleeves, publicity stills,
gallery walls or the matte-finished pages of retrospective anthologies. It took

ROLAND CHARLES: CURATOR, THE BLACK GALLERY

close to forty years for Douglas to assemble his shots for public consumption; the negatives remained in yellowing wax paper sleeves, the prints protected in scrapbooks or frayed cardboard boxes. Douglas, who worked in L.A. in 1948, was encouraged by a local photographer and gallery curator, Roland Charles. 'I was too busy making a living to worry about stuff like that. I used to run with musicians. Liked the people and what they were doing and saying in their music. Those were some of the happiest days of my life.'

Bob Douglas's story is not an uncommon one. With the exception of black photography deities Roy DeCarava and his moody meditations in sooty blacks and grays, Gordon Parks's gritty *Life* magazine photo-documentaries and James Van Der Zee's regal, sepia-toned portrayals of black family life, early black photographers found fame elusive. Even today, they are often relegated to an on-earth purgatory better known as obscurity.

In the early days, making a name in the black community meant serving it. And serving it well. But supporting one's family came first. This required shouldering bags of bulbs, film, cameras, tripods and lights and shooting any-thing from family portraits, weddings, balls and cotillions to the occasional funeral. Rising above and beyond the usual photo pinch hitter depended on how entrepreneurial and innovative the photographer was. Charles Williams, for ex-ample, took bread-and-butter photography to new heights – employing a team of leggy ladies to snap club patrons at fifteen nightspots around the L.A. basin. He performed darkroom chores on site, delivering the finished product by set's end. Pulling out of the club business in 1947, Williams, with the help of some friends, started his own school. The concentration, 'basic, general photography', guaranteed that students could support themselves upon com-pletion.

'They were responsible for documenting the African-American experience', explains Roland Charles, co-curator with Calvin Hicks of Los Angeles's Black Gallery. 'And the lack of recognition that blacks received in society parallels the plight of the black photo-artist.' In the shadow of the newly remodeled Baldwin Hills-Crenshaw Plaza, the Black Gallery, a small, well-lighted spartan space is squeezed between a barber shop and stationery store in an outdoor shopping mall on Santa Barbara Plaza. Since July 1984, supported by grants and out-of-pocket donations (mostly Charles and Hicks's own), the gallery has attempted to serve and encourage this neglected com-munity of black artists.

In November 1983, the Black Photographers of California organized and sponsored an installation at the California Museum of African-American Art in Exposition Park. 'The Tradition Continues' was the first major exhibit featuring the work of roughly sixty black California photographers, saluting photo pioneers Frank Herman Cloud, Vera Jackson, Harry Adams, Jack Davis, Fred Cooper and Howard Morehead. It was this exhibit that gave birth to the Black Gallery. 'It's all about sharing the history', explains Roland Charles. 'Images of black culture are being recorded by nonblacks. The jazz idiom has been well-represented; it's *very* in vogue. But it seems curious that only black *images* are popular. And for some reason, it's very difficult to get shown if you are a black artist depicting those very same images.'

'It's been a struggle', Calvin Hicks agrees, 'and we've gotten some flack over the gallery's name, but it's important to stress that we are open to *all* photographers, and to *all* ethnic groups. Foremost, we are the first gallery in the black community dedicated to black photography.' A meeting ground and sounding board for community artists, the gallery is sometimes transformed into a fifties boho basement coffeehouse – soft-lit and bathed in patchouli – offering poetry and jazz and interpretive dance. For the more 'practical', there are a monthly slide night, summer tech workshops and an annual photo contest.

L.A.'s underground talent and neglected environs were brushed off and decked out for the gallery's most recent show: 'Life in a Day of Black Los Angeles'. With over 120 prints shot on Martin Luther King Day, it is the first body of work documenting a black population in the West. Drawing from a cross-section of communities – Pasadena, Watts, Beverly Hills – the ten photographers recorded the full social spectrum – from the grassroots to the bourgeoisie.

Thomas Wright, who heads his own film and television production company, Barefoot Productions, worked hand-in-hand with Roland Charles coordinating the project. 'We were brainstorming, trying to do something for Black History Month. Then we got to thinking about the fact that there hasn't been a current assessment of the community. It led to this possibility. We had a wide range of photographers – photo-artists to hard-core news photographers – like Akili [Ramsess]. I was anxious to see what they would bring.'

Ramsess, influenced by Gordon Parks, W. Eugene Smith and many of the depression-era WPA project photographers, has been shooting professionally for about six years. A staff photographer for the *Herald Examiner,* her job requires that she trade many hats, covering fast-breaking, hard-news events or sprinting courtside (seven and half months pregnant) during last year's Lakers playoffs. Going into the 'Life in a Day' project, Ramsess says that the focus for her was easy – documenting the changes in L.A.'s once-booming black cultural center, Central Avenue.

'As much as I enjoy and appreciate the written word, I feel that it is the photograph that is the most powerful and lasting.' The images are gritty, confrontational, favoring stark blacks and whites. She plays with hard lines; dissects figures with cool, clean shafts of shadow. Her lens reveals and details the unflattering remains of the 'Jewel of Central Avenue', the old Dunbar Hotel, then pauses on a quiet moment with an elderly man standing in early morning shadows beneath a crumbling burger joint awning, his face all but concealed save for the sad glint in his eyes.

'Most of it can be captured in their eyes', Nathaniel Bellamy explains. Bellamy chose L.A.'s acute homeless problem as his concentration. He wandered the tangle of side streets and congested main thoroughfares that make up downtown L.A., capturing in the sobering image of a vagabond youth bent over a Bible in silent study the despair as well as the hope. 'In their eyes you can see the embarrassment, the sadness. If they had their druthers many of them wouldn't be on the streets. I tried to focus on the cause as well as the effect. I encouraged dialogue with the subject before I started shooting. Paid careful attention to the foreground, background. There's *so* much of the random photograph – everyone coming through snapping pictures, without thinking about how people may feel about it.'

The goal is to communicate a universal – the life experience – while adding something personal and unique: black culture and lifestyle – the black experience. 'Society places a lot of imposing mental restrictions', Roland Charles confides. 'There are so many black photographers whose families threw away their work. They didn't know any better. These men and women left behind a legacy; they fill the gap. Growing up in New Orleans, the only images of blacks that I saw were sharecroppers. I didn't know we had a history and culture above and beyond that. We're descendants of a proud people *captured* into slavery, not simply descendants of slaves. We'd like to change that view. It is as important to us as it is important to the next generation to come.'

1989

CHAPTER 18

THE SPOOK WHO SAT BY THE DOOR: WALTER MOSLEY SHADES THE *ROMAN NOIR*

Harlem-based photographer James Van Der Zee, in the first decades of this century, made a name for himself documenting the dead — more precisely black folks' bodies forever stilled, shells recently relieved of their souls. Few archivists felt it necessary to carefully document the paths of African-Americans — dead or alive, spirited or spiritless. So many lives had been rendered shadows, barely hugging the margins, full identities lost or out of focus, hovering just out of frame or time.

Later, urban documentarist Roy DeCarava froze a moment, then turned it into extended metaphor. Toying with this notion of shadow play, his 1956 photograph 'Dancing' catches midstep, in filmy silhouette, the herky-jerky face-off between two wiry black men in a near-empty New York ballroom. They are urban hieroglyphics; their contorted figures work through a late-night medicine dance: exorcising demons? An abstract expression of cleansing? Release through exhaustion? We don't know for sure who or what inhabits these shadows: just another one of black urban life's mysteries.

Who bothered to document on the page this sense of invisibility? Richard Wright, Ralph Ellison, James Baldwin all eloquently wrote of that Southern-cum-Midwestern-cum-East Coast, race-game frustration turned to rage. They articulated it with the same passion those two men danced out in the heat of Saturday night revelry.

Chester Himes wrote his letters from the Coast. His first dispatch, *If He*

Hollers Let Him Go, was disappointing. Not because of style or execution, but because its content forced those seeking refuge out West to revise their detailed wish list. The West Coast didn't offer heaven on earth at the end of the line. As always, the dream fulfilled was sweet for some, mere chimera for others. 'When I came out to Los Angeles in the fall of '41, I felt fine. . . .' So testifies Himes's protagonist, Bob Jones, whose weighted preamble forecasts his eminent decline, his melding with the shadows. Jones, whose defense industry job is a series of slow-building indignities, often wakes disturbed by the violent drift of his dreams: discrimination, outcast dogs as larger symbols, visions of eternally pounding the pavement in search of the elusive 9-to-5. He's haunted by surreptitious racism, sometimes gleaned in the far corners of a smile, an antagonist difficult to confront because here in Los Angeles it is seldom completely unmasked. 'It was the look on the people's faces when you asked them about a job. Most of 'em didn't say outright they wouldn't hire me. They just looked so goddamned startled that I'd even asked. . . .'

How dare a shadow speak.

Easy Rawlins, Walter Mosley's reluctant private eye, prefers the margins. He's grown accustomed to negotiating them, feels secure in the comfort of their limitations. He has made them his own. With Himes's Bob Jones as his literary antecedent, Rawlins actively presses toward a different sort of invisibility — not one forced on him, borne of neglect and victimization, but one he strives for, an approximation of a calm John Q. Public life complete with house, lawn, wife and child. He would just as soon get lost in the passion of a dark lovely or in the mundane but strict routine of ticking off his checklist of chores and looking after his property. A high profile sends up flares, gives you trouble.

The Los Angeles of Easy Rawlins is the humble parallel universe to the one inhabited by Raymond Chandler's Philip Marlowe. Instead of Pico, Sixth Street, and Wilshire's Miracle Mile as glittering landmarks, Avalon, Central, Florence—and the streets of Watts—lead into a trilogy of stories *(White Butterfly, A Red Death, Devil in a Blue Dress)* detailing midcentury black urban life. What pulls Rawlins into this life as a shadow shadowing others is his desire to hold on to the little crumb of stability he has—his symbolic forty acres and a mule:

'[That] house meant more to me than any woman I knew. I loved her and I was jealous of her and if the bank sent the county marshal to take her from me I might have come at him with a rifle rather than to give her up.'

This little house, this emblem of success, sits at the center of the first two Easy Rawlins mysteries, *Devil in a Blue Dress* and *A Red Death*. By *White Butterfly*, Easy appears settled and firm in his financial holdings, but the struggle, nonetheless, has taken its toll. Despite his wife (Regina), his baby girl (Edna), adopted son (Jesus), and the roof over his head, Easy's convictions and direction are beginning to waver, the psychology behind his actions becoming more indistinct. Although he has attempted to walk the straight and narrow, to put a stop to his evenings catting around and dodging bullets, we find him inhaling four fingers of Johnny Walker at some juke joint or stepping out to pick up some Seagrams from a package store, all the while looking to get lost in an alcohol haze.

He's approached by the LAPD's token black cop, Quinten Naylor, to re-enter his streetlife. Naylor, in his East Coast clip, relates the details of a string of deaths that have occurred in The Community, that nebulous area south of Wilshire's high-rises. Corpses of black 'goodtime girls' found dumped in tall grass, with the killer's signature – a cigar burn on the breast – begin to turn up with alarming frequency. Easy, the peace officer's trusty artery into the back-porch-to-barstool network, at first turns Naylor down with a casual 'I cain't help you man.' He suspects what's behind the agency's intent. Easy knows these deaths barely make a ripple, maybe a thumbnail mention buried deep in newsprint.

When Easy does become enmeshed, he is forced inside by circumstance and bristling city nerves: a white bobbysoxer turns up dead, bearing the same markings. And when the law becomes anxious about violence spilling out of working-class black neighborhoods into communities predominantly white and affluent (the pattern hasn't changed – for example, Westwood's 1988 gang shootings), the machine forges, albeit blindly, full-steam ahead. 'As a rule', Easy's PI-interior explains, 'I will not run down a black man for the law.' Yet he must also address the obvious: the slow thaw, the anxious buzz, the alter ego ghosting him who loves the night. 'I hadn't hit the streets since my wedding. I tried to bury that part of my life. . . . Looking for this killer', Easy concedes, 'was like coming back from the dead for me.'

Easy Rawlins doesn't quite fit in either world. Not the rarefied landscape of fifties Company Man, neither is he completely trusted among his own. Unlike the very visible Quinten Naylor, who carries 'the weight of the whole community on his shoulders', and whom 'the black people didn't like . . . because he talked like a white man and . . . had a white man's job', suspicions about Easy are a little more abstract, tending to gestate in the gut. He noses around too much; people tethered to him – even loosely – suddenly die. Easy is a figure incomplete, remote, not always present even when he's present. All of it is simply his ounce of insurance; sensitive to proximity, intimacy, he doesn't trust those outside, either.

Easy has set up an elaborate pose, an ingenious ruse that cuts him more slack, creates yet another security buffer. Keeping his comings, goings and purpose completely enigmatic, he poses as a contented janitor sweeping balconies in the sun. He allows another man (Mofass) to fit the owner profile and collect the rent on the various properties he owns, while Easy hovers in the background, keeping sentinel. Easy's secrets extend far beyond business partners and friends: 'All of what I had and all I had done was had and done in secret. Nobody knew the real me.' (Did *he*?) 'Mofass knew something but [he wasn't a friend] you could kick back and jaw with. . . . I had lived a life of hiding before I met Regina. Nobody knew about me. They didn't know about my property. . . . I felt safe in my secrets. . . .'

Silence undoes his marriage and works at the seams that secure his tenuous relationship with his mute adopted son, Jesus. Regina implores him to show her the 'weak parts', to help save and nurture what little has passed between them. But he can't find the words to explain why he sits and broods in his existential silence; why he's still haunted by his participation in the violence of a white man's war overseas. 'Defeat goes down hard with black people; it's our most common foe.' Leaving a trail of lies, or half-truths, ensures that there isn't much of anything to follow. But amid all the trickery and fancy deceits, will he lose himself forever? 'You can't hide', Regina warns, 'in your own house. . . .'

The armor that Easy, Quinten Naylor and Easy's sometimes-sidekick (from his Texas days), Raymond 'Mouse' Alexander, have worked to fortify isn't easily let down. Easy has equipped himself for the 'instinctive disrespect' with which white racists attempt to bait him; he's steeled himself so that much of it barely registers or truly matters ('I turned away and he was gone from my life.') Yet the numbness has gradually settled to the bone, affecting all facets of his life. He stares blankly into a dark void, seldom moved.

In daylight hours, Easy's pent-up night visions only feed his rage. The anger, just in check, struggles out of these black men (not friends, but foot soldiers sure in their path) in different ways: exboxer, now local bartender, Joppy Shag in his heyday drew big crowds who marveled at the 'violence he brought to the ring'. The red tinge just beneath the surface of officer Quinten Naylor's skin registers, to Easy, as the 'shade of rage'. Only Mouse has perfected his own way of confronting and working through anger. His resolution technique is pat response augmented by an absence of guilt or remorse – 'You want me to kill him, Ease?'

These novels work far better as pieces of social history than as hard-boiled mysteries whose plot twists are, in retrospect, thin and forced. The turns in Easy's detective path are not nearly as compelling as the everyday mountains he must scale. The nuts-and-bolts elements of the *roman noir* are overshadowed by Easy's small acts of survival. How he'll get himself out of conflict with police and G-men or pay the rent is more interesting than who's a threat to the American Way (*A Red Death*); who killed the bobbysoxer (*White Butterfly*); or where an errant white girl's gotten to (*Devil in a Blue Dress*). Rawlins's foils are large, monolithic and persistently hot on his tail – the IRS, the FBI. He takes cases to pull himself out of a hole (his house note) or a fine mess (back taxes), not to refine his skills as a P.I. striving for a downtown address.

The hitch in this smooth step is Mosley's attempt to let Easy define his larger role in words: 'I had a reputation of fairness and the strength of my convictions among the poor'; or the long didactic speech about the white librarian with a heart of gold and her unwitting (though inherent) disdain for black English that takes up precious pages without advancing *White Butterfly*'s already complex, multilayered plot.

Easy's pace moves at a clip when we're allowed to simply tail him as he cuts through the morass, decoding clues hidden within the landscape. At the same time he clutches desperately at his personal store, afraid that it might all suddenly hurtle from his grasp. Easy's blind treadmill brings him always to the same clearing, confronting the same crossroad: considering the composition of his path toward independence, a semblance of self-sufficiency. 'Money bought everything. Money paid the rent and fed the kitty. . . . I got the idea somehow that if I got enough money then maybe I could buy my own life back.'

'California', Easy Rawlins reflects, 'was like heaven for the Southern Negro. People told stories of how you could eat fruit right off the trees and get enough work to retire one day. The stories were true for the most part but the truth wasn't like the dream. Life was still hard in L.A. and if you worked everyday you still found yourself on the bottom.'

Even when sodden with drink, bruised and beaten, Philip Marlowe never seemed truly at bottom – not the kind of 'bottom' that visited Easy Rawlins in his dreams. That same, clear-headed arctic cool doesn't inhabit Rawlins's countenance; his dispassion is a barely contained frustration that masquerades as calm silence. It is only a harbinger of rage. Where Chandler's fictional 'Bay City' offered a cool breeze, a trip outside a complex city maze, Rawlins's brief trip to Santa Monica in *A Red Death* finds him tense, lunging at shadows and working overtime. Reckless eyeballing on the other side of familiar boundaries will get him lynched, drowned or, at the very least, made a broken example.

But despite the danger, the silence of death a heartbeat away, Rawlins too is captivated by this city's beauty, still perplexed by the folly of the promise. And still, he drinks in its poetry. Where Chandler would read the red winds, Easy decodes the listing palm trees: 'Their silhouettes rose above the landscape like impossibly tall and skinny girls. Their hair a mess, their posture stooped. I tried to imagine what they might be thinking but failed.'

Easy Rawlins is forever trying to meld into that dusk, that trick of light that turns those trees into silhouettes whispering urgent messages (Regina's, possibly). The narrow space he's allotted for his life is like the cell he occasionally finds himself tossed into when he fails to 'cooperate' with the law. Jail proves a sacred place where he contemplates solitude: '[While in jail] I could become the darkness and slip out between the eroded cracks of that cell. If I was nighttime nobody could find me; no one would even know I was missing.' If he melds into the night, it would be a step closer to complete anonymity, inconspicuousness, some state or form that won't attract or bait harm.

He could get lost in a river of drink, or in rough, purging sex, but he always has to surface, wrestle out of the brief pause of an artificial dream. 'Nobody knew what I was up to and that made me sort of invisible; people thought that they saw me but what they really saw was an illusion of me, something that wasn't real.' What would lead a man to this, on a no-holds-barred journey toward nothingness? The goal: a shell that could walk the earth barely discernible to the naked eye, and therefore completely unhindered and able to soar. Easy Rawlins and his like-minded foot soldiers pass through life made to feel this way — or that — looked through or past, their pleas unheard, needs unmet. In a climate where race invades every thought and action, determines the texture and path of one's existence, extending the time between cradle and grave provides the intricate architecture of suspense. Finding your way from one end to the other is the most compelling element of the story, the blind curves of life, the real mystery.

August 1992

ESSAYS

CHAPTER 19

CITY OF SPECTERS

A teacher here recently gave a vocabulary test in which she asked her students to provide the antonym of *youth*. Over half the class answered *death*.
Truman Capote, "Hollywood"

They worship death here. They don't worship money they worship death.
Raymond Chandler on Hollywood

Death is only a word, it is an abrupt absence that has reality.
John Clellon Holmes

Some mornings, from a majestic set of sooty garret windows, Moss will watch downtown's concrete fall then slowly rise. With black coffee in hand and Joe Turner sassing on the stereo, he daily makes note of the city's slow progress – aborted elaborate projects, radically altered plans. Most evenings he is mesmerized by the strict configuration of windows, light, and ledges that metamorphose into surreal though solemn faces. Like sacred ceremonial masks, they loom stoic and unblinking in the vast night sky. This warehouse space squats unobtrusively beneath a black argument of electric lines and is cordoned off by a set of railroad tracks that seem to wander nowhere. It's been years since I've settled down on these scarred wood floors, since Moss has opened the door, his mouth, or his heart to friends.

When I first met Moss through his girlfriend, Inez, he was new to town. I'd met Inez while I was still shelving and selling bestsellers to attorneys and junior film executives at a small bookstore in Century City. Some evenings when I worked late, I'd see her draping mannequins in expensive, exotic clothes. She stopped me one afternoon when she saw me carrying a slim portfolio while waiting in line for lunch. 'Student?' she asked glancing through black-and-white still-lifes. I nodded. 'Good stuff. It'll get better.' She had given up on photography – the smell, the cost. After hours she dressed windows for a chain of Westside department stores; from dawn to dusk she fretted over huge canvases in her downtown loft. With time she offered the use of her forsaken darkroom as well as a critical eye.

In those days, Moss had only just begun curiously prowling empty side streets at all hours, carefully sidestepping the limp bodies of homeless women and men. He would stoop to check a pulse at the temple or the rhythm of halting, shallow breaths – once leaning over to share his air with a little girl whose lips and lids had gone blue. This ritual continued until he was shaken down at dusk near Al's Bar at Traction. Now he seldom talks or slows his stride for any thing or one.

Some say now he is a ghost. Standing a shade over six feet, rail-like, from a short distance within dusk's half-light, Moss looks like nothing more than a haphazard stroke mark leaning against a gray wall. He hasn't the need for a telephone; even an urgent knock at his door goes unanswered. I've often wondered how, within this shroud of secrecy, of ambient solitude, he spends the measure of his days.

There used to be busy, intricate structures occupying floor-to-ceiling space at four corners of this reconverted warehouse. Dark, heavy pieces of menacing industrial sculpture, fabricated from found fragments of iron, steel, aluminum, old hubcaps or wire hangers. He welded works of art together from piles of castaway remains. On ambitious days, he'd take long rides as far south as Long Beach or as far north as Goleta on 'collecting trips'. Since there are no trees, he waited to hear the rustle of newspaper skidding across asphalt before beginning his evening's work. At street side, three stories below, you could catch occasional sparks, a warm glow, and flickering shadows as they moved along the farthest wall. Not much remains of those days: just a few blistered spots in the floor where the heat became too intense, and a faint gray scar running the length of Moss's arm, starting just above the wrist and terminating at the bend of his elbow.

Only once was I asked along on one of Moss's elaborate scavenger hunts. The invitation surprised me, since he was generally mysterious about his work and seldom had words for me. I'd been downtown working in the darkroom and visiting Inez, who'd been floored with the flu. Moss kept bringing in burnt slices of wheat toast, which Inez rejected with a regal flutter of the hand. When she drifted off to sleep, I gathered my things to head back west. 'Where you off to?' he asked over a sink of dishes. 'I think I need a second set of eyes.' We drove out to the beach, taking congested surface streets, Moss chewing gum and twisting radio knobs all the way. Finding a place a half-dozen blocks from the shore, he pulled out a net, some soiled-stiff work gloves, and slipped out of his shoes. With each step we sank deeper into white-hot sand. He rescued odd bits of metals that peeked out from just beneath the surface. The bounty was scarcer than he would have liked; it seemed hardly worth the ride through smog and traffic. 'It'd been nice', he said with his eyes on the road ahead, 'to save a little bit more.'

There was the occasional show. There were modest local reviews. There was a community opening up within the shadow of City Hall, as local artists moved from studio spaces near the sea to work spaces just east of Little Tokyo. They settled within a collection of dark suspicious streets – Traction, Rose, Third, Second, Center, Vigness, Santa Fe – that made up an ersatz SoHo, populated by blue-and-orange-haired Otis Parsons and Art Center grads.

Moss immigrated from Illinois by hand-me-down Ford Falcon. He flopped in a hole-in-the-wall motel on the easterly fringes of Sunset Strip, with the hourly rates hastily scrawled in pencil and posted on the back of the door. Being an emigre was not information Moss offered freely, but cowboy tans or 'pulling calves' would occasionally swirl to the surface in toxically induced reveries. At clear moments he offered instead his sober, polished line: 'I was surely dead in Illinois.'

Shedding small-town shyness, Moss relaxed gleefully into big-town anonymity, carefully collecting a shimmering cluster of friends. His closest was a painter named Aaron, a native, who had an infectious booming laugh that began somewhere deep inside his five-foot-six-inch frame and ended in a high, maniac titter. Moss met him on a midnight constitutional. Both frequently waged battles with insomnia; they rose in the small hours to walk off jangled nerves. In a thin-lapeled, antique tuxedo and black Converse high-tops laced with glittered strings, he would drag Moss to boring Hollywood parties – 'BHPs', he called them – where they would stand around in tight private circles laughing and tossing copper pennies into heated turquoise pools. He would then spirit him off again in his pumpkin-colored Rambler to a 'real' celebration in Echo Park or Silver Lake where the music, heavy on bass and drum, made the floorboards groan and tremble and the hot air floating in smelled heavy-sweet like ancient gardenias.

Moss lived a few buildings away from the neighborhood's sole celebrity – singer/songwriter Peter Ivers, the flamboyant host of the cult cable show 'New Wave Theater'. Ivers, a Harvard graduate in classics, came to L.A. in 1971 to try to break into the music business. Eleven years later, and still far from a household word, he settled into a sixth-floor loft downtown, where he sometimes entertained friends with his own blues harmonica stylings or on a whim invited a random mix of musicians over for a rooftop twilight jam session. He spent many quiet afternoons in meditation or engaged in yoga. Among friends and casual acquaintances he was known as carefree, idealistic, and above all trusting. The first time I saw Ivers, Moss pointed him out at a cramped and smoky downtown party. He was shrugging out of a too-small tailored jacket as someone put a friendly arm around his shoulder, then ushered him into a distant, darkened room. Moss would often brush against him at noisy openings, or exchange a quick nod behind black shades while traveling in daylight down Traction. The next time I saw Ivers, his grainy face filled the front page of an L.A. free weekly – he had been found on March 3, 1983, bludgeoned to death in his sleep. His body tangled within the folds of sheets damp with his own blood.

Daily patterns changed. An unspoken, unofficial neighborhood curfew was quickly imposed. Residents traveled in loud packs at nightfall, and thin voices offering comfort crossed over thinner telephone wires. People traded stories about the forty-five minutes it took for police to arrive; about the failure to seal off the murder scene; about the cheap lock on Ivers's front door. Neighbors waited silently for murder motives, for officers to assemble follow-up clues.

But Aaron grew tired. Moss remembers a bristling, electric impatience. After a handful of weeks he was bored with sipping black coffee with friends, waiting to hear if it was safe to roam neighboring side streets at night. After a noisy display, Aaron ventured out of the neighborhood, to the beach, 'for inspiration'; his body was found the following morning in a littered alley behind a dumpster, a few blocks from the Venice boardwalk. He'd been relieved of $20, a cracked Timex, and his glittered shoestrings.

Most agreed that the streets had gotten mean. 'The romance went out of it after that', Moss recalls. 'I mean you felt kinda foolish trying to hang on to any of it.' The neighborhood began to change after the city rezoned these industrial work spaces as live-ins. Downtown became a neighborhood in transition. Earthquake proofing and proper plumbing put these last refuges for many local artists financially out of reach. Moss sublet his place to one of the many up-and-coming actors who were venturing into the neighborhood for a 'funky place' to throw a memorable grand fete. He rented a U-Haul, packed slides of his work, Levis, T-shirts, hot plate, and books into the trunk of his Falcon and headed east.

'I stopped sculpting', Moss says as he pulls proof sheets, prints, and negatives from black boxes, then spreads them on a gray blanket close to the light. I recognize some faces: Inez, her cotton-white hair pulled away from her face with a foamy smoke-colored scarf, scowls out of frame; Aaron, at the beach in shabby thriftstore layers, shivers through a huge gap-toothed grin.

Moss says, flipping through proofs, that he roamed New York without the energy to pester a soul. He first took a train to Chicago, then rented a truck and traveled to Evanston, Illinois, where he says he sat on the day-porch with his father smoking cigarettes, reveling in the scented silence. This was life for a while. 'Just couldn't seem to work with my hands. They just wouldn't cooperate. And when I did it seemed I'd have dreams. Angry dreams. That's why I stay awake.'

We wade through more photos. Box upon box of matte-finished black-and-white images – people, buildings, sky, ragged terrain. Some have amoeba-like ocher stains where the fixer wasn't completely rinsed away. Most are underdeveloped and have a somber gray cast. Lack of color, Moss explains, provides necessary distance. 'Otherwise it's all too confrontational.'

Since these photos remain in narrow black boxes parked beneath his bed, I ask Moss what he does for money. Odd jobs drawing espresso at local coffee bars, pumping gas, working in darkrooms at professional photo labs in Hollywood. He's grown accustomed to the isolation. 'If you drop out of sight in L. A., people don't always assume you're dead, I've learned. Rather they assume you've only moved out of carphone service distance. Or that you're busy . . . thus happy and healthy.'

I talk him into taking a walk, to move out of the shade of his living quarters. Maybe pick up a roast beef sandwich at Philippe's, or a warm sake in Little Tokyo – just like old times. We walk along deserted but wide-open stretches of Alameda – the same path we'd take to Aaron's summer evenings just before nightfall. We move slowly toward the cluster of wispy palm trees and stucco clock tower denoting Union Station in the distance. We pass a lone transient with a rusted shopping cart filled with a careful selection of grimy rags and broken glass. He has stripped completely nude. His hair has clustered into a dry forest of auburn dreadlocks, his skin so smooth and dark it looks more like cool onyx than charred flesh. He blesses the corner of Alameda and Second with a wave of open palms, then bends head first toward the sidewalk in an extended stretch that looks more like a mystic yoga posture. Moss and I stand motionless as he pauses for a moment, raises his arms, and shouts into the sun.

In junior high school we went to more funerals than weddings. My friend J. remembers solemn autumn rosaries that began just after sunset, giving us little time to climb out of dusty chinos and Earth Shoes and into more somber, respectful attire. These deaths were often careless accidents; macho posturings or random, mercuric moves made in fits of anger, that most times followed a red blur of words. Best friends played fatal games with loaded guns, and Cuban 'car club' members met with grisly, mysterious demises that drastically rewrote the lives of survivors.

The first funerals my classmates attended were for close friends, all under eighteen. 'I didn't go to an old person's funeral until my grandfather died', J. recalls. By then it was a ritual that had grown darkly familiar. For shortly before her grandfather slipped away, her stunned family buried her older brother, the summer of his sixteenth year.

Around campus, J. was often mistaken for a blond-haired, blue-eyed Cuban, since her circle of friends, except for me, was almost exclusively Latino. Like the 'homegirls', she adopted a belligerent slur to her speech, a fluid ease to her style. In her I saw an inner calmness, a worry-free veneer that I worked hard to master. Yet she too, like me, possessed an eager, insatiable curiosity. We both had grand though pragmatic aspirations of being well respected yet quite possibly only modestly successful writers. We spent weekends outside of Culver City, a quiet, tidy community just on the edges of L.A. proper, exploring what lay beyond. We gathered ideas to store in looseleaf notebooks. We collected city color.

Summer 1977, J. and I abandoned Venice Beach and took to tangled Sunset

'RUGGED TERRAIN'

Boulevard. Of that summer, I remember an odd jumble of mismatched details — a wash of faces and light that bloomed on either side of the wide stretch of boulevard. Music was changing on the radio and in the streets. Heavy distorted guitars and epic song-cycles were being replaced by frail, tinny strings backed by even flimsier English voices. These were the new British coif bands that my friend Larry was hyped to join. They would be his magic ticket out of L.A. Others were simply looking to mobilize within city limits, resurrecting junked husks of automobiles to rebuild and eventually call their own. My summer's master plan, to read, eat hothouse tangerines, and watch Lucille Ball four times a day in various sitcom incarnations was undermined by my parents, who quickly filled afternoons with piano lessons at USC and art classes in the hills above Hollywood where I learned to use a potter's wheel.

What I don't remember about that summer were important details. J.'s actual words — what they were or in what order they were spoken. Those have all blurred and faded with years and numerous tellings and retellings. What has stubbornly remained is the flat tone of her voice — distant, matter of fact — as if she were reporting what was playing at the Culver Theater or reading a list of prices from a coffeeshop menu.

She passed on what little information she had at the time — that her brother's battered body had been found within the tall yellow grass in the canyons behind UCLA just above Sunset. Years later I learned that he had been shot full of heroin and that the coroner found several bullets lodged near his heart.

No arrests were ever made.

At the time I mutely sifted through comfort words. I'm not all that sure if I said that I was sorry, or if I even knew that I was supposed to. For the first time in our friendship, I felt a frustrating, sinking sense of helplessness, uselessness. For I had no words or Lucy Ricardo/Ethel Mertz scheme to change the circumstances or erase this reality. I felt in an unforgivable way that I was letting her down. There was some elusive thing to say, floating and swirling just out of reach, that would, if not change things, alleviate some of the confusion and grief. But I was at a loss to find it.

Her brother remains vague in my mind — an adolescent indifference, an impatient grunt, and a closed bedroom door. His death at sixteen sat uncomfortably within my newly formed fourteen-year-old perceptions of life. Old and very sick people died, not sixteen-year-olds. I assumed they were all mistaken, all wrong. I think in the back of my mind I truly believed that he would reappear and laugh the laugh that softened his eyes into slender crescents like his father's. I never told J. this, but I persistently thought it. Sixteen-year-olds didn't die. They still had too much to do.

Over the years, I know that J. found strength and purpose in caring for others, her instinctive need to be strong for everyone else. I'd always been reluctant to ask her how she felt about what happened, but she'd always come to mind when my brother had his own unsettling series of near misses: slipping fifteen feet down an abandoned coal shaft in Colorado; falling asleep at the wheel early one Easter morning just before slamming into a telephone pole. Four a.m. waking nightmares that only confirm how tenuous all is.

Only recently, just a handful of days before our ten-year high school reunion – with J. married and with me easing my way into a commitment to journalism – did I sense that there was the distance to beg for closure. Her thoughts materialized slowly in murky fragments, like Moss's jumbled scrapbook stored in a box: a procession of priests in whispering robes; doves nesting in a front-lawn shade tree; her mother losing a single stone in a ring representing the lives of her children; a teacher who brought by classroom poetry penned in her brother's awkward hand.

With this event, she separates childhood from adulthood. It is her jagged break with innocence. 'Because it has to be.' It has taken some time, but I realize that I do as well. That it has quickened my pace, skewed my view of the world. Sometimes I run so fast that nothing at all comes into focus. And at times amid my mind's white noise, I hear well-intentioned but to me threatening comfort words: 'Slow down, you. We've got to slow you down.'

J., who's grown weary of being strong for everyone else, in marriage has found an anchor. A peace. Sitting in summer skirts, in winter sun, staring out into the gray sea, I remember J. attempting to call up an image of her brother. 'I know he'll never be here the same way I knew him. And not a day goes by that I don't think about him.' But sometimes, she confides, no matter how hard she tries, it's difficult to resurrect a face, a form. 'It's more like a feeling. A presence. Not a physical shape. More a spirit, I hope to never lose.'

Tonight they are dropping poison from the sky. Around the neighborhood there are photocopied notices hastily taped to the windows of all my favorite morning haunts – the bookstore near Franklin Avenue, the coffeehouse on

Vermont – 'Come to the Anti-Malathion Rally at Pioneer Market!' boxy, black letters implore.

At 6 p.m. there's a less-than-impressive assembly shaking angry placards at motorists stopped in gridlocked traffic near Echo Park Avenue. By 7 p.m., not even remote traces of minor civil disobedience remain. Commuters speed by with air-conditioners blasting. Some pause at the corner and slip folded bills through a narrow opening in the window to purchase plastic covers from sidewalk vendors for their cars.

I wake to the voice of a rabid crackpot who's been doing double duty on the radio recent mornings. He drank down a tumbler full of the solution diluted in water a handful of years ago and is still alive to tell of it. He can't understand why a city whose skies are often a brown smear of smog would be so testy over 'a little bug repellent' that just *might* save the state's crops. But as my friend Donna pointed out as I was trying rather unsuccessfully (and against the wind) to tape down a makeshift plastic cover over my car, 'Ever notice they never spray in Beverly Hills.' I hadn't made the conscious connection, not that I was surprised.

I live above one of the less-glamorous stretches of Sunset Boulevard, just after it snakes belligerently, in fits and starts, off its course from the shore to downtown. Outside my picture window a decapitated yet otherwise seemingly healthy palm tree looms. At night when the state helicopters aren't spraying insecticide, city choppers track the trail of elusive fugitives with great shafts of white light. During the uncomfortable heat, brought on by a lingering tropical storm named Fausto, helicopters clip through evening stillness well into the first cool of morning. These are the summer evenings, the uncomfortable waves of heat, that usually don't wrestle with us until the final days of August or early September. I spend early evening bent over a weary rotary fan ten years my senior and listen to the humid voice of Billie Holiday. At night the jasmine, thriving in abundant clusters near my bedroom window, blooms so strong that it often enters my dreams.

Friends call late at night without apologies because with the heat they have lost all hope for sleep. We prepare for the late summer months when acquaintances from out of town will descend. At their request, we embark on macabre foot tours to the site where a lovely starlet expired after leaping from her elevated perch atop the Hollywood sign; or to the barstool at Musso and Frank where F. Scott Fitzgerald swam in his dry martinis. They want to see just where the nocturnal specter takes its noisy ride down Sierra Bonita; where Marilyn Monroe ate Nembutal and crawled into a final, dreamless slumber. There is the ride through Silver Lake as it dips into Atwater, offering an idyllic panoramic view of Forest Lawn Memorial Park in Glendale. For others there is the obligatory stroll along Hollywood Boulevard near the stretch where anxious throngs still fit their soles within grooves set in cement at Mann's Chinese; or those who instead choose to stare into the now equally famous blank eyes of runaways tirelessly parading the boulevard.

Whipping through the canyons, clipping hairpin turns through arroyo-gashed hills on Mulholland Drive, I explain to my disappointed charges that James Dean didn't take his fatal spill along this stretch of road. They accept with little argument, though I sometimes catch them surreptitiously searching for invisible skid marks in the asphalt ahead. Instead we end up in Griffith Park with the rest of the straw-hatted tourists and bored teens on cheap dates, staring up at the bronze James Dean bust just west of the observatory. They study the inscription, snap a few shots, then ask to move on.

There is a dead-man's curve with which I am more familiar. The one that reckless students risk on any given weekend. Because it is not yet world-famous it is not the one that houseguests ask to see. This sinister, serpentine stretch of gray concrete between Pacific Palisades and Brentwood offers blind curves that open up onto glimmering, startling city views. Sunset becomes a densely foliated backwood pass, and one of the drives most negotiated – tanked up and flying – on a dare. The other, 'Top of the World', is a narrow ribbon of road leading up to a flat mesa, where students smoke pot, drink, then extend the rush by driving full speed down this narrow, curving grade.

'They are consumed with having fun. Having a good time', local teachers have explained. Many seem oblivious to consequence. 'They just want to have a good time. It is their impression of The Good Life.' A couple of years ago the cover of the *Los Angeles Times* 'Metro' section featured a shot of Palisades High School students slumped in hysterical tears. Four members of the student body had been killed in an automobile accident on Halloween night. The driver had been drinking and ran headlong into a tree on San Vincente Boulevard. The car exploded into a forest of flames that dramatically lit the night sky. Those standing close by could hear the screams, but the heat was too fierce to admit assistance. Astonished onlookers heard the cries grow faint then die away.

Most student deaths recorded on this campus perched high above Malibu's palm-lined strand are often fatalities stemming from instances of violence. Too many are DUIs, either unlucky victims or blind perpetrators. Former Palisades administrator Roselynd Weeks puts the average at about five a year: 'The Halloween accident seemed to be the most traumatic. There was a longer mourning period. But by junior/senior prom time it was back to business as usual.' Bronze plaques go up along main corridors, memorial pages are set aside in class annuals, and classroom discussions spawn promises to mend old ways, but old habits are slow to change.

They've begun bringing wrecked automobiles onto campus to startle errant students, to shock them into some semblance of responsibility. They've placed them conspicuously in the quad for the day – crumpled masses of wrecked and charred metal, which once represented shining pride. They sit stoically in the sun like precious museum pieces on loan. Some students fall by to marvel at the remains, to imagine the condition of bodies pulled from the amorphous mass. At first some parents and faculty wondered about the appropriateness of this gesture. Some saw it as a tasteless sideshow sensation rather than a drunk-driving deterrent. After a more recent fatality, no one blocked the way.

It is sometimes difficult for teachers and administrators to determine whether some of these accidents are simply an elaborate way to camouflage a flirtation with suicide. Like an elderly shut-in's failure to take life-sustaining medication, it could be a passive, covert form of taking one's own life. Teachers and administrators keep careful watch on troubled students and their black moods. They intermittently explore precarious emotional states in constant flux. Close friends will sometimes duck in to alert a trusted teacher or counselor about the words and needs of a distraught friend.

Creative expression is often a key, a hairline artery leading deep inside – a bleak poem composed in a writing class or a brooding pen-and-ink sketch handed in at an art workshop may have subtle allusions to death eloquently stowed between the lines or intricately laced within its borders. Deep depressions bloom out of everyday disillusionment – disappointment in love, low self-esteem, lack of attention from significant loved ones. These dark moods expand, color existence a sooty gray. Eventually thoughts move from vague, indistinct meditations on depression to concrete contemplations of quick ways out.

For many young people of this generation, the concept of life has never been more ephemeral, the scope of a lifespan more abstract. Worries hover around the planet – environmental and international issues and the future of the human species. More and more, adolescents construct a blueprint for the future that doesn't carve out a place for spouse and/or children. 'They see the big picture more', explains Roselynd Weeks, 'how the system works. And in that sense they are much more mature than generations preceding them.'

There is, despite the abundance of sunshine and wealth, an oppressive sense of doom about an indifferent and chaotic world. A profound emptiness and a gray despair are both cradled snugly within this vast lap of luxury. For some, it only becomes increasingly apparent everyday – there is no need nor time to pace and fret over a future that may never be.

Taking the Harbor Freeway south, the 91 east, I watch a fine drizzle fall. It is the first gray day in months. On the radio, newscasters impart strange tales that seem to wander in from remote dreamscapes: a Latina, after unloading the morning groceries, steps outside her Huntington Park home and sets herself afire. Across town another woman walks toward a car and into the whirl of smoke and hot flame engulfing it. A skull and bones are found beneath a condemned building along the Wilshire corridor. Another medfly discovered, this time in the Compton area. To protect the season's crop, there are plans to send helicopters into these skies in strict, arrowhead formation.

Along Santa Fe, in Compton, the sidewalks and structures rising from them emerge in monochromatic grays. These wide stretches of open road and industrial buildings don't offer much consolation. Traveling north, I watch warehouses unfold into boarded-up apartment buildings, then to chain-link fences enclosing lots of full of rust and weeds, and finally plot upon plot of tiny churches boasting grand and inspirational names: Living Water Fellowship, Compton/Samoa Seventh Day Adventist, Mount Pilgrim Baptist, New Jerusalem Church of God and Christ.

For some time the papers ignored this community and others much like it across the Southland. They ignored the residents who, to avoid a stray bullet, curled near the baseboards to find sleep. They ignored children who stepped over stiff, bloodied bodies on their way to homeroom. They ignored young mothers who worked themselves to the quick to keep their children in private schools, off the street and hidden from harm.

They ignored the survivors.

Both of my parents taught in these innercity classrooms. Some Mondays the police would stop by with stills of the most recent 'Jane Doe' for my mother to identify. She'd stare at the face, search for a familiar glimmer in the eyes, then shake her head. With a nod of thanks they would quickly depart. 'Those were the most resilient kids', she often recalls. 'They all seemed to be blessed with short memories. Life would jump up and slap them down but they'd quietly collect themselves. They were always ready to take more.'

Two years ago, when the 'Gang Problem' spilled out of the ever-widening media-labeled 'South Central L.A.', and into the affluent community of Westwood near UCLA, the papers finally took notice. Police were unleashed on these neighborhoods by the hundreds to 'sweep' the streets clean. City government responded by looking into other vague 'emergency programs' – all BandAid efforts to cure only one of the many problems that have been chipping away at this community for decades.

In spite of the efforts, the statistics remain chilling: the black infant mortality rate is the highest in the county. Black males in the United States between the ages of fourteen and twenty-five have a one-in-twenty chance of being shot. In 1990, 364 gang-related homicides were reported in this city alone, and the number almost doubled in 1991.

As a reporter, I've sat in on community meetings held within exquisite eighty-year-old church sanctuaries. After bowing their heads in prayer, the congregation furrows brows and searches sagacious eyes for the answers. From AIDS to random drive-by shootings, they are a people besieged. Some only shrug shoulders. Others whisper genocide.

Here it is sometimes difficult to gauge what is feared most – the ominous threat of death or the uncertain properties of life. 'Some put up a front, a bravado, to get them through', I've listened to teachers muse. 'They will tell you they're not afraid. I think some of them fear death. Those with conventional values. A good number of them have the loftiest of ambitions – doctors, lawyers, actors, singers, athletes but then there's also the element that has nothing to lose. Those who simply exist.'

You see those empty eyes, those clouded, spiritless faces all over. Yet I'm still struck by the chill that returns a well-intentioned smile. Along this stretch of East Compton Boulevard, this chill moves through the core. More gray buildings, more steely faces; the only splashes of color I see for blocks are Moorish and Byzantine structures containing the mausoleums of Angeles Abbey

Memorial Park.

'We've lost the ability to love, especially the black race. We just can't seem to love ourselves', says Jean Sanders, who is vice president/general manager of Angeles Abbey, the second-oldest black cemetary west of the Mississippi. In a busy week, Sanders sees ten to twelve families in her small, orderly office papered with inspirational messages clipped from magazines and color snapshots of various government dignitaries. The winter months are the hardest, she says. Especially Christmas. 'The joyous times are often the saddest. People just can't cope. The county stats go way high.'

Sanders, whose grandfather was a mortician in Arkansas, carries the tradition a third generation. She is the first black woman to be appointed to the state's Cemetery Board. She digs graves, works in the crematory, and when short-handed, operates the tractor, but most importantly, she explains, her purpose is to listen and console. She's grown use to the fact that when families arrive they are often surprised to see her. Those grieving expect instead a grim old man in an ill-fitting gray suit, but when he fails to greet them, they seldom bother to hide their amazement. Soon their faces will relax with her presence, with the gentle cadence of her voice and the sincerity of her eyes. 'I have women who come in to work on their son's graves. In the process, they will be able to accept their child's death. It's taken one woman seven years. A seven-year death. She's just beginning to focus on her family. People here die slowly, inwardly, for a long, long time.'

It wasn't too long ago that finding a plot of soil to bury a black body posed a problem in Los Angeles. In some areas, private charters blocked these interments as late as 1966. African-American families, in black veils and ash-gray suits, loaded caskets onto streetcars and rode to Evergreen Cemetary in East L.A. It is where three generations of my family have been laid to rest. Sanders remembers hearing those stories. She has watched this neighborhood change three times – from predominantly white until Watts went up in flames in 1965, then predominantly black, and now Latino.

Angeles Abbey has had to adjust to the community's changing face: the Gypsies who throw noisy feasts and roast pigs in honor of the newly departed; the Vietnamese who fill caskets with the loved one's earthly possessions, then decorate the grounds with ripe fruit and flora. The gang funerals, she says, despite what you read in the dailies, have been low-key and uneventful. 'They come in, do their thing, and then they leave.'

'These kids are more afraid of the known than the unknown', Sanders explains. 'They live with the known everyday. Live with a father on crack or a mother on welfare, maybe a brother in the gangs. They take their hostility out on buildings — mark it up with graffiti, break windows. They take their hostility out on people. They take human lives.'

Staring in the face of all this can spiritually drain you, Sanders tells me. It is a job that is diffcult to term 'enjoyable', but Sanders admits she does what she can to strengthen and uplift. She likes people. She gives them hope. 'I had a lot of babies coming in recently. A *lot* of babies, and that's hard. Young adults with gunshot wounds — victims of violent crime. The hatred and hostility is troubling. These dying spirits. I sometimes stop and ask them what they're hungry for. And when they answer, it seems so basic, so simple when you stop to think about it — happiness. That's all they want, "Happiness in the house".'

My old roommate from my days north has recently moved in to town. She is just beginning to get a grip on the rhythm of the city, but its heat and size still daunt her. Just as she traveled two buses with me to buy a proper winter fedora for February's gusts and lightning storms, I carefully instruct her to place cool compresses on her pressure points — then to lie in a darkened room 'cadaver still.'

We often share notes for survival.

She has taken a movie job, a low-budget travesty that required a scene in a cemetary. The crew set up on a patch of green and started digging a shallow grave. After awhile they turned up dry bones. Caretakers turned their heads. The remains glowed ivory white in the dusky earth.

My mind's eye quickly processes these spare details into flickering clips from campy fifties' horror movies; an endless montage shot from oblique angles and captured in powdery half-light. I visualize men and women intently lobbing sun-scorched bones. Tibias and ulnae sail gently through cloudless skies. Yet as in the movies, in varying shades of gray, the eyes don't look so urgent or frightened, the expressions not nearly as desparate as they would, or often do, in real life.

As my friend imparts her tale, we stand in front of 'The Original' Miceli's Italian on Las Palmas. We wait along with a small cluster of others for a table near the bar upstairs where a graying rhythm section runs through an impressive collection of standards — 'Night and Day', 'Stella by Starlight', 'Body and

Soul'. A bewildered drifter, with upturned palms, slows his pace as he nears the line forming near the front doors. Muttering, he works his way north toward the neon and noise of Hollywood Boulevard, shaking his head, his face stretched into a wild, delirious smile, he is saying, 'I'm not dead yet, I'm not dead yet. *I'm not dead yet.*'

July 1990

CHAPTER 20

MY END OF THE BARGAIN

Whenever I hear the stories – whether broadcast news or casual scuttlebutt – about erupting campuses and communities, about racial hate and the violence it breeds, I find that even now I think of 'Mary Jane'. Books-pressed-to-her-chest Mary Jane, the solemn-eyed Negro schoolgirl, would stare off into gray space on the cover of a yellowed paperback that was part of my teacher/mother's classroom lending library. I remember only fragments of Mary Jane's story – a slim fiction paralleling historic events that occurred in Little Rock, Birmingham, Selma. Mostly I remember the wall of angry words, the random, rabid hate.

In Southern California, there were color lines to cross as late as 1972. Almost immediately after my parents purchased our new Westside home, a sterling symbol of broadened, post–civil rights opportunities, we were told stories about cross-burnings in the hills around us. At one time you could see the glow from the flames for miles, one chatty neighbor confided. 'But that was a long, long time ago. . . .' She waved the words away along with her cigarette smoke and left us with a cheery welcome-basket full of overripe fruit that sat neglected, then after a short time shriveled beneath the cellophane.

The summer before I was to start my new school, I became obsessed with Mary Jane. Her image sat at the top of a growing pile of books that I would prop open on my lap during humid August evenings. Prodigious titles weighed down our living-room shelves: *Before the Mayflower; I Am the Darker Brother; Tear*

Down the Walls; Great Negroes Past and Present. Bruised and bloody faces, police dogs loosed on freedom marchers. I didn't understand the hatred, nor could I even begin to comprehend its motivation, but I feared that those disquieting images would come to life. Other photographs lent hope in soft, carefully measured glimmers – Rev. Martin Luther King, Jr in a black stingy-brim and white button-down shirt, Rev. Ralph Abernathy at his side, both wide-eyed, smiling. I understood, at that time, in the vaguest of terms, that their work was meant for me. The duty was complete and my part was simple: not to let what was gained slip from my grasp, always lifting others as I climbed.

What I could have been losing troubled my parents: my 'Black Identity'. Worries were traded across the kitchen table: I wouldn't be properly social-ized; my self-esteem would suffer. But the schools in the old neighborhood were beginning to get 'rough'; tenured teachers were begging out at an astonishing rate. Moving, then, meant more than better schools, it meant an expansive future, a better shot at reaping the rewards.

My nocturnal visions of grown-ups hurling blunt and ugly words didn't occur. No one screamed epithets or carved profanities on my desktop. I eased myself in quietly, into a routine, into work, into casual schoolyard friendships. Subtle episodes confronted me: assigned, unblinkingly, to a slow-moving read-ing group, I was handed books, despite my protests, that I had read two years before. My mother demanded a battery of placement tests. It was the first time I realized that I would always have something to prove. I had to keep up my end of the bargain. I couldn't fail, because so much was at stake.

'The fury of the color problem', as James Baldwin once wrote, for me is not something easily shaken away. I find it still demands notice in achingly familiar ways. I've seen it ascending an escalator, within the cool gaze of a San Francisco commuter, resting a hand on his wallet moments after trading a brief glance with me. I've even heard it screamed from automobiles bulleting along East/West thoroughfares toward the Pacific.

The Civil Rights Movement rendered a new world. I could vote, though my candidates would seldom win; I could catch a movie, yet rarely would I see images familiar to my experience on screen; I could even have the audacity to aspire to a profession for which I would often be reminded in small ways that I was not 'genetically' qualified. What the Movement couldn't do, I have come to realize over the years, was guarantee tolerance. It couldn't remedy ignorance, it couldn't obliterate hate.

LEGACIES

In college I was among two or three of 'the quiet ones' scattered un-threateningly within huge lecture halls. I always did more than was expected: doing extra credit was mandatory. I refused to fit anyone's stereotype: lazy or shiftless, an underachiever. The reward for hard work and persistence was summed up by a cherub-faced professor who, with a hearty pat on the back, just wanted to let me know. 'Most black and Latino kids don't usually do as well as you've done. You should feel proud.'

In my early twenties, I filled the back of my best friend's Toyota with heavy books and winter sweaters, then headed north to the Bay Area for graduate school. I had hand-picked this 'radical' campus noisy with demonstrations and unceasingly papered with urgent petitions. In writing classes I was dissected and tossed about in discussion like an absent third party, informed that my fiction wasn't 'like Toni or Alice's'; that I didn't address tenements or sharecropping, nor did I shed any light on the 'suffering' implicit in the black experience. There were 'problems' with my autobiographical pieces, according to one workshop member: 'Your being black might add some drama to this. . . . Did "blackness" add *no texture at all* to your young life? . . . Do you *never* suffer a moment's torment that you weren't born with soft, golden hair and blue eyes? Didn't the little white boys prefer little white girlfriends?'

Is this what people truly believed I wished for? What we – black people – felt would 'get us over'? Would set us free? If 'blackness' failed to fit these narrow parameters, I found they had no use for it. No use for me. I found it more than frustrating or insulting. I found it lamentable.

Though I didn't participate in sit-ins, wade-ins or a march on Washington, I have come to realize that, like my parents, I must be resilient. The Reagan years, as too many people have pointed out, made racism comfortable. It wasn't until 1984, for instance, that anyone called me 'nigger'. Bigotry cropped up in all sorts of sly ways. Kindly (shiny) old Uncle Ben made his way back on the rice box, sportscasters marveled at Michael Jordan's 'natural' talent. And though giving up has never been an option, sometimes I can't help but feel that I will always be fighting for something that will remain forever out of reach.

March/April 1990

CHAPTER 21

'WHO'S YOUR PEOPLE?':
LA TO L.A. – THE CREOLIZATION
OF LOS ANGELES

'. . . do you know what it means to miss New Orleans . . .'

There is no shingle outside Desvigne's. No neon sign or weathered wooden placard, just a rubbed-out barber pole decal sitting in the center of the front door's filmy glass panel. In other words, you'd have to be in the know to know; which is just about how most everything is down here.

The actual blue, red and white column is stowed inside, up above the doorway, gathering a thick coat of dust on a shelf just out of eyeshot. 'An accident', Mr Desvigne tells me. A few years back, a woman's car sailed through the plate glass at some uncertain speed and hour in the morning. She was trying to keep from hitting a dog that had wandered into her way. Mr Desvigne still shakes his head slowly at the memory.

Stepping inside is like walking into a long sigh – or backward into a dream. The heat, so vivid and still, carries its own color and texture. Summer. Mr Desvigne unlocks his door only three days a week. This 'new schedule' once provided free hours for him to care for his ailing wife. Because she has since passed away, Mr Desvigne has been thinking about resuming his old schedule – five days, with just Sundays and Mondays off for rest.

'Got *sick* of your hometown. N'awlins. . .', Mr Desvigne says to Mark Broyard, who stops in occasionally to have the hairline at the nape of his neck rendered razor-straight, his mustache trimmed and shaped. Taking a seat in one of the vintage brown barber chairs, Mark puts his panama hat in his lap and waits his turn. He always passes by with questions, is always collecting stories and artifacts from the past – about home, about New Orleans. 'Haven't *ever* been back', Mr Desvigne says; the metal clip-clipping, filling the backspace: Hand to forehead, then to neck. Clip, clip. Clip, clip, clip. Mr Desvigne turns to fish something off the counter amid the cans of Gillette shave cream and a jar of combs: a color photo of a smiling Mayor Tom Bradley.

'I think he's afraid to show his face down there', says the reclining customer in madras shorts, from his chair. 'What does "Creole" mean to you, Mr Desvigne?' asks Mark. Mr Desvigne waves his comb and smiles: 'They talk all that gumbo. That Creole. They all broken up.'

Mark asks Mr Desvigne's current customer, a MediExpress driver, for his definition: 'They were those light-skinned blacks that spoke that Creole in New Orleans. The Geechies, weren't they the dark-skinned one's?'

'I had *so* many', Mr Desvigne cuts in, 'who had moved here from Louisiana, from New Orleans. *All* my trade was from Louisiana. Now they're all sick. In rest homes. Moved or passed away. Or back in New Orleans.' He peers over his bifocals, clipping some stray pieces at the crown: 'Some of them are doin' it themselves. Hair growing straight up in the air.' He stops clipping to illustrate, holding his hand with the shears at least a foot into the heavy air. 'It's a new generation, not much you can do about changing their attitude.' He stands back, admiring his handiwork, then takes a Newport from a crumpled package. 'I'm always workin'.' He routs around for a lighter, but settles for a match. 'But times are changin'.'

A lot of it started in the barber shop, while sitting around trading the *cant* – the talk, the gossip. If it wasn't Desvigne's, it probably was Leon Aubry's place, ('King Creole', as some of the neighbors have dubbed him) just a little farther west down Jefferson Boulevard. Or Harold and Belle's while it was still just a sandwich and beer joint. Or the Grotto. Maybe 5-Cs at 54th and 2nd Avenue. Or kicking back at Sid's over on Exposition. Just some place to go to catch up with Louisiana folk. To 'get up-to-date' with what's going on at home. A place to tend to family matters, an antidote for homesickness.

They say that they came by the thousands – 15,000 Louisianans to be exact, just after the Second World War. According to the *Los Angeles Times,* 'L.A. has the second-largest community of Creole descent in the country' – after New Orleans. Evidence is everywhere. You just have to know where to look, who to ask. Much noise has been made about the 'LA to L.A.' connection;

about the mystique, about the curious course of the Louisianan's trail. But why people came is really no mystery. Louisianans came, as did most Southerners or Northerners, or Easterners looking to cash in on the 'Land of Opportunity'. They came for work; they came to escape Jim Crow. With a shortage of building materials and thus a moratorium on residential construction, as well as the decline of the dock business and the slow deterioration of the central business district after the Second World War, jobs in New Orleans became scarce. Those who could packed their things and ventured North to peddle their passed-down trades. But California, so immense and largely unconquered, offered a better crack at success, boundless opportunities for the many who brought with them master-craftsman skills in construction, bricklaying or contracting. They could help to house the migrating masses, already arrived or sure to follow. Single-line postcards said it all, and often said it best: 'You must come and see it for yourself!'

Either you motored, or you booked passage on the train – the Southern Pacific's *Sunset Limited* with its all-diesel engines and its spanking new Pullman cars ('Travel and Sleep in Safety and Comfort') could whisk you across the country in just a few days no worse for the wear. You joined your people – a sister or brother, aunt or uncle, an 'ace boom'. Or you were the trailblazer; the rest would filter their way toward you, share a room, flop on a pallet on the floor.

A lumpy mattress by a drafty door wasn't really hardship, considering what was left behind. Herman Roque, a local C.P.A., recalls the day when he and his father took their seats on a bus in their hometown, Abbeville, and the driver pulled a gun. 'My father sat in the wrong place. It was a small town and everybody knew who was what. That was just the way it was in those days.'

When the City of Angels boomed during the Second World War, wartime industry welcomed eager numbers with open arms. Shipyards hired strong, able bodies, and there appeared limitless opportunity if you were crafty, resourceful and delved deeply enough. 'L.A. was a pueblo when my parents came here in 1917', says community activist Leo Mouton. 'I was born in Watts. A lot of my relatives were involved in various types of business: my uncle cleaned hats, I had another who had a cleaners, one who was a tailor – all on Central Avenue.' But you learned early not to be charmed by the fool's gold of shady, get-rich-quick opportunities; and not to stumble alone into off-limits areas. 'Off-limits' for people of color in Los Angeles ran the gamut and took the pin to that well-rendered dream: not West of Main, not Glendale after dusk, never ever Fontana and its dusty flatlands dotted with burning crosses.

People made do, assures Mouton, in their little corner of L.A. 'Leaving Louisiana, where the KKK, tar and feathering and lynching were common, was easy. A hard life, just an absolutely hard life. Creoles here were all in the family mode, and no one was competing against each other. There were no Joneses to keep up with.' But California, in all its spaciousness and leisure, wasn't anything like the Big Easy. You got homesick, maybe a little lost, so far away from your routine, your people. When you sent your child to the corner store for fresh bread, there was no *lagniappe*, a little something extra, to reward her for the errand. There were no doubloons or carnival beads raining from the sky come Shrove Tuesday. Not a lot of rain at all, for that matter. What to make of this curious desert?

If you can't go home again, why not replicate it? And so it happened. Many Louisianans cooked up lofty schemes to elaborately refabricate home. Transplanted carpenters, bricklayers, plasterers and entrepreneurs would provide their fellow emigrés with familiar outposts, physical structures that could call up memories: Pete's Louisiana Sausage could just about satisfy longings for Eddie Vaucerson's potent hot-links; Girard's or the Louisiana Fish Market often stocked the same brand of crab-boil and fish-fry as the old Circle Market back home. Then too came something else. The Little New Orleans that grew up around Catholic churches in zones not affected by restrictive housing covenants held onto many traditions from 'Home'. Family values (long before George Bush took them up as part of a campaign platform), social clubs, frothy cotillions, noisy LaLas, the frenzy of Mardi Gras, fragments of the *patois,* the lilt of a voice ('the *R*-eaters', 'foist' for *first* and 'hoid' for *heard*). But most important, they held onto the long pause on Sundays to give thanks that they had made it this far, spirits intact.

Insulated but not hermetically sealed, the ways and customs of the Louisiana Creoles are sometimes up for inquiry and careful scrutiny. Outsiders are always curious, and they never completely understand. They want the most subtle nuances put into plain words: 'So what does "Creole" mean anyway?'

The definitions have driven the wedge; they start (or often put an abrupt end to) heated discussions of race, ethnicity, and culture. Everyone has his or her own explanation, a sure-fire way to elucidate those lost in the dark about these Gulf Coast matters. Some definitions come detailed with elaborate coats-of-arms, others with intricate family trees that contain a swarm of French names sounding like a Bizet aria. Everyone has his or her theory, so many that they're difficult to catalog, to accurately assemble – certainly too many, it becomes apparent, to arrive at a happy consensus. Argued well or passionately enough, all seem watertight, plausible, definitive. These raps on race and culture, tradition and lineage, packed tight and carried the distance from Louisiana, all prove to be so much heavy baggage. One can only imagine what lies inside; the crucial bits and pieces still to be unearthed.

My mother arrived on this wave. First or second, depending on which part of the lore you subscribe to. In 1952, she boarded a train at New Orleans's Union Passenger Terminal. With a wicker basket full of food and a list of last-minute cautions, her parents – Frank and Hazel – saw her off. While on the platform, not so on-the-sly, her father paused to ask his friend musician Paul Gayten a favor. Gayten, no doubt, was on his way to sing a few glamorous dates on the coast, but Frank just wanted to know if he wouldn't mind taking a little time out to 'keep an eye on the baby'. Just when he had a moment, from time to time. My mother, in new patent-leather pumps, pristine cotton gloves and traveling suit, sank into her seat, embarrassed at the sheer absurdity of the request. Two thousand miles at the other end of the line, her Aunt Bay waited with a firm bed, some room in the chiffonier and a pot of red beans and rice warming on a back burner. In a few months her mother followed dotingly after her.

This, I've been told lately, is 'typically Creole.'

Growing up, I had a vague understanding of what that meant. Creole. When I was younger, it was the short-hand explanation for why my family in New Orleans had skin shades that ranged from aged ivory to burnt sienna; why all those French names occupied lines in the family Bible; why all those 'white' people on the mantelpiece had posed, smiling, in formal old portraits; why I couldn't quite catch certain words my grandfather ran past me, lightning fast. Beyond that, the whole matter was a mystery. It was certainly nothing I considered, in Los Angeles, on a day-to-day basis. Later, I understood that my grandfather's complex dialect had a fancy name—*patois*—and, as Mr. Desvigne pointed out, those bloodlines down there are 'all mixed up'. But my grandfather—despite the lyric *patois,* the golden complexion, and the wavy, blue-black Gene Krupa curls—considered himself a 'Negro', a 'colored man'. For my family, 'Creole' has been more cultural component than sticky question of ethnicity. For us it explained the importance of extended family, the food, the language, the ritual, and why even after a trail of hurricanes and race storms my grandfather could never leave 'Home'.

But this, I've come to learn, is not how everyone sees it.

One point everyone agrees on: Creole is not Cajun. The Cajuns, descendants of the Acadians (from *Acadie*, now Nova Scotia), were expelled by the British in 1755 and made their way into the Louisiana countryside. Since Cajun chef Paul Prudhomme 'burned a fish' (as Beausoleil's Michael Doucet once put it), the tendency has been to meld the definitions of two outwardly similar yet strikingly different Louisiana cultures. For both Cajuns and Creoles, it is one of the worst *faux pas* an outsider can make.

Attempting a quick-gloss, blanket definition for Creole, however, is walking a mine-field full of incendiary misnomers. Some choose to emphasize the French/Spanish/Native American strain. Others look to Africa. The International French Creole Cultural Heritage Society was created recently to celebrate the culture and attempt to launch an aggressive movement to have Creole culture recognized as its own ethnicity, while others still prefer not to discuss the subject at all.

Taking it all the way back home, the word 'Creole' – from the Spanish term *criollo* (native to the place) – loosely defined those native-born persons who claimed French and Spanish ancestry in *Nouvelle Orleans*. As eighteenth- and nineteenth-century New Orleans grew, so did the complexity of class/culture stratifications, which created strict distinctions, a surfeit of subdivisions, and fancy labels to designate the various bloodlines that converged, commingled and ran as free as the Crescent City's tangle of waterways.

Fair-complexioned, *gens de couler libre* (free people of color) were not considered the same as blacks of 'pure' African lineage. The city's gentry followed a strict pecking order of Griffes (the child of a Mulatto and a black, three-fourths black), Mulattoes (half-black), the Quadroons (one-fourth black), and the Octoroons (one-eighth). The mix only became more complex when Native American, Italian, Cuban, West Indian or just about anything else that wandered into the territory became part of the melange.

The Quadroon Balls of the nineteenth century were held almost nightly by the white Creole gentry, the most lavish of them in the Old Orleans

Theater and Ballroom behind the St Louis Cathedral near the *Vieux Carré*. These opulent events served to secure even more firmly the place of free people of color as a buffer class. They excluded black men as well as 'pure' white women. After choosing one of the bedecked free women of color, these gentlemen (white Creole as well as the French and Spanish gentry) would see to it that their mistresses would receive preferential treatment; their male offspring, trade training; a convent school education for the girls. Others, whose bloodlines didn't measure up, were used for work in and around the antebellum homes along the River Road. Many scholars of Creole culture today believe that the stigma of being a buffer class is at the root of the racial/cultural tensions surrounding Creole-ness that persist today.

G. Reginald Daniel, a professor of Latin American Studies at UCLA, puts yet another spin on the complexity of racial designations in his essay 'Passers and Pluralists: Subverting the Racial Divide':

> This . . . is part of the [Anglo-American] strategy for preserving their dominant status. [They] have enforced a 'policy of hypo-descent' that has designated as Black everyone who is not 'pure' White, and have maintained both legal and informal barriers restricting the contact as equals between individuals of African descent and Whites in the public as well as the private sectors. . . .

Color caste distinctions then gave way to such spiritually detrimental practices as 'brown-bag' or 'fine-tooth-comb' tests, which once determined entry into some of New Orleans's more elite Creole social clubs and placed worth and approval on the shade of one's skin or the texture of one's hair.

Making an already muddy mix that much more confounding, what group can rightly claim the appellation 'Creole' is still a matter of debate. Definitions slide. Webster alone cites seven. The list includes everything from piquant food to the stutter-step *patois* spoken in the West Indies. The French, African-American Spanish and Native American mix that made its home amid the iron lace balconies and Spanish moss trees in *Nouvelle Orleans* is the most visible and often-referred-to designation in Los Angeles. There is, though, still a school of thought like that of Lyle Saxon, whose much-lauded, much-quoted book on Louisiana folklore and legends, *Gumbo Ya-Ya* (1945), denotes 'Creole' this way:

> No true Creole ever had colored blood. This erroneous belief still common among Americans in other sections of the country, is probably due to the Creoles' own

habit of calling their slaves 'Creole slaves' and often simply 'Creoles'. Too, there are proud light-colored families in New Orleans today who are known as 'Creoles' among themselves. But Creoles were always pure white. Any trace of *café au lait* in a family was reason for complete ostracism.

The special privileges that *les gens de colour libre* received from the time Jean Baptiste LeMoyne, Sieur de Bienville, set foot on marshy Louisiana soil slipped away after the Civil War; their prominence and birthrights began to fade. According to Lyla Hay Owen and Owen Murphy's *Creoles of New Orleans*

> After Reconstruction, the prejudice against the Negro race as a whole began to gather momentum in the South. The Jim Crow policies were enforced and to be black was to be enslaved once more; but this time in a more insidious manner. There was suddenly no such person as 'a free person of color', if indeed there had ever been, for the whites considered them to be black and the blacks considered them to be white. They were, however, told to sit in the 'for colored only' sections along with those of 'pure' black ancestry. . . .

For those who were accustomed to moving relatively freely among the upper crust, who could stroll comfortably along the grassy median of Esplanade Avenue near the *Vieux Carré*, and who could earn an impressive salary at a trade, the sudden shock of circumscribed privileges was confusing, if not painful. But if their gray or hazel eyes, fair complexion and light, fine hair could propel them, they could journey over to the 'other side'. To *passe blanc,* to take on new jobs, a new town, a new life. To add an 'h' to the surname or drop an 'e'. Sometimes it was as quick as overnight; as yesterday. No family gatherings at Christmas, no weddings, or paying last respects at funerals. It meant cutting all ties of blood and love: to vanish.

'Faith of our fathers living still. . .'

'The first bond was the bond of blood, the second bond, of course, was of faith', says Father Charles Burns, sitting across from me in St John the Evangelist's sunny conference room. Father Burns, whose short sleeves and generous smile offset the formal collar, has headed St John's congregation for nine years. This neighborhood, within earshot of the hum of the Crenshaw strip, is considered by Louisiana emigres to be the 'St John's Parish'. The designation gives a nod to the old ecclesiastical divisions in Louisiana.

St John's is one of a little over half-dozen parishes – St Bernadette, Transfiguration, Holy Name, St Francis Cabrini, St Anselm, St Eugene, and St Odilia – that have or have had over the years strong Creole leadership. St John's is known for its gumbo-flowing, two-step-inspiring, Louisiana-style LaLas (soirees) in its parish hall, as well as for hosting the first Creole Liturgy and Creole Eucharist. Both events, Father Burns explains, are attempts to highlight the cultural contributions of Creole Catholics. St John's walls are lined with this legacy – priests and bishops and spiritual missionaries – including a black-and-white photo of the first class of men of color who received all of their seminary education in the United States. 'It's interesting to note', says Father Burns, 'that in the first class of four, there were two Creole candidates.'

Along with the more showy accoutrements of celebration or concrete artifacts that Crescent City Creoles brought with them was a sense of faith and commitment to the church. Removed from the Mississippi, Texas, Arkansas, Tennessee Bible belt, New Orleaneans assumed what had been the territory's 'State Faith', Catholicism, established by *Nouvelle Orleans* founder Governor de Bienville within the 1724 *Code Noir* (which among other legislation set standards for both masters and slaves in New Orleans).

'It's amazing how few people know the history of the Creole Catholic and the church', says Father Burns. 'I think like all ethnic groups who migrate, family looked for family and family looked for friends. That was true also of the Creole migration to California.' They tended to settle around one another in same residential areas, and worship at the same local parishes. One glance around the streets surrounding St John's will attest that the church is caught up in the quick drift of demographic change in Los Angeles. Father Burns's firmly Creole congregation has thinned and opened up to include immigrants from Mexico and Central America. To better serve the ever-growing 1,000-plus families who make St John their church home, he and his associate perform masses in both English and in Spanish.

'It's now a lot more difficult for the younger generation because you really don't have the neighborhood cohesion that once existed in New Orleans. What is happening in L.A. is that their children move to the Valley, or Riverside County. You don't have the presence of the grandmother anymore, or grandfather. So just by geographical separation a lot of the cultural/religious cohesion is being lost. and I know it's a big concern to the parents.'

After the move is made into largely Anglo neighborhoods in L.A.'s broadening cache of bedroom communities, these young couples lose the social comforts of the church. 'Many are finding the same kind of racism and discrimination in the Valley and the Inland Empire as [their parents] found when they first settled in the Archdiocese of Los Angeles. And that is cause for concern.' This drift away is much more significant than it first appears. 'When some of the younger generations don't have that same deep-rooted faith as their fathers or their grandparents, and when they encounter racism [in the community and in the church], some of them react by simply not going to church at all.' It is yet another piece of Creole culture slipping further away, something else that struggles to survive the span of time and stretch of miles.

I've been warned that people may be 'shy' – about talking to me; about discussing the origins of their social clubs or cultural heritage organizations; about sharing details of their journey west.

Over the phone, in recent weeks, I hear something else. Something much more potent than shyness. Distrust. Skepticism. About the press, 'Who've gotten it all wrong in the past', they tell me. 'Who've burned us before.' There has been a spate of chilly 'We don't want to be includeds' and one rather brief-and-to-the-point receiver slammed down, the fury of which still reverberates. I've explained in even tones that I respect the quest for and right to privacy. And when I tell them that this project is about migration, about sturdy family structure, about culture, about surviving, some budge a fraction. 'Are you from Louisiana?'

'No. My mother is, though. New Orleans. . . .'

'Oh. Who are your people?'

'Bowers, Prevost, McGhee, Breaux, Williams. . . .'

Some thaw with the list of Louisiana names –'Oh yes, I know Prevost. . . .' They soften as if these words were instead an incantation. They open a few squeaky doors – but only a crack. The necessity for this isolation, what has been perceived as 'clannishness' and 'cliquishness', is slowly revealed over time. To Angelenos *Creole* was curio, as Herman Roque began to understand when he took his post office job here in 1953. 'They really didn't know what Creole was. You're either black or white.' In Los Angeles there was no in-between.

Almost forty years later, the space between hasn't widened any. In a city charged with racial issues and live-wire tensions, and in a time when so many are forced to state their claim to one side or another, Creoles who keep careful watch over their unique bayou culture feel disinclined to choose. It is with this philosophy in mind that there have been, since the beginning of the migration, a proliferation of L.A.-based social clubs that celebrate the culture: the Socialites, the Jolly Jokers, Autocrat West, the Crescent City Lodge. For many there is comfort in being among 'your own'. It alleviates tensions, precludes questions about black/white bloodlines and obviates the pressure of identification. Nowadays, to *passe blanc* and bypass the Creole designation altogether indicates a systemic dilemma of race and equality and bloodlines in modern society. 'If America wasn't such a racist country', offers Creole historian Marion Ferreira, 'this wouldn't be an issue.'

Bearing one of the most historically prominent Creole family names, Louis Metoyer, editor of the newspaper *Bayou Talk,* was determined to provide a constant cultural record, an outpost that could provide a dynamic community dialogue. The paper, which offers a routine mix of articles about culture, updates on local LaLas and picnics, birth and death announcements, as well as historical essays and family trees, has a loyal readership of about 10,000. Its 5,000 copies are printed in San Bernardino, but Metoyer answers the mail and pours over the grids in an office space he's set aside in his West Covina home. 'We're so spread out', says Metoyer who explains that in addition to delivering stacks to local Creole restaurants or festivals, the bulk of the distribution is provided through subscription, with a mailing list that includes pockets in Hawaii, Seattle, and Chicago as well as the folks back in New Orleans. 'Creoles are very family-oriented, and this is the way that we could continue to keep in touch with family and with one another. That's important to survive.'

Metoyer uses the pages of *Bayou Talk* to dispel what he believes are misconceptions that the general public has long held about Creoles and Creole culture. 'One of the well-known myths that seems to be very prominent today is that people think that all Creoles are black. You can look at me and see that I'm not 100 percent black. I have French in my cultural background, I have American Indian in my cultural background, I have Caucasian in my cultural background *and* I have African-American in my cultural background. . . . For me to stand up and say "I'm black" would be denying the other three cultural backgrounds. I can't honestly do that, and I think that you'll find that most Creoles are the same way. They want to be known as Creoles – not this ethnic group or that ethnic group. They want to be what they were told that they were [by] their ancestors, not what a book said or gave a description of. I find that myth a mystery combating me almost [on] a daily basis.'

Merrita Hawkins, founding member of the Jolly Jokers, who co-wrote the Creole Liturgy with Metoyer, shares Metoyer's rationale: 'We come from a unique community where the priority is family. We received something very special from living in a slow-growing community. We have a responsibility to give it back to our kids. I'm proud of who I am and where I come from . . . . I don't want anyone to pigeonhole me. Someone else doesn't designate who or what I am. No matter what Webster says.'

'I see myself as Creole. But I see myself as African', says Shaka Aubry. Aubry (nephew of King Creole himself, Leon Aubry), was born in Los Angeles of New Orleanean-immigrant parents, and now co-owns an African art and clothing space, Bak-Tu-Jua, in Leimert Park. 'The language was important. I'm very interested in the African aspects of Creole culture', says Aubry. 'The Creoles upheld the finer parts of African culture — the extended family, the language. Even "gumbo" is an African word.'

'The whole Creole thing — the *patois* that they call "gumbo" — that uses African syntax', says Florence Borders, co-editor of the *Chickory Review*, a New Orleans–based journal that celebrates the enigmatic culture and language of Afro-Louisianans. Borders has been attempting to better understand what else grew out of the close-quarters shared among the French, the Spanish and the African in Louisiana. 'The way the French arranged the words and the way the Africans arranged the words came out differently. So instead of saying, for instance, *Je vous aime* or *Je t'aime* to say 'I love you', it's *Mon l'amie tois*. The pronoun and the word order and everything changed. So the Africans just made the language serve them; they accommodated the language to their tongues and taste. The people who wanted to communicate with them — the whites for whom they worked and with whom they came in contact — learned to speak with *them*.'

Like Borders, Shaka Aubry believes that not enough time has been spent drawing these parallels, and that too much time has been spent running away from these African connections, or sweeping them under the rug. 'Those African genes would pop up now and then — full lips, a broad nose, the curly hair — *la tête crotet*. People would go to great pains to keep the child's hair cut short. But if you had a girl . . . well, that was another problem.'

Between two worlds, amid a wash of several distinct cultures, just where did one fit, or pledge allegiance? Much like the Mexican Spanish designation *mestizo* – mixed blood – it meant roaming around without real place. 'Creoles weren't really comfortable around whites, or for that matter other blacks. They wanted to be their own thing', says Aubry. 'They would experience a lot of attacks from blacks, people who equated Creole and light skin with this oppressive system. My family was never comfortable with the dark skin/light skin [caste system]. But they didn't want to confront it. That was just how things were.'

He admits that it has taken him awhile to understand, to work toward an appreciation of the French element of his heritage. 'I've felt proud of being Creole, of what had been preserved, the extended family, the *nainaine* and *parrain* [godparents], who really supplemented your father and mother.' Too often the strength of the Creole family structure goes unnoticed; in troubled times, it is seldom held up as an example of a unit that works. 'Here in L.A.', says Aubry, '[the role of godparents] is more symbolic. The structure is there, but everything is more dispersed. It wasn't just color; it was a cultural thing.'

'The third generation became very tribalistic', says Salah Abdul-Wahid, a local activist and documentary filmmaker. 'In fact, the big question that's always asked when people know you're from New Orleans is: 'Who's your people?' When the Creoles emigrated to L.A., Salah explains, they brought with them their tight and intricate family structures. 'In New Orleans you had a strong male and female image in the household. You didn't have fragmented families like you did in Mississippi, where you had miscegenation laws, where people had trouble tracing their fathers or their uncles – the roots of what we're still seeing today, the makings of the black male ghost image.'

Salah can't remember a time when he didn't have a role model in or around the house, someone to show him how to make a fishing net, someone else to take him crabbing. 'My parents, Martinez and Carmel Hewlett, came here prior to the Second World War. They both wrote for the *California Eagle,* the only black paper west of the Mississippi. I was given a work ethic and a philosophy of family. I was taught to hunt at a very early age. Going crayfishing so that you could make gumbo was a very positive, bonding thing.'

In these pockets, nestled around fabulously ornate Catholic churches, these families did their best to recreate the rhythm and family feel of the Quad

– New Orleans's Seventh Ward. 'Especially in this area of L.A., around Sid's, I couldn't walk ten blocks and not meet people I knew', says Salah. 'I threw the *L.A. Times* around here for years. My grandmother was a cook at Sid's, my aunt Bessie gave big gumbo parties in her backyard and visiting musicians would come here and play – Louis Armstrong, Sidney Bechet, Trummy Young. My job was to check the ice and keep the Jax beer cold.'

Celebration was built into the strict work ethic. Some sweat in the sun was always handsomely rewarded. 'All these men had some type of trade, whether it was working with concrete or carpentry. So they had what would be equivalent to a Midwestern barn-raising. If you needed an addition to your house 'cause you had more kids, everybody would show up on weekends and chip in. All you had to do was cook gumbo or red beans and hot sausage and the work would get done and people would help each other. [Our parents] took their hard-earned money and made sure you went through private school, in many cases, Catholic schools. My generation never really learned the language completely, we never really picked up the crafts, we were busy going to UCLA or other things. So a lot of those bayou arts are lost.'

But Salah has been perplexed by some of the things that have survived the long journey, some of the other 'old ways' that grew out of Louisiana soil: 'I remember men telling me that when you have to fill out this form and it says "black", "white", "other", put "other", "because there's black people, white people and then there's us." Not being fully politicized or educated, [they] brought this mentality, knowing only that they had to hold on to the positive side of their culture.'

But L.A. was not New Orleans of 1941, 1955 or 1962. No posted Jim Crow. No Octoroon, Quadroon, Griffe distinctions. 'When I came up my reality was not their reality. You'd go home or you'd go to the funerals or the weddings or the parties, and you'd listen to all the *cant* about who's doing what and how come so-and-so's growing an afro and how come so-and-so is going out with this black girl. That was *their* reality. But I lived in these streets around here and what they brought from New Orleans didn't always work for me. I respected them, they were my elders, they gave me a good sense of family, but their politics were off – for L.A.'

These issues have only become easier to broach and candidly confront, Salah believes, since the younger generations have become politicized and socially aware. (Salah himself made a controversial stand by leaving the religion of his youth to undertake the study of Islam.) The Watts uprising in 1965 shook many Angelenos awake if they had been dozing, dreaming under the trees. 'It was sort of like a watershed even for Creoles in the city because people had to make some decisions. You had to either stand up and have some heart and fight for what is right, calling an injustice an injustice, or you just went into a little buck-and-wing Dixieland Creole thing and ignored it all. Which is what some people did.'

Salah, with straight hair and keen features and skin the shade of coffee smoothed with milk, knows that many Creole women and men like him have encountered racism in its most blatant form. It's emblematic of a larger problem, that the sobering reality of social change is far from complete, and that the freedom these Louisianans traveled 2,000 miles for is still a long way off. 'I have been in situations with white people where they have been in their subconscious "no black people around" [mode]. They've taken me for white and without my soliciting anything from them, they have come out with some of the most vile, hateful, racist remarks in the world. I identify myself as a person of color. And if I were to internalize that, I would just turn up my internal rage. You have a lot of Creole men walking around who have had those experiences and they don't have a way to channel that. This rage *has* to be dealt with.'

Setting the culture separate and apart from the raging race problem in this city and beyond, Salah believes, moves people further away from solutions, further from dealing with their rage. 'Some people will try to paint the whole Creole thing as even another race, or try to romanticize and idealize it. It's a comfort zone for them to say "I'm not black, I'm not white, I have my own culture." They *have* their own culture. There are a lot of things out of Creole culture that are unique. To say "I'm Creole", sometimes these people are saying, "Leave me out of it." I think it's a way of marginalizing their African-American brothers and sisters and it's also a way of marginalizing themselves.'

What to keep, what to lose. Nowadays these artifacts of culture are better passed informally — verbal family trees, just-so stories, and neighborhood gossip all inexplicably seem to stick when there's no pressure to remember. In Los Angeles, Jase's (still better known as Sid's Cafe) is one of the best gathering places to collect the stories of home. Handed from one Sidney to another (Gaigner and DesVignes) now to Aquilla Jase, this loud and friendly Exposition Boulevard restaurant with Dixie on tap (no more Falstaff or Jax) and a wire rack stocked with back issues of the *Louisiana Weekly* on the counter plays tricks with the psyche. With a shrimp po' boy and Jase yelling broad boasts from behind the kitchen's deep fry to a bar full of afternoon regulars, instead of the rusted railroad ties unrolling toward some unknown destination you expect to see the muddy Mississippi, or maybe the busy traffic trundling along St Bernard Avenue.

What has been most responsible for keeping the language – the cadence and color – alive (both the Creole as well as Cajun *patois*) are the songs. The music heats up the gymnasium at Watts's Verbum Dei High School's LaLas, where the formalized version of the Louisiana celebration got its start here in Los Angeles. This music, zydeco, with its frenzied *froitoir* and accordion trademark, may not be to city folks' taste. Those who prefer later incarnations of the hot jazz that brewed out of Basin Street, then later Rue Bourbon, look elsewhere for the short suites dreamt up by Lord Jelly Roll and his Red Hot Peppers, Buddy Bolden or the late, great Satchmo. But the music serves its purpose as historical record like nothing else. LaLa fixture Joe Simien sings in the Cajun French of his Lawtelle, Louisiana youth. 'If I played by myself at dances I think people would throw bananas at me. I don't sing in English. All my songs are in French. These country folks all wanted to Americanize them-selves so much, *ces vous aime des Americains.* You went to the city, you had to be American.'

A similar assimilation game is quietly played out today here in Los Angeles, yet most times it's echoed in other, subtler ways. 'The people who came out here sort of wanted to get the ways of the California people who were probab-ly transplanted from other places too', says Carmel Hewlett, who stepped out on L.A. soil for the first time in 1942.

She, too, was taken at first glance by its tropical beauty, a different kind of ease and gentleness, quite unlike Southern gentility. 'I don't think I know anybody who really wants to come out here now. I think L.A. lost its charm when people came out and discovered that things were not too different – that there was just as much bigotry, there was just as much segregation.' So much energy went into winding through L.A.'s curious maze that the more intangible mementos of home slipped away. 'It isn't as strong a hold as in the fifties or sixties', says Carmel: the family structure, the language, crafts and trades. But these old ways creep out now and again. They gather life in bits and pieces of language, in the ritual of food and in the long reminiscences with friends. Carmel says, though she may not always express it, that she's happy to see her daughter preparing the dishes of her childhood, a deep *roux* gumbo or a jambalaya, adding her own California accent here and there. She builds on the influences, the tradition. 'I have felt proud that we have such a mixture', she says. 'We get a lot from a lot of people. You go to Africa and some of the things that they eat there sound very much like what we've been accustomed to cooking in New Orleans. It came from a lot of different cultures, and there's a French word that envelops that – a whole big mixture – *courtbouillon.*

I spoke to the river and the river spoke to me. *Percy Mayfield*

I expect to see a stingy-brim straw fedora hovering over the rest – over the audacious panamas, the fancy baseball caps slashed with an X, or the floppy neon sunhats. For a minute I think I see him – a flash of white-cotton, suspenders, *café-au-lait,* silky, silver hair. Just someone else's grandfather, walking the walk, smiling the smile, talking the talk – 'How you do, *chère?*'

'MSY'. The tags on my bags loll in the river breeze as I wait on the *banquette* for my ride. MSY: the travel code for New Orleans – has, since I can remember, meant 'Miss You' to me.

I'm traveling with George Washington Cable, reading a well-worn copy of his *Old Creole Days* and thinking about what my friend Masizi said about my grandfather: 'He will be with you. He will help you with your task, while realigning his spirit with yours. This is a feast. Don't say it out loud. Ask him in your mind, early in the morning. He will know that you are there.'

I expect the heat to be furnace-like, hot against my face, like a pair of old cradling hands, but the breeze throws me, relieves me for number of reasons. It's been ten years since my last visit to New Orleans. Before that I'd spent many Augusts here, with scores of mosquito bites tracing my arms, legs and eyelids to prove my tenure. The last time was to attend my grandfather's funeral, little of which I remember except the rain; people sitting, filling space in the dark living room with laughter; my mother blank-eyed, without words. I'd vowed that time would be my last.

The breeze and mystery of a new location, of different digs where I'll rest my bags and take my bed, will make this trip easier, keep me better focused on my task. This time I'm staying in the Ninth Ward with my cousin Katherine Prevost, instead of the Seventh, far away from my grandfather's house and those memories of him. Katherine, who moves even faster than she speaks, is fair and light-eyed. I'm closer (though darker) in hue to her eldest daughter Che, medium brown with hints of crimson, like Camellia brand red beans. I'm having trouble keeping up, with all of my journalist trappings – books and microcassettes, notepads, maps, tape-recorder. 'Hey, *chère?*' she smiles. I pile it all in, she turns the air-conditioning on full blast, and only then I think that I can say 'I'm fine.'

We motor past a veldt of green – moss and oaks and crepe myrtle.

I'm here to collect stories, but mostly I feel like I'm chasing ghosts. In the morning I crack open the phone book just to survey the number of Bowers names, to wonder about the connections, but I am startled, thrown, when I find my grandfather's 'Frank, D.' and his Paris Avenue address listed with all the rest. I wonder why after ten years it still survives here in black and white, creating an illusion of a tangible connection, playing mischievous tricks.

Cousin Kitty creates a diversion, giving me patient lessons about how to pry into a huge pile of crayfish, removing the heads first. I'm a mess of gooey fingers, stained walking-shorts and, with hunger unabated, very little show for my efforts. Setting to our task over dinner, she runs through tales of the sugar mill in Baldwin, Louisiana, my grandfather's long swims down at Lake Pontchartrain, how Hazel, his wife, my grandmother (who died when I was very young, but whose melancholy eyes I inherited) would hover timidly at shore. Over the next few days there is the parade of pictures: the deliberate stare of my great grandmother Edna Prevost; Kitty's brother Anno's earnest attempt at a facile afro; the starched formality of my uncle Dr Charles H. D. Bowers, one of the early members of the Original Illinois Club; my grand-mother's father in felt fez, playing a shiny French horn, leading a brass band on Mardi Gras Day. We hardly look related, this rainbow of shades. Then the suc-cession of streets: Rocheblave, Tonti, Dorgenois, St Bernard, Miro, Claiborne – all arteries into a past, long before my own. I hear them all in my grandfather's voice. Songs in *patois* about 'M'sieur Banjoe', the stories about a young Louis Prima, who lived a few doors down on St Peter, stopping in to watch his father, Frank, Jr tinker with radio sets. Some of it is vague, slipping away like some of the ghostly images on daguerreotypes: the grandfather (many times removed), a Frenchman 'Jean-Louis', whom no one speaks very much of. And working to remember the proper answer to my grandfather's rapid inquiries, turned playful taunts — *pas connais*. I don't know.

Los Angeles hangs close by, at every turn it seems. Everyone's got L.A. on the lips. Got blood or near-blood on the coast. 'I was in L.A. for thirteen years', our Greyhound tour guide tells me as we board on Rue Decatur, alongside the Mississippi, 'till a lady ran me out the state.' And the patchouli-scented woman drawing Dixie from the tap at the Old Absinthe House on Rue Bourbon talks about how during jazz fest Aaron Neville told the crowd that L.A. was on fire. He asked for a moment of silence. 'Everybody started crying, shaking hands, giving each other high-fives. It just gave us all chills. . . .'

'Chicago was heaven in the thirties and the forties. It was L.A. in the fifties and sixties, but you know, Heaven is what you make it', says the Dooky Chase Restaurant owner, Leah Chase, who brought the wooden chairs and downtown soft-lit glamour of the *Vieux Carré,* to her folks and friends in the neighborhood near the St Bernard Projects. 'The people who went to L.A. didn't often mix. They stayed to themselves. Didn't spread out, didn't blend in. They created their own community. The culture was *good*', says Leah, 'but you don't lord over others with it. Do you see the condition of the Seventh Ward? A disaster. Thank God for the American Negroes, thank God for them.'

'The Civil Rights Movement saved us. It liberated us', says Harold Baquet after welcoming me home, and then into his air-cooled space cluttered with slides, film and prints at Loyola University on St Charles Avenue. 'It got rid of class distinctions. Not many people my generation consider themselves Creole any more. We're black. I went through my identity crisis a while ago. Before then we had no identity. I did it when I was seven. You didn't want to risk being archaic.'

Baquet offers a glib definition, with a smile: 'The Creoles were the ones who lived in the Seventh Ward, went to Corpus Christi Church and had pianos in their living rooms. . . .' But the smile disappears when he speaks about what he terms 'The Exodus' — with all the Biblical connotations, he assures me, that come along with it. 'We can't blame ya'll. Some people think you copped out. Let us fight the Civil Rights Movement for you. You missed the struggle, but we don't feel slighted.'

Baquet cooly articulates an emotion many of our Crescent City cousins share about the Great Flight to California and subsequent shades and repercussions of abandonment. For those who have wandered away, Baquet has been carefully documenting folk life in New Orleans, preserving the faces, eyes and hands. 'Your barbershop alone is an archive', he says. 'They escaped something terrible. Going to California was like going to the colonies. A lot of them left for jobs, the economy was so depressed. If you didn't want to pass for white, you just didn't work.' It's taken some time, Baquet admits, but 'we're proud of our family who left.'

At Treme and Basin streets, you can hear the drums on Saturday afternoon just outside Louis Armstrong Park. With all that *charivari*, that rough music, these are not ghosts, or the charms of *vaudaux* braving broad daylight. Inside, the gates, the swirl of cobblestone at the edge of green is the historic Congo Square, where on Sundays New Orleans's slave population was free to play its drums, dance its dances and give thanks to its gods.

When I arrive, the six-foot wooden silhouette of Africa that usually stands in the middle of the square has fallen. It takes two men to carefully upright it, to place it in its proper place, at the center. Che and her daughter Alana pick up empty cans, bottles, and go-cups scattered around the area, but you can still smell the trash overflowing from the city-neglected bins, fermenting in the sun.

Luther Gray, one of the founding members of the Congo Square Foundation, holds a drum clinic every Saturday afternoon from two to four. Along with working to get the square declared a national monument, the clinic is part of larger attempt to bring Africa back to New Orleans. Participants gather along a circular bench under the generous shade of cypress and oak trees with their drums, sticks and a single *shekere*. Luther helps them find links to understand the turns in the road back to Africa, like the *Bamboula* beat that he pounds out on his conga, which echoes the bass drum line of the celebratory New Orleans second line. Luther was at first discouraged by the small numbers who ventured out in the hot sun and humidity – but like anything else new and unfamiliar, 'It was slow, but the idea is catching on.'

I take, for want of a better term, the scenic route, to Ashton's Shatto, cruising around my old neighborhood, past the pastrami place, Hungry Harold's, and the Kentucky Fried Chicken that used to be a car-hop hot spot called Teddy's. Actually, of late I've found myself checking up on the rebuilding, the clean-up, the spirits. Even though the Boys Market at Crenshaw and Slauson is open and sparkling, owners of smaller stores still don't seem to feel comfortable enough about taking those hand-penned signs down. N'Awlins West has its sign prominently displayed, so did the Louisiana Fish Market over on Vernon and Arlington, at least a couple of weeks ago. Businesses loudly proclaimed, 'Black Owned'.

At the Shatto, people are filing in to the whine and wail of the Nevilles, as well as Professor Longhair, Antoine 'Fats' Domino, and Joe Liggins signatures, all wrapped around the scent of cayenne pepper. Low tables made to look like altars, set with votive candles and jars of filé powder, stray carnival beads and red-hot pepper sauce, define the space designated as stage. When the room fills, the lights dim, it's Louis Armstrong singing about the saints, but who comes marching in? Two wiry figures in baggy suits and black masks, carrying umbrellas, waving brilliant handkerchiefs, and of course throwing carnival beads – 'Lord, have moicey, it's a second line!' Hands keep time, cheers let up. This duo dances and mugs until the trumpet sails far, far away. 'Hold that for me, *chère,*' Mark Broyard, says entrusting his black brolly to a woman in the front row. First up is 'brown paper bag test'. Mark holds one lunch-sack-size bag against Roger Guevneur Smith's beige skin, carefully scrutinizing the hues. 'Am I all right?' Roger asks nervously. 'All right?'

After a long pause, Mark concedes. 'All right', he says with a nod.

The brown bag is put away only to reveal a fine-tooth comb, prompting more laughter. Will it run, unhindered, through the dark, wavy locks? Holding their breath, both take turns with the comb, passing the test without question or hitch.

The meeting has begun.

Inside the Creole Mafia is a performance piece that both Mark and Roger, quite unwittingly, started researching when they were still Cub Scouts. 'Although my family is not Creole, I first became exposed to the whole Creolismo because I went to Catholic school', says Roger. 'During lunchtime at Transfiguration, I remember, there was an ongoing dispute in the schoolyard about who was Creole and who was Negro. This was the sixties, and people were trying to develop their psychological and racial allegiances.'

This potent performance piece, which came out of a series of conversations about the community, rattles Creole culture's skeletons and takes well-aimed solid knocks at sacred cows – from the brown paper bag test and the

HAZEL AND FRANK BOWERS, CANAL STREET, 1940s

proper way to make *café au lait* (what comes first: the coffee or the milk?) to an outrageous yet poignant segment depicting a wandering soul's tearful and terrified visit to 'Creole Anonymous'.

'We definitely wanted to inspire debate', says Roger. 'I think there is one extreme which embraces Creole culture above all other cultures and elevates it to an almost racial status, then you've got the other extreme of people who reject the Creole community – I'm talking Creoles and non-Creoles alike – who see it as anti-black, anti-African, and who get upset when people start talking about anything Creole. So somewhere in there there's got to be a way of sustaining and enjoying the culture without allowing it to inundate your political and social agenda. That's the struggle we're trying to embody inside this piece.'

'It's theirs. It's their piece', says Mark Broyard. 'It's to let these Creole people know they've done something we're proud of and to let America know the diversity of our culture. We're not one hue. We did it with our own sense of style. It's multicultural, and it doesn't even know it.' Broyard hopes that the piece will lift up a culture 'not in an arrogant way, but in an artistic way. It is a chance for these people to see their culture on stage as glorified and celebrated.'

Mark, born in New Orleans, is the silver voice that fills St Bernadette's sanctuary at Sunday evening Mass. A community fixture, he sings songs of joy at weddings, songs of consolation at services for the deceased. Much of the clannishness comes out of a need for protection, a safe harbor, Mark has learned. Not everyone understands the complexities of the culture.

While growing up Mark heard the weighted inquiries, the ever broadening inventory: 'You're not all the way white, *are* you, Broyard?'; 'white boy'; 'Mexican'. 'We still don't recognize ourselves', he points out. 'In sixty-five, I realized that I looked different, but I never knew we were part of something.' His mother cautioned him to 'soft-pedal that Creole thing'. Instead, he started writing it all down. And when that wasn't enough, he went beyond – foraging for sentimental objects, building small altars to his forbears, all of which has grown into a large multimedia sculpture he's titled 'Why Did We Come? What Did We Bring?'

'In order for a culture to exist, there have to be artifacts', says Broyard. So he squirrels them away, relieving neighbors of their throw-aways: Zatarain's crab boil and root beer boxes; a roadmap that traces I-10 from New Orleans to

L.A., doubloons, CDM Coffee, L.A. maps with pushpins demarcating salient points: Pete's Louisiana Sausages, Marin's, Ashton's Shatto, Larry Aubry's Barber Shop, Desvigne's. . . .

Broyard has been able to trace his line back to a striking and symbolically poetic image – five faceless silhouettes departing North Africa: 'I wonder about those five Moroccan brothers on that boat. Were they exiles? Were they dissidents? How did they spell their names?' At thirty-four, Broyard understands that he must start now, passing these traditions down to his children, so that they become part of their daily lives. 'I want to see the places that my grandfather went. I want to do the things he did. He went to nine churches on Good Friday. I want to go to nine churches on Good Friday. I want to immerse myself in it. It's *my* stuff. My baggage. . . .'

At my own home in Echo Park, I've been slowly erecting my own little altar: there are candles and family familiars, a small collection of antique frames filled with serious sepia-toned faces. In the largest one, purchased near Union Station, here at the end of the line, stand my grandparents Frank Dixon Bowers III and Hazel Rose McGhee Bowers, on Canal Street, some time in the forties. Summer. Frank's hat is straw, not a felt fedora. On Sunday, my mother believes: 'See the bag?' she says. That would be for one of my great-grandmothers – maybe Edna, or Lodie. Dinner, cooked and packed away. Now the long stroll on a humid night.

'I think about my grandfather every day', says Mark, sliding me gently out of my reverie.

I don't say it, but I know: I'm surprised at all my antique baggage, surprised at what I'm still unpacking, though so neatly arranged, the space it occupies, the history and struggle it represents.

I know. I understand. But still don't find the words to tell him that I think about mine, too.

ABOUT THE AUTHOR

Lynell George was born and raised in Los Angeles. A graduate of Loyola Marymount University, Los Angeles, she is currently a features reporter for the *Los Angeles Times*. Her work has been published by the *LA Times* Syndicate, *LA Style* magazine, *Utne Reader*, *San Francisco Bay Guardian*, *New Left Review*, and *LA Weekly*. She won the National Association of Black Journalists Award in 1992 for Hard Features—Outstanding Coverage of the Black Condition. She lives in Los Angeles.